CAMBRIDGE T
HISTORY OF

FRIEDRICH NIETZSCHE
Writings from the Early Notebooks

CAMBRIDGE TEXTS IN THE
HISTORY OF PHILOSOPHY

Series editors
KARL AMERIKS
Professor of Philosophy at the University of Notre Dame

DESMOND M. CLARKE
Emeritus Professor of Philosophy at University College Cork

The main objective of Cambridge Texts in the History of Philosophy is to expand the range, variety, and quality of texts in the history of philosophy which are available in English. The series includes texts by familiar names (such as Descartes and Kant) and also by less well-known authors. Wherever possible, texts are published in complete and unabridged form, and translations are specially commissioned for the series. Each volume contains a critical introduction together with a guide to further reading and any necessary glossaries and textual apparatus. The volumes are designed for student use at undergraduate and postgraduate level and will be of interest not only to students of philosophy, but also to a wider audience of readers in the history of science, the history of theology and the history of ideas.

For a list of titles in the series, see end of book.

FRIEDRICH NIETZSCHE

Writings from the Early Notebooks

EDITED BY

RAYMOND GEUSS
University of Cambridge

ALEXANDER NEHAMAS
Princeton University

TRANSLATED BY

LADISLAUS LÖB
University of Sussex

CAMBRIDGE
UNIVERSITY PRESS

CAMBRIDGE
UNIVERSITY PRESS

University Printing House, Cambridge CB2 8BS, United Kingdom

One Liberty Plaza, 20th Floor, New York, NY 10006, USA

477 Williamstown Road, Port Melbourne, VIC 3207, Australia

314-321, 3rd Floor, Plot 3, Splendor Forum, Jasola District Centre, New Delhi - 110025, India

79 Anson Road, #06-04/06, Singapore 079906

Cambridge University Press is part of the University of Cambridge.

It furthers the University's mission by disseminating knowledge in the pursuit of
education, learning and research at the highest international levels of excellence.

www.cambridge.org
Information on this title: www.cambridge.org/9780521671804

The selected material in this volume is used and re-translated from Friedrich Nietzsche, SÄMTLICHE
WERKE, edited by Giorgio Colli and Mazzino Montinari, by arrangement
with STANFORD UNIVERSITY PRESS

© Cambridge University Press, for this edition 2009
First published 2009
5th printing 2018

A catalogue record for this publication is available from the British Library

Library of Congress Cataloging in Publication data
Nietzsche, Friedrich Wilhelm, 1844–1900.
[Selections. English. 2009]
Friedrich Nietzsche : writings from the early notebooks / [edited by] Raymond Geuss, Alexander Nehamas,
Ladislaus Löb.
p. cm. – (Cambridge texts in the history of philosophy)
Includes bibliographical references and index.
ISBN 978-0-521-85584-6 (hardback) 1. Philosophy. I. Geuss, Raymond. II. Nehamas, Alexander,
1946– III. Löb, Ladislaus. IV. Title. V. Series.
B3312.E5G48 2009
193–dc22 2009005335

ISBN 978-0-521-85584-6 Hardback
ISBN 978-0-521-67180-4 Paperback

Contents

Contents

Abbreviations

KGW *Friedrich Nietzsche, Samtliche Werke, Kritische Gesamtausgabe,* ed. G. Colli and M. Montinari (Berlin: de Gruyter, 1967–77)

KSA *Friedrich Nietzsche, Kritische Studien-Ausgabe,* ed. G. Colli and M. Montinari (Berlin: de Gruyter, 1980)

BT Friedrich Nietzsche, *The Birth of Tragedy,* ed. Raymond Geuss and Ronald Speirs (Cambridge University Press, 1999)

DK *Fragmente der Vorsokratiker,* ed. H. Diels and W. Kranz, 2nd edn (Zurich: Weidmann, 1996)

DL Diogenes Laertius, *Lives of Eminent Philosophers,* trans, E. Hicks, 2 vols. (Cambridge, Mass.: Harvard University Press, 1959)

GSD Richard Wagner, *Gesammelte Schriften und Dichtungen* (Leipzig: Siegels Musikalienhandlung, 1907)

KR *The Presocratic Philosophers,* ed. G. S. Kirk, J. E. Raven and M. Schofield, 2nd edn (Cambridge University Press, 1983)

WWR Arthur Schopenhauer, *The World as Will and Representation,* trans. Ernest Payne (Indian Hills, Colo.: The Falcon Wing Press, 1958)

Introduction

No modern philosopher has been read in as many different ways or appropriated by as many diverse schools of thought, social and political movements or literary and artistic styles as Nietzsche – perhaps, Plato's towering figure aside, no philosopher ever. Notorious during much of the twentieth century as a 'precursor' of German National Socialism, he was also an inspiration to left-wing and avant-garde radicalism in the century's early years as well as to the European and American academic left toward the century's end. Denounced by some for undermining all traditional faith in truth and goodness, he has been praised by others for confronting honestly and truthfully the harmful and deceptive ideals of a self-serving past.

Nietzsche's almost irresoluble ambiguity and many-sidedness are partly generated by his style of writing – playful, hyperbolic, cantering and full of twists and turns – and by his fundamental philosophical conviction that 'the *more* affects we allow to speak about a thing, the *more* eyes, various eyes we are able to use for the same thing, the more complete will be our "concept" of the thing, our "objectivity"'.[1] Nietzsche was intentionally a philosopher of many masks and many voices. His purported objectivity is also due to the fact that most of his writing (more than two thirds of his total output, not counting his voluminous correspondence) has come to us in the form of short notes, drafts of essays and outlines of ideas and books he never published – fragmentary texts that allow great latitude in interpretation. These unpublished writings – his *Nachlass* – were

---

[1] Friedrich Nietzsche, *On the Genealogy of Morality*, trans. Carol Diethe (Cambridge University Press, 1994), III. 12, p. 92.

mostly inaccessible until the recent publication of the standard edition of his works.[2] His readers had to rely on a series of different editors who, beginning with his own sister, selected the texts to be published according to their own preconceptions, arranged them in idiosyncratic ways, and sometimes attributed to him ideas and even whole books he had never himself contemplated.[3]

Because of their intrinsic interest, their bulk, the role they have played in Nietzsche's reception so far and the role they surely should play in trying to come to terms with his sinuous engagement with the world, Nietzsche's unpublished writings deserve serious study and reward careful attention. But, in order to be read at all, these texts – fragments that range from the casual to the polished, from the telegraphic to the discursive, from the personal to the detached, and address, sometimes in considerable detail, topics and problems that preoccupied him throughout his life – must first be placed within a context.

I Reading strategies

This volume contains an extensive selection from the notebooks Nietzsche kept between 1868, just before he was appointed Professor of Classical Philology at the University of Basel in Switzerland at the age of twenty-four, and 1879, when he resigned his position because of his health and devoted himself full-time to his writing.[4] During that time, Nietzsche composed and published *The Birth of Tragedy* (1872), his four *Untimely Meditations* (1873, 1874, 1876) and *Human, All Too Human*, volumes I and II (1878). Ten years later, in January 1889, Nietzsche collapsed in a public square in the Italian city of Turin and never regained full control of his faculties until his death in 1900. These notes, then, represent his philosophical reflections over more than half of his creative life. They address questions that were central to Nietzsche's early philosophical views: the relative importance of music, image, and word to art

---

[2] Friedrich Nietzsche, *Sämtliche Werke, Kritische Gesamtausgabe*, ed. G. Colli and M. Montinari (Berlin: de Gruyter, 1967–77) (KGW).

[3] The most famous among them is the compilation of notes published by Elizabeth Förster-Nietzsche and her collaborators under the title *The Will to Power: Attempt at a Revaluation of All Values*, first in 1901 and then, in expanded form, in 1906. English translation by Walter Kaufmann and R. J. Hollingdale (New York: Random House, 1968).

[4] With one exception: a set of notes on Schopenhauer from 1867–8 which are crucial to the material that follows.

and life; the role of ancient Greece – Greek tragedy in particular – as a model for a renewed German culture; and the nature of genius. But they also raise issues with which he grappled throughout his life – the nature of truth, knowledge and language, the connections between art, science and religion, the ancient Greeks' attitudes toward individual and collective goals, the role of philosophers both then and now, and the nature and function of morality. They also reveal different sides of Nietzsche's life-long involvement with his two great 'educators', the composer Richard Wagner and the philosopher Arthur Schopenhauer.

Before we try to look at this material in more detail, though, we must ask how one should go about reading such a collection of semi-independent texts, which shift abruptly from one subject to another, try different tacks only to abandon them and do not generally aim to establish a clear conclusion. The problem of 'reading Nietzsche', a centrepiece of Martin Heidegger's monumental study (published in Germany in 1961),[5] has given rise to a complex debate over whether each of Nietzsche's many voices speaks on its own, independently of the others, whether one among them is authoritative or whether they all harmonise in expressing a single overarching way of looking at the world. The debate was joined by the French philosopher Jacques Derrida,[6] who focused on a sentence, ' "I have forgotten my umbrella" ', appearing (within quotation marks) in a notebook from 1881–2. Derrida argued that it is impossible to determine precisely the sense of such a sentence and suggested that not only Nietzsche's fragmentary notes but all his writings present a similarly inscrutable face to their interpreters: 'To whatever lengths one might carry a conscientious interpretation', he wrote, 'the hypothesis that the totality of Nietzsche's text, in some monstrous way, might well be of the type "I have forgotten my umbrella" cannot be denied.'[7] On the basis of that hypothesis, Derrida took issue with every attempt to establish a coherent overall interpretation of Nietzsche's work.

The trouble, though, is that, in order to support his reading of this passage, Derrida himself had to place it along with other passages in which, he claimed, Nietzsche expressed similar ideas (for example, sections 365

5 Martin Heidegger, *Nietzsche*, trans. David Farrell Krell, 4 vols. (San Francisco: Harper & Row, 1979–82).
6 Jacques Derrida, *Spurs: Nietzsche's Styles*, trans. Barbara Harlow (University of Chicago Press, 1979).
7 Ibid., p. 133.

and 371 of *The Gay Science*). In so doing, he conceded that it is impossible to read anything without bringing some other text – if only the sentences that precede and follow it – to bear upon it. And that, in turn, means that no sentence or statement stands completely on its own, impervious to the pressures of its context. That is not a matter of choice, particularly in the case of Nietzsche's often haphazard notes. Choice enters only when we ask, as we now must, how to select a context within which to read them so as to be able to say something significant about them – even if that is only that they lack all specific meaning.

It won't do, that is, to take each note as a small work in its own right. Consider, for example, note 7[166]:

> Euripides and Socrates signify a new beginning in the development of art: *out of tragic knowledge*. This is the task of the future, which so far only Shakespeare and our music have completely appropriated. In this sense Greek tragedy is only a preparation: a yearning serenity. – The Gospel according to St John.

The problem here is that, on a theoretical level, it seems close to impossible even to process the words of this passage (unlike the simpler ' "I have forgotten my umbrella" ') without thinking of what *The Birth of Tragedy* and various other notes have to say about tragedy, Euripides, Socrates, Shakespeare and German music (that is, primarily, Richard Wagner). Each of these passages, in turn, invites (and requires) a reading in the light of still others. For instance, in note 7[131] we read: 'Euripides on the path of science seeks the tragic idea, in order to attain the effect of dithyramb through words. Shakespeare, the poet of fulfilment, he brings Sophocles to perfection, he is the *Socrates who makes music*.' What, then, are we to make of Walter Kaufmann's view that the 'Socrates who makes music' in section 15 of *The Birth of Tragedy* 'is surely an idealized self-portrait: Nietzsche played the piano and composed songs'?[8] And even if we stop that line of questioning there, the reference to the Gospel of St John continues to resist understanding. Why shouldn't we, then, take into account note 7[13], 'The *Gospel according to St John* born out of Greek atmosphere, out of the soil of the Dionysian: its influence on

[8] Friedrich Nietzsche, *The Birth of Tragedy*, trans. Walter Kaufmann (New York: Random House, 1966), p. 98, n. 10.

Christianity in contrast to Judaism', which will necessarily send us in ever-new directions?[9]

On a practical level, taking each note as a tiny essay in its own right makes it impossible to keep it securely in mind once we have moved to the next (or the next after that, and so on). Almost as soon as we have read one note, the previous one will have disappeared from memory (try it). Nor again does it improve matters to take the opposite tack and try to read the notebooks as discursive works, containing a more or less unified presentation of interconnected topics in good expository order. In most cases, it is simply impossible to establish such an order and the net result is that the notes fail to make a lasting impression and fade away soon after we have read them.

That is not just an abstract hermeneutical problem: it has affected directly the way in which Nietzsche's notes have been published. Earlier editors, for example, addressed it in the following manner.[10] In his correspondence during the decade 1870–9, Nietzsche often referred to an ambitious project that would combine his university lectures on early Greek philosophy with further material in his notes into a work on the cultural significance of philosophy in ancient Greece compared to its role in contemporary Europe. He never settled either on a title or on a structure: his notes contain many different plans and projected outlines, several of them included in this volume. Accordingly, and based on the method Nietzsche's sister Elisabeth used in compiling *The Will to Power*, some of his editors selected various notes and arranged them in several thematically connected groups, as if they were early or unfinished versions of larger works which might have eventually been incorporated into a *magnum opus* treating these issues. And so, in addition to more polished essays like 'On the Pathos of Truth' and 'On Truth and Lie in an Extra-Moral Sense' (both included here), Nietzsche was credited with the following 'potential' works: *The Philosopher: Reflections on the Struggle between Art*

---

[9] Here is one of them: the Gospel according to St John is not only a Greek legacy to Christianity, it is also 'the most beautiful fruit of Christianity' (10[1]) – a description that cannot be deciphered without following the tangled webs of Nietzsche's views on Christianity, the Dionysian and beauty.

[10] The method is followed, with some individual differences, by the editors of both *Nietzsches Werke* (Leipzig: Kröner, 1901–13) – known as the *Grossoktavausgabe* – and *Nietzsches Gesammelte Werke* (Munich: Musarion, 1920–9) – the *Musarionausgabe*.

and Knowledge, The Philosopher as Cultural Physician, Philosophy in Hard Times and *The Struggle between Science and Wisdom*.[11]

That way of providing a context for Nietzsche's notes does not only depend heavily on editorial discretion but is also, in a serious sense, circular: it uses as *evidence* for Nietzsche's views 'works' constructed only on the basis of a previous *interpretation* of those very views – how else could one select and order a series of discrete passages into a coherent whole? There is, however, a further difficulty: although Nietzsche might have planned to use a note in a work he was considering at the time, it is impossible to know whether he would have kept it, revised it or even rejected it for the work's final version.

In place of such an 'internal' or 'vertical' approach to the notes, linking them to others that precede or follow them, it might be better to provide them with an 'external' or 'horizontal' context. Without overlooking the notes' internal connections, we should read them alongside the works he published during the 1870s, using both to cast light on one another, add complications to his views or generate uncertainty where only confidence was visible before. The unpublished material can provide us with 'more eyes with which to see the same thing' and thus increase the 'objectivity' with which we can address his intricate, manifold views.[12]

II Intellectual background

Let's begin by considering three topics that preoccupied Nietzsche during the years when he was thinking about, and writing, *The Birth of Tragedy* and, in one way or another, during most of the rest of the 1870s: the philosophy of Schopenhauer, the music of Richard Wagner, and the importance of ancient Greek art and civilisation for a renaissance of German culture.

1 Schopenhauer

By far the most important source of philosophical inspiration for the young Nietzsche was the thought of Arthur Schopenhauer (1788–1860),

---

[11] That material, along with some of Nietzsche's plans and outlines, appeared (before the relevant volumes of KGW had been published) in an excellent English version, *Philosophy and Truth: Selections from Nietzsche's Notebooks of the Early 1870's*, translated and edited with an introduction and notes by Daniel Breazeale (New Jersey: Humanities Press, 1979).

[12] That should also not exclude other published works, which some of the notes may anticipate, reinforce or, sometimes, contradict.

whose major work, *The World as Will and Representation*,[13] Nietzsche read while studying Classics at the University of Leipzig in 1865. 'Here', he wrote in a later autobiographical sketch, 'every line cried Renunciation, Negation, Resignation, here I saw a mirror in which I caught a glimpse of World, Life and my own Mind in frightful splendour,'[14] while in 'Schopenhauer as an Educator', the third of his *Untimely Meditations*, he confessed that, 'though this is a foolish and immodest way of putting it, I understand him as though it was for me he had written'.[15] Nietzsche admired Schopenhauer intensely as an exemplar of what a philosopher should be, and was particularly influenced by his metaphysics, his views on art and his all-encompassing pessimism.

Schopenhauer saw himself as the true heir of Immanuel Kant (1724–1804), who had argued that the objects of our experience are necessarily located in space and time, subject to the law of causality. But space, time and causality apply to things not as they are in themselves but only as they appear to beings like us: they are, so to speak, the filters through which the human mind necessarily perceives and understands the world.[16] The objects of experience, therefore, are not things as they are in themselves, independent of any experiencing subject, the world as it really is, but only things as they appear (to us) – mere 'phenomena' or 'representations'. But while Kant had concluded that 'how things in themselves may be (without regard to representations through which they affect us) is entirely beyond our cognitive sphere',[17] Schopenhauer was convinced that the real, 'inner' or 'intelligible' nature of the world remains unknown only as long as we limit ourselves to an 'objective' (scientific) standpoint and look at things, *even at ourselves*, from the outside. But in addition to that standpoint, we can also adopt a 'subjective' point of view, and, when we do, when we look at ourselves so to speak from the inside, we find something else: *Will*. It is the will, he argues, that accounts for what from the outside

---

[13] WWR; originally published in 1819 and twice revised by Schopenhauer. English translation by E. J. Payne, 2 vols. (Indian Hills, Colo: The Falcon Wing Press, 1958).

[14] 'Rückblick auf meine zwei Leipziger Jahre', in Karl Schlechta, ed., *Werke in Drei Bänden*, vol. III (Munich: Carl Hanser Verlag, 1960), p. 133.

[15] Friedrich Nietzsche, 'Schopenhauer as Educator', in *Untimely Meditations*, trans. R. J. Hollingdale (Cambridge University Press, 1983), p. 133.

[16] A place in space and time makes each thing distinct from every other and causality allows it to interact with every other. The world of experience is subject to the principles of 'individuation' and 'sufficient reason'.

[17] Immanuel Kant, *Critique of Pure Reason*, trans. and ed. Paul Guyer and Allen W. Wood (Cambridge University Press, 1998), A190/B234, pp. 305–6.

looks like mere bodily movement, an inexplicable succession of stimuli and reactions, and makes it intelligible as a series of actions aimed at satisfying our needs and desires. What *appears* as body and movement when seen from without is an 'objectification' of the will which constitutes our inner reality. In our awareness of ourselves as will, then, we have at least one instance of a direct, unmediated interaction with a thing-in-itself.

For various reasons (some better, some worse), Schopenhauer generalised that conclusion to everything in the world – not only human beings but also animals and plants and even, most surprisingly, to inanimate objects. He thought of objects as spaces filled with force and of will as the ultimate metaphysical nature of the world as a whole. Will was for him beyond 'individuation' and 'sufficient reason' – without distinct position in space and time and not subject to the laws of causality. And, most important, it was 'blind': without rhyme or reason, as experience testifies, it is always destroying some of its own parts in order to satisfy the others; the world is finite and if anything is to come into being something else must provide its raw materials.

The will, whether we think of it as nature itself or as it is manifested within each one of us, is eternally dissatisfied, in pain as long as it lacks what it pursues and bored as soon as it obtains it, swinging inexorably between these two sources of suffering – and to no purpose. Schopenhauer's pessimistic conclusion is that nothing in life has a point: all effort is a failure as soon as it succeeds, nothing can affect the world's monstrously indifferent chaos.

Art and beauty, however, can offer a temporary liberation from the will's 'fetters'. Taking the commonplace idea of aesthetic absorption in the most literal terms, Schopenhauer writes that, confronted with a beautiful object, 'we lose ourselves entirely in [it]; in other words, we forget our individuality, our will, and continue to exist only as pure subject, as clear mirror of the object, so that it is as though the object alone existed without anyone to perceive it'.[18] At that point, 'all at once the peace, always sought but always escaping us on the former path of the desires, comes to us of its own accord, and it is well with us. It is the painless state Epicurus prized as the highest good and as the state of the gods.'[19] On a more permanent level, what Schopenhauer called 'salvation' is a cessation

---

[18] WWR, vol. I, p. 178.
[19] Ibid., vol. I, p. 196.

or denial of willing, accomplished, if at all, only through an ascetic life, a constant effort to overcome the very temptation of striving, a realisation that all goals are completely insignificant and that striving itself is never more than a source of new, continuous suffering.

2 *Richard Wagner*

Nietzsche's love of Schopenhauer's philosophy was matched only by his devotion to the controversial music of Richard Wagner (1813–83), whose equally controversial cultural politics became a source of inspiration for the young scholar. The two met in Leipzig in 1868, where Wagner, himself under the thrall of Schopenhauer, invited Nietzsche to visit him at his house in Tribschen, Switzerland – an invitation that marked Nietzsche's life for ever, since Tribchen was close to Basel, where Nietzsche moved in 1869, and his frequent visits led him into a fateful personal and intellectual friendship with the fiery composer.

In large part, Wagner admired Schopenhauer on account of his view of music. Unlike the other arts, which represent the knowable elements of the everyday world (the Ideas), music – which is non-verbal but nevertheless a vehicle of communication, a 'language' in its own right – is an 'immediate ... copy' of reality, that is, the will or the thing-in-itself.[20] Schopenhauer's belief that music (not language) came closest to capturing what the world is really like was a perfect fit with Wagner's contempt for traditional opera, which he accused of subordinating music to language and using it, often deforming it in the process, primarily to illustrate or emphasise the action on the stage. By contrast, Wagner's own music drama (to which denial of the will became a central theme – think of *Tristan and Isolde* or *The Ring of the Nibelung*) made music – the representation of the structure of the will – pre-eminent and used language only to provide its audience with illustrations of the possible objects and activities on which the pure feelings expressed in the music might become focused.

Wagner was convinced that his music drama – artistically genuine, philosophically correct and true to the German 'spirit' – would give its audience a direct experience of the nature of the world, their place within it and the bonds of will which, transcending their individual identity,

---

[20] Ibid., vol. I, p. 257.

tied them together into a single, unified people (*Volk*). His monumental faith in himself aside, though, was it reasonable to imagine that music, or any art, was capable of such a grandiose metaphysical, cultural and social role? Nietzsche, who, having taken on Wagner's aspirations for a rebirth of German culture, asked that question, believed its answer lay in 'the tragic age' of ancient Greece. What the Greeks had accomplished, especially as it was manifested in the great works of Attic tragedy, established that Wagner's dream was possible and provided a model for the regeneration of the decadent culture of modernity.

3 *The Greeks*

In contrast to most of his contemporaries, Nietzsche wanted philology to shed its scholarly carapace and return to its eighteenth-century origins, when, animated by a sense of kinship between modern Germany and ancient Greece, it studied the Greeks in order to show the emerging German nation how to understand its authentic character and forge a new, unified culture. But, in contrast to its great eighteenth-century admirers, Nietzsche refused to find the heart of Greek culture in what Johann Joachim Winckelmann (1717–68) had famously characterised as 'noble simplicity and quiet grandeur' (*edle Einfalt und stille Größe*). His view of the Greeks was immensely more complex.

In the high points of Greek culture Nietzsche found not a seamless harmony but a host of deeply conflicting tendencies – among them, love of freedom going hand-in-hand with an acknowledgement of the necessity of slavery and devotion to the social unit counterpoised by overweening individual ambition – joined and held together in a dynamic unity. Greek culture was for Nietzsche 'artistic' because it incorporated such oppositions into the balanced structure that is characteristic of great works of art and because the creation and appreciation of art was, as he saw it, its most valued endeavour: 'The Greek artist addresses his work not to the individual but to the state; and the education of the state, in its turn, was nothing but the education of all to enjoy the work of art' (7[121]). The pinnacle of Greek art, in turn, was Attic tragedy, in which the two deepest and most radically opposed tendencies of the 'Hellenic soul' – a deeply pessimistic insight into the real nature of life and the world and a joyful desire to live life to the fullest – found their clearest expression and their final reconciliation. In his interpretation of Greek tragedy Nietzsche combined his interest in Schopenhauer's philosophy, his admiration for Wagner's art and politics, and his devotion to the study of Greece into a radical, extraordinarily ambitious programme for the revival of German culture and, more generally, of the culture of modernity as a whole.

III The notes

It is impossible to give a comprehensive survey of the material in this volume here. Instead, I will discuss a few specific issues relevant both to Nietzsche's notes and to his published works in order to indicate the various ways in which each kind of writing can cast light on the other. The notes are divided into three sub-periods, corresponding, roughly, with his writing *The Birth of Tragedy*, the *Untimely Meditations* and *Human, All Too Human*.

1 1867–1872

In his 1886 Preface to a second edition of *The Birth of Tragedy*,[21] Nietzsche insisted his early work had already moved well beyond Schopenhauer's thought despite the fact that it still relied on his terminology. In some respects, he was quite right. He was right, for example, that, while Schopenhauer believed that morality – which depends on identifying with others and sharing their suffering – is one of the highest expressions of what it is to be human, his own 'instinct turned *against* morality at the time [he] wrote this questionable book':[22] morality plays no role either in explaining or in justifying life in *The Birth of Tragedy*. He was also right that Schopenhauer could never have imagined such a thing as 'the metaphysical solace which … we derive from every true tragedy, the solace that in the ground of things, and despite all changing appearances, life is indestructibly mighty and pleasurable'.[23] Schopenhauer's pervasive pessimism was much more closely aligned with what in *The Birth of Tragedy* Nietzsche calls 'the wisdom of Silenus', whose advice to human beings was that 'the very best thing is … not to have been born, not to

---

[21] 'An Attempt at Self-Criticism', in *The Birth of Tragedy*, trans. Ronald Speirs (Cambridge University Press, 1999), pp. 3–12.
[22] Ibid., sec. 5, p. 9.
[23] *The Birth of Tragedy*, sec. 7, p. 39.

be, to be *nothing*. However, the second best thing for you is: to die soon'.[24] Nietzsche, who was unwilling to accept such a nihilistic view, found much to celebrate in the fact that, even if only 'by means of an illusion spread over things, the greedy Will always finds some way of detaining its creatures in life and forcing them to carry on living'.

That illusion is most forcefully illustrated in tragedy. By combining the Greeks' 'Apollonian' love of the ordered world of individual objects with their 'Dionysian' exaltation in a loss of identity through which (as in communal singing or dance) one is merely part of a larger whole, tragedy offered its audience 'the metaphysical solace that eternal life flows on indestructibly beneath the turmoil of appearances'.[25] Contrary to Schopenhauer's claim that art allows us momentary respite from the torture of willing, Nietzsche sees in it a rekindling of the will: it is precisely at the 'moment of supreme danger for the will [that] *art* approaches as a saving sorceress with the power to heal'.[26]

Why does art spread an 'illusion' over that insight? The reason is that, although Nietzsche rejects Schopenhauer's pessimism, the metaphysical picture that underlies his effort to show that 'only as an *aesthetic phenomenon* [are] existence and the world eternally *justified*'[27] is Schopenhauer's through and through. *In reality*, there is only blind will, working without rhyme or reason, manifesting itself in the individuals and cultures that it will itself eventually destroy. Only through the illusion that the will's creatures provide it with a beautiful spectacle can we come to think of ourselves as *both* creatures (represented by the Apollonian hero on the tragic stage) and creator (represented by the Dionysian chorus in the orchestra whose vision the hero is). And only through that illusion can we be seduced into believing that effort, any effort, is worth making in so far as it provides – for us and for 'that original artist of the world' – yet another beautiful spectacle.

At this point, we can see why it is important to take Nietzsche's notes into account. For there is among them a discussion of Schopenhauer, composed in 1867–8, before he had even met Wagner, in which he makes a set of devastating criticisms of Schopenhauer's metaphysics and, in particular, of the notion of the will (pp. 1–8 below). Nietzsche's

---

[24] Ibid., sec. 3, p. 23.
[25] Ibid., sec. 18, p. 85.
[26] Ibid., sec. 7, p. 40.
[27] Ibid., sec. 5, p. 33.

criticisms begin with an objection to the legitimacy of the concept of the 'thing-in-itself' that Schopenhauer had adopted from Kant. He goes on to argue, however, that, even if we were to grant that concept to Schopenhauer, we would still have to ask why he believes he can identify the thing-in-itself with the will. 'The will', Nietzsche writes, 'is created only with the help of a poetic intuition, while his attempted logical proofs can satisfy neither Schopenhauer nor us' (p. 3).[28] Further, even if we allow that the thing-in-itself is the will, it is not at all clear how the will, which is beyond experience and therefore altogether unthinkable (since thinking necessarily presupposes the categories of time, space and causality), can be one, eternal (timeless) and free (not bound by reason).[29] Schopenhauer, Nietzsche argues, attributes these features to the world as will only because the world as representation is multifarious, temporal and subject to causality. But, he continues, the realm of the in-itself is not contrary to but incommensurable with appearance: no opposition is possible between them, and none of these features can apply to it.

Nietzsche finds Schopenhauer's system 'riddled [with] a species of extremely important and hardly avoidable contradictions'. He discusses these contradictions in some detail and concludes that Schopenhauer sometimes, when it suits him, thinks of the will as a transcendent thing-in-itself and sometimes, again, as one object among others. Nietzsche, of course, retained his admiration for Schopenhauer himself and for many of his philosophical ideas. This passage shows, though, that from a very early time Schopenhauer's metaphysical picture was not among them. There are, in fact, indications that *The Birth of Tragedy*, without explicitly announcing it, presents an original development of Schopenhauer's view and not a straightforward application of it. And it is possible to argue that, taking advantage of the ambiguity he had himself noted, Nietzsche interprets the will not as the ultimate reality of the world but as the primary manifestation of that reality, itself lying still further and, in itself, completely unknowable.[30] At the same time, though, it is impossible not to wonder why Nietzsche avoids all criticism of Schopenhauer on this

---

[28] For a sympathetic exposition, and measured criticism, of Schopenhauer's arguments on this and many other issues, see Julian Young, *Schopenhauer* (London: Routledge, 2005), pp. 53–88.
[29] I believe 'reason' here refers to the principle of sufficient reason, i.e., causality, which Schopenhauer believed to be incompatible with freedom.
[30] See the excellent discussion in Henry Staten, *Nietzsche's Voices* (Ithaca, N.Y. Cornell University Press, 1990), pp. 187–216 and James Porter, *The Invention of Dionysus: An Essay on 'The Birth of Tragedy'* (Stanford University Press, 2000), pp. 57–73.

issue and why the work seems almost designed to give the overwhelming impression that it follows faithfully in his footsteps. We might, in fact, begin to suspect that Nietzsche may have made a strategic decision to proceed in a way that would not alienate the work's first and ideal reader – Wagner, to whom the work is dedicated and whose friendship with Nietzsche was cemented on their mutual admiration for the philosopher of metaphysical pessimism.

That Nietzsche's decision was in fact strategic is made more likely by another difference between his notes and the published version of *The Birth of Tragedy*. In a notebook dating from the beginning of 1871, there is a long continuous passage which, although originally intended as part of the book, was not included in the final version.[31] The passage contains several views about Greek culture and culture in general that became progressively more prominent in Nietzsche's writings, but not until well after his break with Wagner – most notably the idea that a genuine culture is impossible without a large labouring class, if not a class of actual slaves. This, however, would have seemed intolerable to Wagner, whose vision of a future German culture excluded every vestige of the *de facto* slavery to which capitalism condemns the largest, wage-earning segment of society – and that could certainly be a reason for Nietzsche's tactfully avoiding the issue in a book dedicated to the realisation of the composer's vision.

Whatever the final answer to these questions, it is clear that we cannot avoid asking them once we take, as I believe we should, Nietzsche's notes into account along with *The Birth of Tragedy*. Taken in conjunction with the published works to which they are related, the notes are indispensable to the interpretation of his philosophy.

2 1872–1876

Nietzsche had hoped *The Birth of Tragedy* would have a direct and profound effect on public discourse regarding the culture of the new German *Reich* but, in the event, the book's reception proved a bitter disappointment. It is true that Wagner and his circle were delighted with it, but their numbers were much too small to satisfy Nietzsche and, in any case,

---

[31] A different version of that passage, with the title 'The Greek State', was (along with 'On the Pathos of Truth', included in this volume) part of Nietzsche's 'Five Prefaces to Five Unwritten Books', a Christmas gift for Cosima, Wagner's wife, in 1872.

their admiration did not remain a source of unequivocal pleasure for long. Wagner himself moved his family to Bayreuth in April 1872 and devoted himself to building a theatre exclusively dedicated – as it still is – to the performance of his works. Nietzsche, to be sure, remained close to him and visited Bayreuth several times, but relations between two men gradually became cooler. In 1876, when Nietzsche arrived for the inauguration of the theatre with the first full performance of *The Ring of the Nibelung*, what he saw, far from a modern equivalent of the ancient dramatic competitions, was just yet another occasion for the display of German bourgeois philistinism – *fast habe ich's bereut* ('I have almost regretted it'), he wrote to his sister, with a characteristic pun on the town's name.[32]

Personally and intellectually, these were difficult years for Nietzsche. By the standards of the next decade (the last of his productive career), which saw the publication of at least fourteen books and various other pieces, this period of his life is relatively barren, although his notes indicate that he contemplated several different works. One was a series of thirteen essays, collectively entitled *Untimely Meditations*, only four of which – his total literary output for these years – appeared. The first was an attack on David Strauss, who had combined a demythologised portrait of Jesus with continued faith in the precepts of Christianity, and on the philistinism Nietzsche took him to represent. The second addressed the contributions of the study of history, positive and negative, to the life and flourishing of society, and the third and fourth were accounts of his views on Schopenhauer and Wagner respectively.

Nietzsche's notes of the time reveal his increasing interest in philosophical problems of metaphysics and epistemology as well as in the history of Greek philosophy. He is concerned with the role of philosophy, both in the ancient world and in his own day, within culture – prompted, perhaps, by his own failure to intervene directly in the cultural politics of Germany. He worries about the connections between philosophy, art, science and religion, and speculates on the origins of the desire for knowledge and truth and its effects on life in general. And while he does not abandon the main themes of his earlier years – Schopenhauer, Wagner and the Greeks – he begins to look at them with new and different eyes. Above all, his notes testify to a preoccupation with his writing style and

---

[32] Nietzsche improved on his joke in later years: 'Typical telegram from Bayreuth: *bereits bereut* [already rued]'; see *The Case of Wagner* (1888), included in *Basic Writings of Nietzsche*, ed. and trans. Walter Kaufmann (New York: Random House, 1968), p. 641.

his determination to acquire a voice of his own and, although his language does not yet achieve its later brilliance, it becomes progressively simpler and more straightforward. His 1886 confession that *The Birth of Tragedy* was marred by being framed in the language of Kant and Schopenhauer[33] is clearly anticipated in a note from just this period: 'Everything must be said as precisely as possible and any technical term, including "will", must be left to one side' (19[46]).

Although morality, which was to become one of Nietzsche's main pre-occupations, plays no explicit role either in *The Birth of Tragedy* or in the *Untimely Meditations*, his notes show that it was already on his mind well before it burst forth in *Human, All Too Human* and the works that follow it. Nietzsche is sometimes positive about it – when, for example, he associates it with Schopenhauer's idea of identifying with the suffering of others or with the Christian ideal of love of the neighbour, which he contrasts to the prudential origins of justice (19[93]; see also 19[63]). Sometimes he thinks of it in terms that anticipate 'the morality of custom', which emerges most clearly in *Daybreak* (1881): 'If we could create custom, a powerful custom! We would then also have morality' (19[39]). More often, though, his interest in morality emerges indirectly, particularly in his many discussions of the practical source of those most theoretical of human desires: the 'drive' for knowledge and the 'pathos' of truth.

Along with the problem of the role of philosophy in antiquity and today, with which it is closely connected, the question of the origins of these drives is probably the most important theme in these notes. It is a theme to which Nietzsche returned again and again. He was convinced that 'our natural science, with its goal of knowledge, drives towards *downfall*' (19[198]) and he contrasted 'σοφία' [wisdom], which 'contains within it that which selects, that which has taste', with science, which, 'lacking such a refined taste, pounces on everything worth knowing' (19[86]).[34] Not quite certain that wisdom gives him the right contrast to knowledge, he tries out various candidates, usually art – 'Absolute knowledge leads to *pessimism*; art is the remedy against it' (19[52]) – or philosophy: 'It is not a question of destroying science, but of *controlling* it. For science in all its goals and methods depends entirely on philosophical views, *although*

---

[33] 'An Attempt at Self-Criticism', sec. 6, p. 10.

[34] 'Science' and 'knowledge' are almost completely interchangeable in such contexts: the German word *Wissenschaft* applies to everything from physics to classics.

it easily forgets this. But the controlling philosophy must also remember the problem of the degree to which science should be allowed to grow: it has to determine value!' (19[24]). His fundamental idea, however, remains unchanged: the unfettered pursuit of knowledge for its own sake, as if everything worth knowing is equally and supremely valuable, leads inevitably to the realisation that knowledge is finally unattainable. The drive to knowledge thus undermines itself and its result is a pessimistic resignation from the pointlessness of life.

Before asking why Nietzsche was tempted by that position, we should note his view that the intellect, the faculty directed at knowledge, is, like all human faculties, primarily

> a means of preserving the individual, [and] unfolds its main powers in dissimulation; for dissimulation is the means by which the weaker, less robust individuals survive, having been denied the ability to fight for their existence with horns or sharp predator teeth. In man this art of dissimulation reaches its peak [so] that there is hardly anything more incomprehensible than how an honest and pure drive from truth could have arisen among them. ('On Truth and Lie in an Extra-Moral Sense', p. 254)

This is one of the earliest expressions of an idea that pervades the thought of Nietzsche's later years. Beginning with *Thus Spoke Zarathustra* and throughout the works that followed it, he launched a vehement attack against the assumption that knowledge of the truth has an unconditional and overriding value. He argued that such a belief could not have been based on experience 'if both truth *and* untruth had constantly made it clear that they were both useful, as they are': 'rather it must have originated *in spite of* the fact that the disutility and dangerousness of "the will to truth" or "truth at any price" is proved ... constantly'.[35] At that time, Nietzsche traced the will to truth to a moral conviction: the principle that deception (even of oneself) is absolutely wrong. That conviction in turn is based on thinking that human beings are radically different from the rest of nature, which depends essentially on deception to accomplish its purposes. Although the essays of the 1870s explicitly reject such a metaphysical picture and insist that we are simply one animal among many, 'On

---

[35] Friedrich Nietzsche, *The Gay Science*, trans. Josefine Nauckoff (Cambridge University Press, 1981), sec. 344, p. 201. Nietzsche expands this discussion in sections 24–7 of the Third Essay of *On the Genealogy of Morality*.

Truth and Lie in an Extra-Moral Sense' locates the origin of the drive for truth and knowledge in our need for social organisation.

The contrast between truth and lie arises because lying, which misuses the valid designations of things, can be harmful to society. That only shows, though, that what we really want to avoid is not the lie, the deception itself, 'but the bad, hostile consequences of certain kinds of deception. Only in a similarly restricted sense does man want the truth. He desires the pleasant, life-preserving consequences of truth; he is indifferent to pure knowledge without consequences, and even hostile to harmful and destructive truths' (p. 255). The origin of the 'pathos' (passion) for truth is therefore profoundly practical: 'Man demands truth and achieves it in moral contacts with others; all social existence is based on this. One anticipates the bad consequences of reciprocal lies. This is the origin of *the duty of truth*' (19[97]).[36] At the same time, though, Nietzsche recognises that telling the truth is not always benign and quotes approvingly Benjamin Constant's statement that: 'The moral principle that it is one's duty to speak the truth, if it were taken singly and unconditionally, would make all society impossible' (29[6]). He seems, that is, to be aware that the obligations society imposes upon us can be no more than partial: both truth and untruth are useful. From where, then, does the pathos of truth derive its claim to absolute authority? Nietzsche answers that question through an examination of the general features of language and representation.

In fact, even those 'valid designations' the rules of language specify as true are in reality radically and completely false – they are all, in the appropriate sense, 'lies'. In reality, we are told in 'On Truth and Lie in an Extra-Moral Sense', it is impossible for any human perception, word or sentence to be faithful to the structure of the world.

First of all, Nietzsche claims, we are never aware of things-in-themselves but only of various stimulations of our nerve-endings, and no inference from the properties of a nerve stimulus, which is internal to us, to the properties of a cause outside us is ever legitimate: the in-itself is not subject to the principle of causality or sufficient reason. Second,

[36] Nietzsche uses the term *moralisch*, 'moral', in a broad sense and applies it indifferently to both moral and prudential interests. He eventually thinks of morality as a much more specific set of rules, values and practices and distinguishes it not only from prudential but also from other ethical institutions. See, for example, the contrast between 'noble' and 'slave' values in the First Essay of *On the Genealogy of Morality*.

he argues, on the basis of a version of Schopenhauer's epistemology, that none of the links in the chain that connects a nerve stimulus to an image (perception) and an image to a sound (word) can be an accurate representation of what gives rise to it. Each imposes 'a complete overleaping of the sphere' to which the previous element belongs: it is nothing but a metaphor, and metaphors 'do not correspond in the slightest to the original entities' they attempt to describe (p. 256).

Things get even worse when we introduce the conceptual aspects of language into the picture: while in reality every experience is 'unique' and 'entirely individualised', a concept, which is meant to apply to whole families of such experiences, 'comes into being through the equation of non-equal things. As certainly as no leaf is ever completely identical to another, so certainly the concept of leaf is formed by arbitrarily shelving these individual differences or forgetting the distinguishing feature' (pp. 256–7). Strictly speaking, then, there is no truth at all – all our representations of the world, sensory, perceptual and conceptual, are in principle inadequate to the reality to which they are supposed to correspond. Why, then, do we value truth as we do? Whence the pathos of truth? Nietzsche answers that it lies in *forgetting*. Above and beyond

> the obligation that society, in order to exist, imposes on us – the obligation to be truthful, i.e. to use customary metaphors ... to lie in accordance with a firm convention ... man forgets that this is his predicament and therefore he lies, in the manner described, unconsciously and according to the habit of hundreds of years – and arrives at a sense of truth precisely *by means of this unconsciousness*, this oblivion. The sense of being obliged to call one thing red, another cold, a third mute, awakens a moral impulse related to truth. (pp. 257–8)

That is, finally, why the unbridled pursuit of knowledge leads to its own 'downfall' (p. xxiv above): we *have forgotten* that the obligations of society are conditional. We have forgotten that both truth (lying according to fixed conventions) and untruth (lying in unusual ways) are useful and, more important, that they are both *lies*, since language is necessarily inadequate to the world. Our overvaluation of truth thus leads us into an indiscriminate pursuit of knowledge and, the more we learn, the closer we come to realising the *actual* truth that the truth is completely inaccessible to us.

Nietzsche's view is deeply flawed, but we can address only two of the difficulties it faces here.[37] The first is with the very idea of forgetting. For if, as Nietzsche acknowledges, society constantly requires both truth-telling and lying, how could we ever have forgotten the usefulness of the lie and attributed all value to truth?[38] The second problem is that his epistemology faces serious difficulties of its own. Very briefly, it is impossible to see how Nietzsche can claim both that 'we believe that we know something about the things themselves ... and yet we possess nothing but metaphors for things which do not correspond in the slightest to the original entities' on the one hand and that 'no leaf is ever completely identical to another' on the other (p. 256). If nothing we say corresponds to the way things are, it is impossible to assert correctly that in reality every leaf (supposing reality contains leaves in the first place) is different from every other. Either language succeeds in describing reality, in which case we can say some true things about it, or it does not, in which case the best we can do is to remain silent. It is not even clear that we can say that our representations can't correspond to the world, because if we knew that we would know *something* about the world – enough, at any rate, to know that we can't possibly represent it: how else could we tell that we can't?

Nietzsche's notes show that he was ambivalent here (e.g., 9[154–63], 29[8]). And that ambivalence, I believe, is why Nietzsche did not publish any of his views on metaphysics and epistemology between 1872 and 1876: he seems to have realised that his extreme epistemic pessimism – the idea that all of our beliefs, from the most abstruse to the most common and banal, are necessarily false – was not a sustainable position; but he also seems to have been unable to see his way to formulating a reasonable alternative to it.

What he published, instead, were four essays that he hoped would give him the public voice he had failed to develop through *The Birth of Tragedy* – three, as we have seen, on specific individuals and one on the way in which the study of history can be put to the service of 'life'.

---

[37] For a detailed examination of the theoretical claims of 'On Truth and Lie in an Extra-Moral Sense', several of their difficulties and Nietzsche's leaving both behind, see Maudemarie Clark, *Nietzsche on Truth and Philosophy* (Cambridge University Press, 1990), chapters 3 and 4.

[38] Ironically, in *On the Genealogy of Morality* Nietzsche dismisses the 'unhistorical' thinking of 'the English psychologists' who argue that the original sense of the concept 'good' – 'unegoistic' – was gradually forgotten with the question: 'How was such forgetting possible? Did the usefulness of such behaviour suddenly cease at some point?' (I. 2–3, pp. 12–13).

By 'life', Nietzsche mainly meant the cultural life of Germany, whose self-satisfaction with its victory in the Franco-Prussian war he considered 'capable of turning our victory into a defeat: *into the defeat, if not the extirpation, of the German spirit for the benefit of the "German Reich"*.[39] In 'On the Uses and Disadvantages of History for Life' he addresses one of the dangers he saw threatening the 'German spirit': an excessive concern with the past, which, under the delusion that history can be studied scientifically and 'without restraint, … uproots the future because it destroys illusions and robs the things that exist of the atmosphere in which alone they can live'.[40] That idea, in turn, bears a complex and illuminating relationship to the notes of this period.

The essay distinguishes three ways of approaching history. *Monumental* history inspires us to 'act and strive' by showing that since greatness was possible in the past it may also be possible in the present; *antiquarian* history shows the worth of the present by tracing it to a past that is perceived with love and loyalty; *critical* history allows us to move beyond our past by 'condemning' various of its parts and loosening their claim to persist: some things – privileges, castes, dynasties – really do deserve to perish. Each makes its own contribution to life but all depend, once again, on a crucial forgetting. A past event appears exemplary and worthy of imitation only by means of forgetting that no effect can be separated from its causes and by wrenching a particular occurrence from a web of relations apart from which it is really unthinkable.[41] One's past appears unique and pre-eminently valuable only as a result of forgetting anything that did not directly contribute to it, by an extreme narrowing of vision that relates the past to nothing else, gives every one of its parts equal value and finally identifies value with antiquity and rejects anything new and evolving.

---

[39] This comes from section 1 of 'David Strauss, the Confessor and the Writer,' the first of the *Untimely Meditations*, p. 3. Nietzsche has clearly moderated his early hopes for the future of the *Reich*.

[40] 'On the Uses and Disadvantages of History for Life', *Untimely Meditations*, sec. 7, p. 95.

[41] Nietzsche insists that 'that which was once possible could present itself as a possibility for a second time only if the Pythagoreans were right in believing that when the constellation of the heavenly bodies is repeated, the same things, down to the smallest event, must also be repeated on earth … but that will no doubt happen only when the astronomers have again become astrologers … [whereas] the truly historical connexus of cause and effect … fully understood, would only demonstrate that the dice-game of chance and the future could never again produce anything exactly similar to what it produced in the past' (ibid., p. 70). That is bound to cast doubt on the popular interpretation of the idea of the 'eternal recurrence', which appears in sec. 341 of *The Gay Science* and in several of Nietzsche's late works, as a theory that declares precisely the sort of repetition that is said to be impossible here to be a necessary natural phenomenon.

The passions, errors and crimes of the past, such as they are, can be condemned only by forgetting that we too are ourselves their outcome and that all the condemning in the world cannot alter the fact that we originate in them and that they are part of what makes us what we are.

History served life in the past only because of such forgetting. But the present is different: the 'constellation of life and history' has been disturbed by 'a mighty, hostile ... gleaming and glorious star' – '*by science, by the demand that history should be a science*' (p. 77). By 'science', Nietzsche understands a particular attitude toward our knowledge of the world, not a particular method of investigation for whose indiscriminateness he feels contempt – 'The drive for knowledge *without choice* is on a par with the indiscriminate sex drive – a sign of *coarseness*!' (19[11]) – and about whose outcome he is deeply pessimistic:

> Historical verification always brings to light so much that is false, crude, inhuman, absurd, violent that the mood of pious illusion in which alone anything that wants to live can live necessarily crumbles away: for it is only in love, only when shaded by the illusion produced by love, that man is creative. (p. 95)

Love, which makes one's own deeds seem more beautiful and greater than they are, is contrasted with justice, which accords each thing the attention it deserves: 'he who acts loves his deed infinitely more than it deserves to be loved' (p. 64).[42] Love, too, requires precisely the narrowing of horizon that allows history to serve life, 'an enveloping illusion' that gives its object pride of place in the world and makes it worth pursuing. That illusion is what science refuses to respect and, in its relentless pursuit of the truth, will reveal for what it is.

Knowledge, so to speak, levels the field. Since it reveals nothing that inspires love and attracts our energy and attention to the exclusion of other things, it leaves us listless, unable to make the choices necessary for forging a path to a new future. It forbids us to forget the injustice of love (one illusion) and disowns both art and religion, which 'bestow upon existence the character of the eternal and the stable' (another). Action, though, is impossible without such illusions; to maintain them we must 'restrain' the pathological growth of the historical sense a scientific approach to history brings in its wake (p. 120).

---

[42] For a contrast between love and justice along a different axis, see 19[93].

How can the historical sense be restrained? The essay itself offers no unequivocal answer, but Nietzsche's notebooks are clear on the direction of his thought:

> If we are ever to achieve a culture, tremendous artistic forces are needed in order to break the boundless drive for knowledge and once more to create a unity. *The supreme dignity of the philosopher manifests itself here, where he concentrates the boundless drive for knowledge and restrains it into a unity.* This is how the ancient Greek philosophers [who lived in the most artistic of cultures] must be understood: they restrain the drive for knowledge. (19[27]; see also 19[24])

Nietzsche sets philosophy 'against the dogmatism of the sciences ... but only in the service of a culture' (23[7]). Culture is the unified and therefore mutually balanced and restrained expression of the drives of a people (19[42]) and it is perhaps the highest task of philosophy to bring such a unity about.

Philosophy is connected both with science, since both depend on a conceptual representation of the world, and with art, because the purpose of both is to articulate what 'greatness' is and to promote it at the expense of everything else. A sense that what matters is not only truth but 'greatness' as well '*restrains* the drive for knowledge' (19[83]) because it forces us to omit, overlook and ignore: 'it has not the same interest in everything perceived' and directs the drive to truth toward what matters (19[67]; cf. 19[33]). Nietzsche is aware of difficulties here. He confesses to a '[g]reat uncertainty as to whether philosophy is an art or a science' (19[62]) and doubts whether, like art, philosophy can create a culture on its own: '[The philosopher] *cannot create a culture*, but he can prepare it, remove impediments, or moderate and thereby preserve it, or destroy it. (Always exclusively by negation)' (28[2]; cf. 23[14]). Not today, he seems to think: 'For us it is no longer possible to produce a succession of philosophers such as Greece did in the age of tragedy. Their task is now performed *by art alone*' (19[36]). Can philosophy, then, reclaim its ancient status and, if so, how can it find a place next to art and religion?[43]

That he had no answer to that question may be why 'On the Uses and Disadvantages of History for Life' leaves the mechanism that turns

---

[43] Nietzsche's notes are important in showing that his attitude toward religion during this period was much more positive than one would expect from a reading of his later work.

history into art relatively obscure. The problem would have been even more pressing when Nietzsche began to work on 'Schopenhauer as Educator' since it might cast doubt on Schopenhauer's own accomplishment and on the claim of the philosopher to join saint and artist in Schopenhauer's pantheon.

Nietzsche resolved that difficulty through a brilliant application of a theme he had introduced both in his notes and in the essay on history. He now located the aim and justification of a genuine culture in the creation of great individuals: 'the *goal of humanity* cannot lie in its end but only *in its highest exemplars*'.[44] Philosophers are among such exemplars because their creative work is not exhausted by their ideas: it includes, crucially, the application of their ideas to life, the demonstration that one can forge a new way of living on the basis of those ideas. But Nietzsche realised that to follow such exemplars could not possibly be to become their disciple: each constellation of views answers to the circumstances, the needs and aspirations of the person who produced it. What exemplary 'educators' can offer to others is a life and accomplishments that, idiosyncratic and unrepeatable as they may be, can be understood as an instance of 'the universal life' which it is everyone's fate – whatever the differences between our specific situations – to live. In his late works, of course, Nietzsche repudiated all claims to universality, which he came to consider pathological,[45] but the present view is not without advantages. It gives philosophy a place next to art because it construes the philosophers' lives and examples as their creative works (see 29[205]). It explains why philosophers can disagree so radically with one another and yet function as exemplars, since each philosophical vision is tied to its creator's own 'want', 'misery' and 'limitedness'.[46] And it allows Nietzsche to proclaim his indebtedness to Schopenhauer at the same time that, on account of such differences, he can also declare himself independent from him. No

---

[44] 'On the Use and Disadvantages of History for Life', p. III; cf. 19[38].

[45] Compare this passage, along with the earlier and more absolutist 'The single outstanding moral man exercises a magic that causes others to imitate him. The philosopher must spread this magic. What is law for the highest specimen must gradually become the law as such: if only as a barrier for the others' (19[113], with section 43 of *Beyond Good and Evil*: the pride and the taste of the 'philosophers of the future' would be offended 'if their truth were a truth for everyone (which has been the secret wish and hidden meaning of all dogmatic aspirations so far)' – Nietzsche's own included. Friedrich Nietzsche, *Beyond Good and Evil*, trans. Judith Norman (Cambridge University Press, 2002).

[46] 'Schopenhauer as Educator', p. 142.

wonder that, many years later, he claimed that the essay 'registers my innermost history, my becoming'.[47]

This discussion has not touched either on Nietzsche's extensive comments on Socrates, which are much more ambivalent than his attack in *The Birth of Tragedy*, or on his treatment of early Greek philosophy, which he admired intensely. We merely mentioned his growing disillusion with Wagner, which made him doubt for a while whether he should publish his essay on the composer's significance and accomplishment. And we ignored a host of other important themes and questions. It is time, though, to take a quick look at the material that dates from the years when Nietzsche was writing *Human, All Too Human*, a work in which he truly found his own voice and articulated a radically new and original set of philosophical ideas.

3 *1876–1879*

Nietzsche's life was in upheaval. His academic career was in a shambles. His health, which had been precarious to begin with, had been further weakened while he served as a medical orderly in the Franco-Prussian war, making everyday life – not to mention writing and meeting his professional obligations – almost impossibly painful. The world around him was brimming with optimism – about the *Reich*, the scientific revolution, technological progress, the successes of capitalism and, variously, both liberalism and imperialism. By contrast, he was convinced that Europe was blissfully unaware of the disastrous collapse, with the erosion of religion during the Enlightenment, of the only authority on which its faith (illusory as it may have been) in the absolute validity of the values that sustained it could be based. But, disillusioned with Wagner and emancipated from Schopenhauer, he was left without a model (illusory as *that* might have been) for an alternative cultural and philosophical project of his own, while his rather vague appeals to 'German youth' in the *Untimely Meditations* had gone, once again, completely unheeded.

It was time to change tack: 'To readers of my writings I want to declare unequivocally that I have abandoned the metaphysico-artistic views that essentially dominate those writings: they are pleasant but untenable. If

---

[47] *Ecce Homo*, trans. Judith Norman in *Friedrich Nietzsche: The Anti-Christ, Ecce Homo, Twilight of the Idols and Other Writings* (Cambridge University Press, 2005), 'The Untimely Ones', sec. 3, p. 115.

one takes the liberty of speaking in public early one is usually obliged to contradict oneself in public soon after' (23b[159]).[48] *Human, All Too Human*, which appeared in 1878, was the record of his first effort to think through his problems without Wagner, Schopenhauer or, to a considerable extent, the Greeks. It represents a radical turn away from looking for comfort in art and metaphysics and a new respect for science and 'the little unpretentious truths which have been discovered by means of rigorous method ... [rather] than the errors handed down by metaphysical and artistic ages and men, which bind us and make us happy'.[49] It proposes to show that both the origins and the consequences of our most hallowed and spiritual aspirations and accomplishments are firmly anchored in the natural world of physics and biology and that instead of having an otherworldly significance they are simply human, all too human.

At the same time, Nietzsche's writing style undergoes an utterly drastic change. The continuous prose of his earlier works gives way to a series of aphoristic passages, ranging from a single line to a few paragraphs, each relatively self-contained, as economical in expression as they are lavish in implication. This style, on which Nietzsche was to depend in most of what he wrote from now on, allows him to look at everything he approaches from many different points of view and gives his thought, despite the confidence of each individual statement, a diverse, multifarious quality that has often been mistaken for inconsistency.

The change in both style and substance is immediately evident in the first notebook from this period, compiled almost immediately following the completion of *Wagner in Bayreuth*. In 1871, Nietzsche had credited the greatest accomplishment of art to 'individuals' who 'are driven ahead ... into that devouring brightness – to return with a transfigured look in their eyes, as a triumph of the Dionysian will which, through a wonderful delusion, bends back and breaks even the existence-denying last barb of its knowledge, the strongest spear directed against existence itself' (7[123]). Now he writes, 'The artist needs the infidelity of memory in order not to copy but to transform nature' (17[32]). The sharp distinction between appearance and reality, the essential conflict between art and science, the necessity of a metaphysical illusion – all that is gone. In

---

[48] I use the letter 'b' to distinguish the notebook in question, included in vol. 8 of KSA, from a notebook that bears the same number in vol. 7.

[49] Friedrich Nietzsche, *Human, All Too Human: A Book for Free Spirits*, *trans.* R. J. Hollingdale (Cambridge University Press, 1996), sec. 3, p. 13.

their place, forgetting, itself shorn of metaphysical garb, provides a natural mechanism for art's transfiguration of the only world we all inhabit.
Forgetting has already become for Nietzsche 'not just a *vis inertiae*, as
superficial people suppose, but ... rather an active ability to suppress,
positive in the strongest sense of the word', to which, he will later claim,
we owe not only art but even happiness, cheerfulness, hope and pride.[50]

Metaphysics, the belief in a world behind every *possible* appearance,
a stable domain of the in-itself in which human beings alone, among
all natural creatures, have an uneasy share, is now interpreted simply as a response to the human need 'to prefer *any explanation* to none'
(19b[107]). But need, Nietzsche writes, 'proves nothing about any reality
corresponding to that need'; however necessary it has become, a belief
may still be false. But – we find here perhaps for the first time an idea
that became central to his thought – to refute a belief created by a need is
not to abolish the need: 'By overthrowing a *belief* one does not overthrow
the *consequences* that have grown out of it' (19b[97]). To show that there
is no metaphysical world (or that, even if there is, it is irrelevant to us)[51] it
is not enough to dislodge our faith that the authority of our deepest views
and values is absolute, as if it did in fact derive from a world beyond the
continual change that deprives the world of phenomena of anything universal or absolute.

Life is partial and limited; it lacks objectivity: 'Love and hate are cataractic and one-eyed, likewise the "will"' (21[40]). But objectivity, the
ideal of impartial knowledge, cannot sustain life. It is incapable of providing it with the preferences and values without which it is unthinkable:
'No *ethics* [a way to live] can be based on pure knowledge of things: for
that purpose one must be like nature, neither good nor evil' (17[100]). But
although we cannot possibly be like nature, we are still natural beings.[52]
What has allowed us to separate ourselves from the rest of nature so far is
religion and metaphysics: 'How would men look without all these sublime

[50] *On the Genealogy of Morality*, II. 1, p. 38.
[51] *Human, All Too Human*, sec. 9.
[52] It is clear that Nietzsche is trying out various paths here: 23[9], for example, proposes a reduc-
tionist view – often wrongly identified with 'naturalism' – to the effect that all that happens bio-
logically 'is determined by chemical laws just as a waterfall is determined by mechanical laws',
while the notion of 'drive' applies only when psychological phenomena 'have not yet been traced
to their chemical and mechanical laws'. But see *Beyond Good and Evil*, sec. 9, for an indication
of his attitude toward that proposal, as well as the opening section of *Human, All Too Human*,
which shows how broadly he understands the idea of 'chemistry'.

errors – I believe, *like animals.*' But what of it? Depending, of course, on the kind of animal involved, 'the *truth* and *animals* get on well together' (23b[21]).

Metaphysics, then, is essentially a collection of errors, but error – everyday, literal error, not the grand illusions with which Nietzsche had been occupied so far – can have the most beneficial results: 'If men had not built houses for gods architecture would still be in its infancy. The tasks man set himself on the basis of false assumptions (e.g. the soul separable from the body) have given rise to the highest forms of culture. "Truths" [he continues, problematically] are unable to supply such motives' (23b[167]). The question, for whose answer Nietzsche was to search for the rest of his life, is how to eliminate the need that gave rise to particular errors yet preserve the useful consequences many of them may have had.

Perhaps we should think of *The Birth of Tragedy* itself as a great work that is based on the most erroneous views. Nietzsche, however, was not so charitable and he focused on its errors more than its greatness. One such error, he makes it very clear, was his overvaluation of tragedy and drama in general: 'Dramatists are *constructive* geniuses, not original finders like epic poets. *Drama* is *lower* than the epic – coarser audience – democratic' (27[19]). And along with his rejection of drama comes his final renunciation of Wagner, whom he now demotes – rather cruelly, perhaps – from 'musician' (or, in Wagner's own terms, 'dramatist of reality' – a dramatist whose raw material is music and whose subject is the world beyond appearance) to 'dramatist' (someone who, in the end, is only capable of representing everyday reality without discerning the fissures through which different alternatives to it appear possible): 'His soul does not *sing*, it *speaks*, but it speaks as the supreme passion does. What is *natural* to him is the tone, the rhythm, the gestures of the spoken language; the music, on the other hand, is never quite natural, but a kind of *learnt* language with a modest stock of words and a *different* syntax' (27[47]).[53]

He describes *Human, All Too Human* as an 'atonement' for *The Birth of Tragedy*, which he suspects, to the extent that it had an influence on Wagner, of having caused him 'some harm'! 'I regret this very much,' he concludes (30[56]). He criticises *The Birth of Tragedy* for the view that the world has an 'author' (30[51]) or an 'artist-creator' (30[68]) who

---

[53] It is important to contrast this note with Nietzsche's earlier views in 12[1]; see also 29b[15], where he claims that both tragedy and comedy supply a 'caricature, not an image, of life'.

provides it with an aesthetic justification, and he even expresses considerable scepticism regarding his understanding of Greek philosophy: was
it perhaps due simply to 'the ears of a man in great need of art' (30[52])?
His self-criticism is relentless and sweeping, clearing the ground for the
immense project he is beginning to set for himself and which he will pursue until the end of his life: how to find a way to live and thrive in a world
that provides no absolute foundation for value, imposes no requirements
and offers no pre-established paths for anyone to follow.

Nietzsche was engaged in this radical revaluation of his own values while,
having resigned his professorship, he was also preparing himself for a solitary,
nomadic life with minimal resources, and his notes testify to that as well:

> I conclude: *Restricting* our *needs*. With regard to these (e.g. our food,
> clothing, shelter, heating, climate etc.) we must *all* make sure that we
> become *experts. Building our lives on as many or as few foundations
> as we can adequately judge* – that is how we promote general mor-
> ality, i.e. we force every craftsman to treat us *honestly* because we
> are *experts.* If we do not want to become experts in any one need we
> must *deny* that need to ourselves: this is the new morality. (40[3])

This is all very serious business, as Nietzsche was always ready to
remind his readers. But he also expected more from them than just earnest
agreement since nothing, including seriousness, is ever good or bad in itself
(23b[152]). As we follow him through his notes' labyrinthine paths and
leave him just as they have led him to the threshold of his greatest accomplishments, we can do no better than keep with us, as our own version of
Ariadne's thread, the world of the very last note included in this volume:

> Shame on this lofty semi-idiotic seriousness! Are there no little lines
> around your eyes? Can't you lift a thought on your fingertips and
> flick it up in the air? Does your mouth have only this one pinched,
> morose expression? Do your shoulders never shake with laughter? I
> wish you would once in a while whistle and behave as if you were in
> bad company, instead of sitting together with your author in such a
> respectable and unbearably demure way. (47[7])[54]

Alexander Nehamas

[54] I gratefully acknowledge Raymond Geuss' comments and suggestions on an earlier version of
this Introduction.

Chronology

1844   Born in Röcken, a small village in the Prussian province of Saxony, on 15 October.

1846   Birth of his sister Elisabeth.

1848   Birth of his brother Joseph.

1849   His father, a Lutheran minister, dies at age thirty-six of 'softening of the brain'.

1850   Brother dies; family moves to Naumburg to live with father's mother and her sisters.

1858   Begins studies at Pforta, Germany's most famous school for education in the classics.

1864   Graduates from Pforta with a thesis in Latin on the Greek poet Theognis; enters the University of Bonn as a theology student.

1865   Transfers from Bonn, following the classical philologist Friedrich Ritschl to Leipzig where he registers as a philology student; reads Schopenhauer's *The World as Will and Representation*.

1866   Reads Friedrich Lange's *History of Materialism*.

1868   Meets Richard Wagner.

1869   On Ritschl's recommendation is appointed professor of classical philology at Basel at the age of twenty-four before completing his doctorate (which is then conferred without a dissertation); begins frequent visits to the Wagner residence at Tribschen.

1870   Serves as a medical orderly in the Franco-Prussian war; contracts a serious illness and so serves only two months. Writes 'The Dionysiac World View'.

1872   Publishes his first book, *The Birth of Tragedy*; its dedicatory preface to Richard Wagner claims for art the role of 'the highest task and truly metaphysical activity of his life'; devastating reviews follow.

1873 Publishes 'David Strauss, the Confessor and the Writer', the first of his *Untimely Meditations*; begins taking books on natural science out of the Basel library, whereas he had previously confined himself largely to books on philological matters. Writes 'On Truth and Lying in a Non-Moral Sense'.

1874 Publishes two more *Meditations*, 'The Uses and Disadvantages of History for Life' and 'Schopenhauer as Educator'.

1876 Publishes the fourth *Meditation*, 'Richard Wagner in Bayreuth', which already bears subtle signs of his movement away from Wagner.

1878 Publishers *Human, All Too Human* (dedicated to the memory of Voltaire); it praises science over art as the high culture and thus marks a decisive turn away from Wagner.

1879 Terrible health problems force him to resign his chair at Basel (with a small pension); publishes 'Assorted Opinions and Maxims', the first part of vol. II of *Human, All Too Human*; begins living alone in Swiss and Italian boarding-houses.

1880 Publishes 'The Wanderer and His Shadow', which becomes the second part of vol. II of *Human, All Too Human*.

1881 Publishes *Daybreak*.

1882 Publishes *Idylls of Messina* (eight poems) in a monthly magazine; publishes *The Gay Science* (first edition); friendship with Paul Ree and Lou Andreas-Salomé ends badly, leaving Nietzsche devastated.

1883 Publishes the first two parts of *Thus Spoke Zarathustra*; learns of Wagner's death just after mailing part one to the publisher.

1884 Publishes the third part of *Thus Spoke Zarathustra*.

1885 Publishes the fourth part of *Zarathustra* for private circulation only.

1886 Publishes *Beyond Good and Evil*; writes prefaces for new releases of: *The Birth of Tragedy*, *Human, All Too Human* vols. I and II, and *Daybreak*.

1887 Publishes expanded edition of *The Gay Science* with a new preface, a fifth book, and an appendix of poems; publishes *Hymn to Life*, a musical work for chorus and orchestra; publishes *On the Genealogy of Morality*.

1888   Publishes *The Case of Wagner*, composes a collection of poems, *Dionysian Dithyrambs*, and four short books: *Twilight of Idols*, *The Antichrist*, *Ecce Homo*, and *Nietzsche contra Wagner*.

1889   Collapses physically and mentally in Turin on 3 January; writes a few lucid notes but never recovers sanity; is briefly institutionalised; spends remainder of his life as an invalid, living with his mother and then his sister, who also gains control of his literary estate.

1900   Dies in Weimar on 25 August.

Further reading

The notes contained in this volume date from the years 1869–79, and the best complement to them are the three major works which Nietzsche published during that period. These works, *Human, All Too Human*, ed. R. J. Hollingdale and Richard Schacht (Cambridge University Press, 1996), *Untimely Meditations*, ed. Daniel Breazeale (Cambridge University Press, 1997), and *The Birth of Tragedy*, ed. Raymond Geuss and Ronald Speirs (Cambridge University Press, 1999), often throw light on the notes, just as the notes throw light on the published work. Some further relevant material that was written by Nietzsche during this period, but not published during his lifetime, is contained in *Nietzsche on Rhetoric and Language*, ed. Sander Gilman, Carole Blair and David Parent (Oxford University Press, 1989).

The standard biography of Nietzsche is in German in three volumes: Curt Paul Janz, *Friedrich Nietzsche: Biographie* (Munich: Hanser Verlag, 1978). Useful one-volume biographies in English include R. J. Hollingdale, *Nietzsche: The Man and his Philosophy*, 2nd edn (Cambridge University Press, 1999), Ronald Hayman, *Nietzsche: A Critical Life* (Oxford University Press, 1980) and Rüdiger Safranski, *Nietzsche: A Philosophical Biography*, trans. Shelley Frisch (London: Granta, 2002). Nietzsche was a strikingly vivid and informative letter-writer and there exist two, not completely overlapping, collections of translations of his letters which can usefully be consulted: *Nietzsche: A Self-Portrait from His Letters* (Cambridge, Mass.: Harvard University Press, 1971), edited by Peter Fuss and Henry Shapiro, and *Selected Letters of Friedrich Nietzsche* (University of Chicago Press, 1969), edited by the poet Christopher Middleton.

Much of Nietzsche's early thinking is informed by his reading of Schopenhauer, whose major work *The World as Will and Representation* is available in a paperback edition in two volumes, translated by Ernest Payne (New York: Dover Publications, 1969). Schopenhauer's two volumes of essays, *Parerga and Paralipomena*, trans. Ernest Payne (Oxford University Press, 1974), was also one of the young Nietzsche's favourite books.

The secondary literature on Nietzsche is so extensive as to be unsurveyable, and the following is no more than a brief indication of some works that are especially suitable for beginning students, with the emphasis on works available in English. The best short, general introduction to Nietzsche's thought is Michael Tanner's *Nietzsche* (Oxford University Press, 1994), or, in German, Volker Gerhardt's *Friedrich Nietzsche* (Munich: Beck, 1992). Karl Löwith gives a good account of Nietzsche's place in the history of philosophy in his *From Hegel to Nietzsche*, trans. David Green (Chicago: Holt, 1984), and Erich Heller's *The Importance of Nietzsche* (University of Chicago Press, 1988) is excellent on Nietzsche's general cultural significance. Three books on Nietzsche's philosophy as a whole that can be strongly recommended are Gilles Deleuze, *Nietzsche and Philosophy*, trans. Hugh Tomlinson (New York: Columbia University Press, 1982), Alexander Nehamas, *Nietzsche: Life as Literature* (Cambridge, Mass.: Harvard University Press, 1985), and Henry Staten, *Nietzsche's Voices* (Ithaca, N.Y.: Cornell University Press, 1990). For more specialised work on Nietzsche's early views about philology and the study of the ancient world, see James Porter's *Nietzsche and the Philology of the Future* (Stanford University Press, 2000). For those who read German, Hubert Cancik's *Nietzsches Antike* (Stuttgart: Metzler, 1995) is required reading. Sarah Kofmann's *Nietzsche and Metaphor*, trans. Duncan Large (London: Athlone Press, 1993) treats Nietzsche's views on language and epistemology. Kenneth Gemes gives an excellent analysis of Nietzsche's views about truth in his essay 'Nietzsche's Critique of Truth', now reprinted in Brian Leiter and John Richardson (eds.), *Nietzsche* (Oxford University Press, 2001). For Nietzsche's relation to Wagner, see the chapter by Dieter Borchmeyer, 'Wagner and Nietzsche', in Ulrich Müller and Peter Wapnewski (eds.), *The Wagner Handbook*, trans. John Deathridge (Cambridge, Mass.: Harvard University Press, 1992). For Nietzsche's relation to Schopenhauer, see Chris Janaway (ed.),

Willing and Nothingness: Schopenhauer as Nietzsche's Educator (Oxford University Press, 1988). Finally, *The Cambridge Companion to Nietzsche*, edited by Bernd Magnus and Kathleen Higgins (Cambridge University Press, 1996), contains much that is of relevance to anyone with an interest in studying Nietzsche.

Note on the texts

Friedrich Nietzsche left a very extensive corpus of unpublished written material, much of it in the form of handwritten entries into various note-books. During any given period of time Nietzsche commonly had more than one project on the go, and used and re-used a variety of notebooks. In the 1930s the editor Joachim Mette assigned signature numbers to these notebooks (and to various folders containing loose sheets of paper on which Nietzsche wrote notes) and these have established themselves as the standard form of reference. Mette also tried to establish a crude dating of the notebooks and folders. In the 1960s two Italian scholars, Giorgio Colli and Mazzino Montinari, undertook a full study of all the existing material and published a new *Kritische Gesamtausgabe: Werke* (abbreviated KGW) of Nietzsche's published and unpublished writings (Berlin: de Gruyter, 1967ff.). This is now the standard scholarly edition. In 1980 Colli and Montinari published a paperback edition of all the published philosophical works and a large chunk of the philosophically relevant unpublished notes; this is known as the *Kritische Studien-Ausgabe* (KSA), and gives all texts in the authoritative form established in KGW. Our edition is translated from the KSA.

The texts published here seem to have been written between 1868 and 1879. In autumn 1869, at the age of twenty-four, Nietzsche took up an appointment as professor of classical philology at the University of Basel and threw himself into a very taxing schedule of teaching, public lecturing and research. He held this position for ten years, before retiring on grounds of ill health to re-commence life as a peripatetic *rentier* in a variety of hotels and *pensioni* in Switzerland, Italy and Southern France. During his time as professor in Basel Nietzsche wrote and published one of his most abidingly influential works, *The Birth of Tragedy*, the four long essays known collectively as *Untimely Meditations*, and, at the very end (1878), the first part of his *Human, All Too Human*. The Basel period, thus, has a certain coherence, and with one exception – the fragment 'On Schopenhauer' which opens this selection, which is slightly earlier (1867/8) but has been included because of its philosophical significance – the material in this volume arose while Nietzsche was actively engaged in the teaching of classics, and this context has left a deep imprint on the texts.

Two of the texts from this period that are included in this volume ('On the Pathos of Truth' and 'On Truth and Lie') have a slightly different status from the others. Although they were not published during Nietzsche's lifetime, he did have them copied out in fair hand and circulated privately. They are printed here at the end of the volume.

The notebooks (and folders) Nietzsche kept during the period from 1869 to 1879 are contained in volumes 7 and 8 of KSA, and this serves as the basis for the present edition. Volumes 7 and 8 of KSA comprise about 1500 pages, whereas the selection given here amounts to no more than 250 pages, i.e., about one sixth of the whole. The text for 'Pathos of Truth' and 'Truth and Lie' is taken from KSA volume 1. The text used as the basis of the translation of 'On Schopenhauer' is taken from *Friedrich Nietzsche: Werke und Briefe, Historisch-kritische Gesamtausgabe*, ed. Hans Joachim Mette and Karl Schlechta (Munich: Beck, 1933ff.): *Werke*, vol. 3: *Schriften aus der Studenten- und Militärzeit 1864–8*, pp. 352–61. This edition was abandoned when war broke out and remains incomplete, but contains some material, including 'On Schopenhauer', which is not available in the Colli-Montinari edition.

In 1979 the distinguished scholar Daniel Breazeale published a selection of Nietzsche's notebooks from the early 1870s with a helpful Introduction and a set of notes under the title *Philosophy and Truth: Selections from Nietzsche's Notebooks of the Early 1870s*; this volume was reprinted in paperback in 1990 by Humanities Press. Breazeale's edition has been out of print for many years now, but it differs in a number of ways from the volume presented here. First of all, *Philosophy and Truth* appeared before the publication of the relevant volumes of the now authoritative text established by Colli and Montinari, which forms the basis of this translation. Second, while this edition contains almost everything in the 150 pages of material by Nietzsche that Breazeale included in his version, it also contains a generous selection of further material from the early 1870s, and extends coverage to include a selection of the notebooks from the late 1870s.

In preparing the notes use has been made of the excellent annotation in Colli and Montinari's KSA, the notes in Breazeale's edition (for those portions of this text that are included in his edition), and the commentary by Barbara von Reibniz on BT, *Ein Kommentar zu Friedrich Nietzsche, "Die Geburt der Tragödie aus dem Geiste der Musik" (Kapitel 1–12)* (Stuttgart: Metzler, 1992), which contains a wealth of information on Nietzsche and antiquity.

The English quotations from Schopenhauer are adapted from *The World as Will and Idea*, trans. R. B. Haldane and J. Kemp, 4 vols (London: Routledge, 1883), *The World as Will and Representation*, trans. E. F. J. Payne (New York: Dover, 1969), and *Parerga and Paralipomena*, trans. E. F. J. Payne (Oxford: Clarendon Press, 1974).

Note on the translation

Most of Nietzsche's texts in this volume are rough notes, occasional jottings, concise *aide-mémoires*, brief sketches of ideas, or clipped aphoristic statements. Apart from a handful of more prolonged reflections, he seems to have written them down rapidly and carelessly, probably with the intention of developing them further at some other time. Their obscurities and ambiguities, jarring associations of words and images, disjointed grammatical structures and abrupt conclusions give them a harsh, jagged quality, which I tried to reproduce as accurately as possible, resisting the temptation to produce a more polished and graceful version. This may be the main difference between my translations and Daniel Breazeale's elegant renderings,[55] which cover the same ground in many cases.

In accordance with Nietzsche's central themes, certain key words recur on numerous occasions. Some of these adhere more or less directly to established philosophical terminology, while others carry meanings specific to Nietzsche's own thought. In both cases they frequently lack precise English equivalents. They may have wider semantic fields, which can be covered as a whole only by a variety of English words, or they may correspond to one of several meanings of a single English word, which will therefore serve to translate a number of different German words corresponding to its other meanings.

Three examples may stand for all those cases where I believe Nietzsche uses established philosophical vocabulary. For *Erkenntnis* I chose the standard epistemological term 'knowledge', even though it lacks the sense

[55] *Philosophy and Truth: Selections from Nietzsche's Notebooks of the Early 1870's*, ed. and trans. Daniel Breazeale (Amherst: Humanity Books, 1999).

of a dynamic process suggested by the German. Similarly, I followed current philosophical practice in translating *Vorstellung* as 'representation', regardless of the strong case that could be made for 'image' or 'idea'. The same applies to *Anschauung*, which in everyday language means 'view' or 'outlook', but which I rendered by the more specialised philosophical alternative 'intuition'.

The need for more than one English word to translate a German word with a range of different meanings may be demonstrated by *Übertragung*. At each occurrence I was obliged to deduce from the context whether what Nietzsche had in mind was correctly interpreted by 'translation' or by 'transference', with 'projection' as a possible alternative for the latter.

Where several meanings of two related terms overlap, the complexity is multiplied in translation. *Kultur* and *Bildung*, for instance, can both be translated as 'culture', but they have further meanings that are not synonymous. Where Nietzsche writes about *Kultur*, referring to the achievements of a whole society, I was able to translate it with reasonable accuracy as 'culture'. However, for *Bildung*, in the sense of the full intellectual and spiritual formation of an individual, only the more limited 'education' was available in English.

The gender-neutral *Mensch* again has several English equivalents. It is often translated by 'person' or by 'human being', but the first seemed too politically correct and the second too cumbersome. In view of Nietzsche's time, outlook and style, my preferred option, for all its one-sided emphasis on the male of the species, was 'man'.

Geist is one of the most notoriously untranslatable German words, not least because it too has a wide range of meanings, acquired through a long history, which cannot be rendered by a single comprehensive term in English. Each time Nietzsche uses it I had to make a choice between 'mind', when he seemed to refer to the human intellect, and 'spirit', when he seemed to invoke what may be described as the animating force assumed to reside in all things.

Nietzsche often reinforces his statements by playing on the sound of words or emphasising the etymological links between them. Where possible, I tried to achieve similar rhetorical effects, but where I was unable to reproduce the form and the meaning together I naturally gave priority to the meaning.

Two examples may show how Nietzsche underlines his message through phonetic devices. A sequence like *Wahn, Wille, Wehe* ('delusion, will, pain') makes its impact through alliteration, while the juxtaposition of *Verstellung* and *Vorstellung* ('dissimulation', 'representation') works through a change of vowels. Typically, in both examples I had to put meaning before sound in translation.

Three other examples may illustrate Nietzsche's method of drawing attention to conceptual affinities by placing words with common roots near each other. I managed to reproduce this on some occasions, but not on others. In *Erscheinung* and *Schein* ('appearance' and 'illusion'), *Missgeburt* and *Missgebilde* ('freak' and 'malformation'), or *Wahn* and *Wahnsinn* ('delusion' and 'madness') the etymological links in German are quite transparent, but I was unable to find any exact parallels in English. On the other hand, by translating *Täuschung* and *Trugbild* as 'delusion' and 'illusion', I was able to include a Nietzschean word game while remaining faithful to the meaning.

A characteristic feature of German is the reliance on compounds, where English tends to prefer periphrasis. Two small but telling examples – *Notlüge* and *Freilüge* – may stand for many. The first, with somewhat more serious connotations than 'white lie', is a lie we tell under duress to extricate ourselves from an awkward situation, while the second is a lie we tell of our own free will, for no particularly pressing external reason. I opted for 'self-protective lie' and 'gratuitous lie', that is, an adjective and a noun in each case, because I was unable to find any appropriate English compounds.

As is usually the case with German, I had to translate Nietzsche's adjectival nouns differently in different contexts. Where the combination of definite article and adjective described an abstract quality, I kept the same structure in English, for example, 'the worlds of the Apollonian and the Dionysian' for *die Welten des Apollinischen und des Dionysischen*. Where the same combination referred to one part of a whole I added a prop word, for example, 'the tragic element in tragedy' for *das Tragische in der Tragödie*. On some occasions I felt it necessary to replace an abstract German term with a more concrete English one, for example, *Tragik* with 'tragedy'. Any attempt to maintain consistency in changing contexts would have produced unidiomatic English.

At the syntactical level, Nietzsche's terse, elliptical notes present relatively few problems for the translator, except where comprehension is made difficult by the absence of links such as articles, conjunctions or even verbs. My policy throughout was to add only the minimum of clarification or amplification, in order to achieve the closest possible approximation to the original. On the other hand, the long, hypotactical sentences that occur occasionally would have been unreadable in English, and I therefore broke them up into shorter, paratactical ones. Where, for the sake of emphasis, Nietzsche starts a sentence with the object, I followed the normal English custom of putting the subject first.

Nietzsche'a punctuation is idiosyncratic, with a profuse repetition of colons, exclamation marks and dashes coming in ones, twos or threes. To convey the rhythm and movement of his thought, I followed him as far as it seemed acceptable in English. However, where this threatened to confuse or mislead, I reverted to more conventional English practices.

I tried to replicate not only the wording, but also the physical appearance of the original. My indentations and alignments, columns of key words, parentheses, headings and sub-headings mirror Nietzsche's manuscript as mediated by the Colli-Montinari edition. One exception is my use of italics, rather than spaced letters, for his single underlinings, and of bold type, either italic or roman, for his double or triple underlinings; although titles and foreign words are also italicised, English-speaking readers will have no difficulty distinguishing between the two kinds. In translating the passages, I took care to omit nothing and to add as little as possible. Apart from the numbers referring to the editor's notes, the additions are minor aids to reading: where the meaning of an unfinished word or clause was less than clear I supplied the missing element in square brackets; otherwise I left the text untouched.

In the texts that follow, a number of significant words are quoted in German at the appropriate point in the footnotes. I hope that these opportunities for comparison will help readers with some knowledge of German gain further insights into Nietzsche's way of writing.

Finally, I would like to thank Raymond Geuss for the exceptional blend of rigour, understanding and sensitivity he brought to the task of improving my translation, Karl Ameriks for his most helpful queries and suggestions, and Alexander Nehamas for his reassurance that I was on the right track. The responsibility for any remaining errors is, of course, mine.

Ladislaus Löb

1

October 1867 – April 1868: On Schopenhauer[1]

An attempt to explain the world under an assumed factor.

The thing-in-itself[2] receives one of its possible shapes.

The attempt failed.

Schopenhauer did not regard it as an attempt.

His thing-in-itself was deduced by him.

The reason why he did not see his own failure was that he did not want to sense the dark and contradictory elements in the region where individ.[3] ends.

He distrusted his own judgement.

Passages.

The dark drive, brought under an apparatus of representation, manifests itself as world. This drive has not found a place under the *princip. indiv.*

---

[1] Arthur Schopenhauer, German philosopher (1788–1860), was a major influence on the young Nietzsche.

[2] Immanuel Kant, German philosopher (1724–1804), distinguished sharply between what he called the thing considered 'as it was in itself' (originally Latin: *res per se spectata*; German: '*Ding an sich*') and the thing as a possible object of human experience. The former, Kant argued in his *Critique of Pure Reason* (1781), could not be known in any way by humans, although it could be an object of mere thought, empty speculation, faith, etc. Few of the Idealists who came after Kant could resist the temptation to think of the thing-in-itself as a reality that stood behind the world of appearances.

[3] Schopenhauer believed that the world of our human experience was a world of things 'subject to the *principium individuationis*' (the 'principle of individuation'), that is, that it was a world composed of objects that were distinct from each other by virtue of their location in space and time. However, this individuated world was the mere appearance, the reality of which was a (non-individuated) will. See *WWR* I. § 23.

I

The title page of the World as W[4] and R already reveals what Schopenhauer claims to have achieved for humanity through this work.

His answer to the yearning question of all metaphysicians – expressed in Goethe's 'whether the spirit would not reveal many a secret'[5] – is a bold Yes; and to ensure that the new insight was seen far and wide, like an inscription on a temple, he wrote the redeeming formula for the old and most important riddle of the world across the face of his book as the title *The World as Will and Representation*.

that alleged solution, then:

To grasp comfortably where the resolving and enlightening quality of this formula is to be sought, it is advisable to translate it into a semi-figurative form

The will, which has neither cause[6] nor knowledge, manifests itself, when subjected to an apparatus of representation, as world.

If we subtract from this proposition what Schopenhauer received as the heritage of the great Kant and what in his grand manner he always regarded with the most proper respect, the one word 'will' with its predicates is left behind. It is a solidly coined, wide-ranging word, intended to express an idea which was so significant and which went so far beyond Kant that its discoverer could say that he considered it as 'that which has very long been sought under the name of philosophy, and which is therefore considered by those who are familiar with history to be as impossible to find as the philosophers' stone'.[7]

Here it occurs to us in good time that Kant too regarded a no less questionable discovery, through the unfashionably ornate table of categories [*illegible*], as a great, indeed the greatest and most fruitful deed of his life, albeit with the character. difference that Kant, after complet. 'the most difficult thing that could be undertaken for the purp[ose] of met[aphysics][8] marvelled at himself as a violently erupting force of nature and was ordained to 'appear as the ref[ormer] of phil[osophy]',[9] while

4 *WWV* is Schopenhauer's main philosophical work.
5 This quotation from Goethe is the motto of *WWV*, vol. I.
6 *grundlos.*
7 *WWV*, Preface to first edition.
8 Friedrich Albert Lange, *Geschichte des Materialismus* (Iserlohn: Baedeker, 1866), p. 260.
9 Ibid, p. 257.

Schopenhauer always feels grateful [for] his alleged find to the prodigious sagacity and visual force of his intellect

The errors of great men are admirable because they are more fertile than the truths of the lesser ones.

If we now set about analytically examining the proposition put forward above, which is the quintessence of Sch's syst[em], nothing is further from us than wishing to harass Schopenhauer himself through such a criticism, confront him triumphantly with the separate pieces of his proofs, and finally ask with raised brows how on earth a man can arrive at such pretensions with a system that is so full of holes.

II

Indeed it must not be denied that the proposition with which we started as the quintessence of Schopenhauer's system can be successfully attacked from four sides.

1. The first, and most general, attack is directed against Schopenhauer only in so far as he did not go beyond Kant where it was necessary. It has its sights on the concept of a thing-in-itself, which it considers, in Überweg's words, as 'only a hidden category'.[10]

2. However, even if we grant Schopenhauer the right to follow Kant along that dangerous path, what he puts in place of the Kantian X,[11] the will,[12] is created only with the help of a poetic intuition, while his attempted logical proofs can satisfy neither Schopenhauer nor us. Cf. I, p. 125. 131.

Thirdly we are obliged to protest against the predicates attributed by Schopenhauer to his will, which sound far too definite for something absolutely unthinkable and which are gained throughout from their opposition to the world of representation; while between the thing-in-itself and the appearance even the concept of opposition is meaningless.

4. Nevertheless, all these 3 instances could be countered in favour of Schopenhauer with a possibility raised to the power of three:

there may be a thing-in-itself, albeit in no other sense than that in the realm of transcendence anything is *possible* that is ever hatched out in

---

[10] Friedrich Überweg was a nineteenth-century historian of philosophy; this is cited from Lange, *Geschichte des Materialismus*, p. 267.

[11] See Kant, *Critique of Pure Reason*, A104–10, A249–53.

[12] *WWR* I. §§ 19–20.

the mind of a philosopher. This possible thing-in-itself may be the will: a possibility which, having come into being from the combination of two possibilities, is only the negative power of the first possibility, which, in other words, amounts to a strong step towards the other pole, impossibility. We reinforce this concept of a continually decreasing possibility once again if we admit that even those predicates of the will assumed by Schopenhauer may pertain to it, because an opposition between the thing-in-itself and the appearance can be thought even though it is unprovable. Now any kind of moral thinking would declare its opposition to such a knot of possibilities: but even this ethical objection could be countered by saying that the thinker, faced with the mystery of the world, has no other means than guessing, i.e. hoping that a moment of genius will place on his lips the word that provides the key to the writing that lies before everyone's eyes and yet has never been read, which we call the world. But is that word the will? – This is the point at which we must make our fourth attack.

Schopenhauer's supporting tissue becomes tangled in his hands, least of all as a result of a certain tactical ineptitude of its maker, but mainly because the world cannot be fitted into the system as comfortably as Schopenhauer had hoped in the first enthus[iasm] of a finder. In his old age he complained that the most difficult problem of phil. had not been solved by his philosophy either. By this he meant the question of the limits of individ[uation].

3

Henceforth we shall closely examine a certain species of contradictions with which Sch.'s system is riddled; a species of extremely important and hardly avoidable contradictions which, as it were, arm themselves to wage war against their mother while still in her womb, and which perform their first deed by killing their mother when they have scarcely been born. They all refer to the boundaries of individuation and they have their $\pi\rho\tilde{\omega}\tau o\nu$ $\psi[\varepsilon\tilde{\upsilon}\delta o\varsigma]$[13] at the point touched on under number 3.

'The will as a thing-in-itself', Schopenh. says, *W as* [*Will and Representation*], vol. I, p. 134, 'is quite different from its appearance and entirely free of all the forms of the same, which it does not enter until

---

[13] An 'initial error' which infects everything that follows from it with untruth.

it appears, and which therefore concern only its nature as an object and are alien to itself. Even the most universal form [of all representations], that of an object for a subject, does not apply to it, much less those forms subordinate to it that have their common expression in the principle of sufficient reason, which, as is commonly known, includes space and time and consequently also the multiplicity which exists and was made possible through them alone. In this last respect, borrowing a term from the true old Scholasticism, I will call time and space the *principium individuationis.*'

In this account, which we encounter in innumerable variations in Schopenh's writings, we are surprised by the dictatorial tone, which predicates of that thing-in-itself which lies altogether outside the sphere of knowledge a number of *negative* properties and which therefore does not accord with the assertion that the most general form of knowledge, being an object for a subject, does not apply to it. Schopen. himself expresses this in *W as W* p. 131 as follows: 'This thing-in-itself, as such, is never an object, because every object is its mere appearance and no longer itself. If it *was nevertheless to be thought of objectively*, it had to *borrow* a *name and concept* from an object, i.e. from something in some way objectively given, and therefore from one of its appearances.' Schopenhauer, then, demands that something that can never be an object be nevertheless thought of objectively: but on that road we can reach only an apparent objectivity, in so far as a totally obscure and incomprehensible x is hung with predicates as if with brightly coloured garments taken from a world that is alien to it, the world of appearances. We are then required to regard the draped garments hung on it, i.e. the predicates, as the thing-in-itself: for that is the meaning of the sentence 'if it was nevertheless to be thought of objectively, it had to borrow a name and concept from an object'. So the concept of the 'thing-in-itself' is secretly eliminated because 'it is meant to be' and we are handed another concept in exchange.

The borrowed name and concept is precisely the will, 'because it is the clearest, most developed appearance of the thing-in-itself, directly illuminated by knowledge'. But that does not concern us here: what is more important for us is that all the predicates of the will too are borrowed from the world of appearances. Admittedly, Sch. makes an attempt here and there to present the meaning of these predicates as totally incomprehensible and transcendent, e.g. *W as W* II, p. 368: 'The unity of that will in which we have recognised the essential nature-in-itself of the world of appearances is a metaphysical one. Consequently our knowledge of it is transcendent, i.e. it is not based on the functions of our intellect and therefore cannot really be grasped by them.' cf. *W as W.* I. p. 134, 132. However, we can see from Sch.'s entire system, and in particular from the first account of it in vol. I of *W as W*, that he permits himself the human and by no means transcendent use of unity in the will wherever it suits him, and basically has recourse to that transcend[ence] only where the gaps in the system strike him as too palpable. For this 'unity' therefore, the same holds as for the 'will': both are predicates of the thing-in-itself, taken from the world of appearances, under which the real heart of the matter, the transcendental, evaporates. What is true of the three predicates of unity, eternity (i.e. timelessness), liberty (i.e. lacking any reason)[14] is the same as what is true of the thing-in-itself: they are tied inseparably to our organisation one and all, so that it is extremely doubtful that they have any meaning at all outside the sphere of human knowledge. But that they should pertain to the thing-in-itself, because their opposites rule the world of appearances, is something that neither K[ant] nor Sch. will be able to prove to us, or even just make more likely, the latter above all because his thing-in-itself, the will, cannot make ends meet with those three predicates and is continually having to raise a loan from the world of appearances, i.e. transfer the concept of multiplicity, temporality and causality to itself.

On the other hand he is entirely right in saying, I p. 118, that 'it will never be possible to reach the nature of things from without: however much we may investigate, we gain nothing but images and names'.

4

The will appears: how could it appear? Or to ask differently: where does the apparatus of representation in which the will appears come from? Schopenhauer answers, with an expression peculiar to him, by describing the intellect as the μηχανή[15] of the will, II. 315: 'But this enhancement of brain development is brought about by the constantly increasing and ever more complicated need of the corresponding appearances of the will.' 'Thus the knowing and conscious self is basically tertiary, since it

---

[14] *Grundlosigkeit.*
[15] instrument; see *WWR* I. § 27.

presupposes the organism, and the organism presupposes the will.' II. 314 Schopenhauer thus imagines a step-by-step sequence of phenomena of the will with continually increasing existential needs: in order to satisfy these, nature uses a corresponding step-by-step sequence of aids, among which the intellect, from scarcely conscious sensations to extreme clarity, has its own place. This view places a world of appearances in front of the world of appearances, if we want to cling to Schopenhauer's *termini* concerning the thing-in-itself. Before the appearance of the intellect we already see the *principium indiv.*, the law of causality, in full effectiveness. The will seizes life post-haste, seeking to manifest itself in every way; it begins modestly at the lowest levels and as it were works its way up from the bottom. In this region of Schopenhauer's system everything is already dissolved into words and images: of the initial definition of the thing-in-itself everything – almost even the memory of it – has been lost. And where this memory steps in once in a while it serves only to bring the complete contradiction out into the full light of day. *Par.* II. 150: 'The geological events that preceded all life on earth did not exist in any consciousness at all: neither in their own because they had none, nor in the consciousness of another because there was no such consciousness. Therefore ... they did not exist at all; or what else does their having existed mean? Basically, it is merely *hypothetical*, that is, *if* a consciousness had existed in those primeval times, such events would have appeared in it. That is where the *regressus* of appearances leads us and therefore it lay in the nature of the thing-in-itself to manifest itself in such events.' They are, as Sch. says on the same page, only 'translations into the language of our intuiting intellect'.

But how, we ask after these sober explanations, was it ever possible for the intellect to come into being? Surely, the existence of the last step before the appearance of the intellect is as hypothetical as that of every earlier step, i.e. this step did not exist because no consciousness existed. And now, at the next step, the intellect is supposed to have appeared, i.e. the flower of knowledge is supposed to have burst forth suddenly and abruptly from a non-existent world. This is supposed to have happened in a sphere of timelessness and spacelessness, without the intervention of causality. But what comes from such a world stripped of worldly qualities must – according to Schopenhauer's principles – itself be the thing-in-itself. Now either the intellect remains eternally joined together with the thing-in-itself as a new predicate or there can be no intellect at all because an intellect could never have come into being.

But an intellect exists: consequently it could not be a tool of the world of appearance, as Schopenhauer would have it, but it would be the thing-in-itself, i.e. the will.

Schopenhauer's thing-in-itself would therefore be at one and the same time *princip. indiv.* and the ground of necessitation: in other words, the existing world. Sch. tried to find the x of an equation: and the result of his calculation is that it equals x, i.e. that he has not found it.

5. Ideas.
6. Character.
7. Teleology and contrast.
8.

It must be noted how carefully Schopenh. avoids the question of the origin of intellect: as soon as we reach the region of this question, hoping that it will now come, he hides as it were behind the clouds, although it is quite obvious that the intellect in Sch.'s sense presupposes a world caught up in the *pr[incipio] in[dividuationis]* and the laws of causality. On one occasion, as far as I can see, this admission is at the tip of his tongue; but he gulps it down in such a strange way that we must examine it more closely. *W. as W.* II 310. 'If we now go back in the objective comprehension of the intellect as far as we possibly can, we shall find that the necessity of, or the demand for, *knowledge as such* arises from the multiplicity and the *separate* existence of beings, that is, from individuation. For if we imagined that there was only *one single* being, it would have no need of knowledge: because nothing would exist that was different from it and whose existence it would therefore have to absorb indirectly through knowledge, i.e. image and concept. It would itself already be all in all, and therefore there would remain nothing for it to know, i.e. nothing alien that could be understood as an object. However, given the multiplicity of beings, every individual is in a state of isolation from all the others, and this is what gives rise to the necess. of knowledge. The nervous system, by means of which the individual animal first becomes conscious of itself, is bounded by a skin; but in the brain, raised to intellect, it crosses this boundary with the help of causality as its cognitive mode, and thus it develops intuition as a consciousness of *other* things, as an image of beings in space and time, changing in accordance with causality.'

Notebook 1, autumn 1869

1[1]

Whoever talks or hears about Aeschylus, Sophocles and Euripides[1] today immediately thinks of them as *littérateurs*, because he first got to know them, either in the original or in translation, from *books*: but this is roughly as if somebody who is talking about *Tannhäuser*[2] means and understands nothing more than the libretto. I want to talk therefore about those men *not* as librettists but as composers of operas. I know that with the word 'opera' I am handing you a caricature, even though only a few of you will initially admit that. But I shall be satisfied if by the end you have been convinced that our operas are mere caricatures in comparison to the ancient musical drama.

The origin itself is characteristic. The opera came into being without any foundation in the senses, in accordance with an abstract theory and the conscious intention to achieve the effects of the ancient drama by these means. It is therefore an artificial homunculus, indeed the malicious goblin of our musical development. Here we have a warning example of the damage the direct aping of antiquity can do. By such unnatural experiments the roots of an unconscious art growing out of the life of the people are cut off or at least badly mutilated. We are shown examples of this by the emergence of French tragedy, which, from the outset, is a

---

[1] Aeschylus, Sophocles, Euripides: These are the three fifth-century (BC) Athenian tragedians some of whose works have survived. Aeschylus, probably born in the 520s BC, was the oldest of the three. Euripides was the youngest, probably born in the early 480s BC, and who died in 406; Sophocles outlived Euripides by about a year.

[2] *Tannhäuser oder der Sängerkrieg auf dem Warteburg*, opera by Richard Wagner, first performed in Dresden in 1845.

9

learned product, designed to contain the quintessence of the tragic, in an entirely pure form, as an abstract concept. In Germany too, since the Reformation, the natural root of drama, the Shrovetide play, has been undermined: attempts at creating something new, up to and including the classical period, have been made in a purely learned manner. At the same time this proves that even in a misguided and unnaturally developed genre such as the drama of Schiller and Goethe[3] an irrepressible genius like the German can find a way; and the same process can be seen in the history of the opera. If the force slumbering in the depths is truly all-powerful it will overcome even such alien admixtures: in the most gruelling, often even convulsive struggle, nature will be victorious, albeit very late in the day. If one is to describe briefly the massive armour under which all the modern arts break down so often and advance so slowly and erratically, it is erudition, conscious knowledge and excessive study. Among the Greeks the beginnings of drama go back to the unfathomable expressions of folk impulses: in the orgiastic celebrations of Dionysus[4] people were driven outside themselves – ἔκστασις[5] – to such an extent that they acted and felt like transformed and bewitched beings. Nor are such conditions entirely remote from the life of the German people, except that they never experienced such a flowering: at least I see the St John's or St Vitus' dancers, who used to wander singing and dancing from town to town in enormous and constantly increasing masses, as nothing other than such an ecstatic Dionysian movement, even though in medicine today the phenomenon is regarded as an epidemic of the Middle Ages. The ancient musical drama blossomed out of such an epidemic;

[3] As Artistic Director of the Court Theatre in the small Ducal Residence town of Weimar in Central Germany from 1791 to 1817, Johann Wolfgang (von) Goethe (1749–1832) was responsible for producing a number of his own plays and plays by his friend Schiller (1759–1805), who also lived in Weimar from 1787 to his death. Nietzsche had three basic criticisms of the kind of drama they wrote during the period of their co-residence in Weimar. First of all, their theatre was consciously an aristocratic *court* theatre, and Nietzsche – at any rate during this early period – followed Wagner in insisting that the best theatre could never depart too far from its roots in a genuine popular culture. Second, as in most of its modern forms, the 'classicism' Goethe and Schiller espoused during their Weimar period had to do more with admiration of an idealised 'antiquity' rather than with any correct apprehension of ancient realities. Sometimes Nietzsche cites this creative idealisation as a strength of the Weimar project (see below, p. 206, 5[167]), but sometimes as a weakness. Third, Goethe, at any rate, despite his many gifts, had one notorious blind spot: he was utterly unmusical with completely philistine taste. This, in Nietzsche's eyes, made him unfit to attain any deeper understanding of drama, which is *essentially* musical.
[4] Greek god of natural vitality and intoxication. See BT §§ 1–2.
[5] The state of being 'outside oneself'.

and it is the misfortune of the modern arts that they do not stem from such a mysterious source.

1[27]

Absolute music and everyday drama: the two parts of musical drama torn apart.

The happiest stage was the dithyramb[6] as well as the early Aeschylean tragedy.

In Socrates the scientific principle intrudes: with it, strife and the destruction of the unconscious.

1[47]

What is art? The ability to create the world of the will without the will? No. To recreate the world of the will without the product *willing*. Therefore the thing to do is to create the will-less through the will and *instinctively*. Consciously, this is called craft. However, the affinity with procreation is obvious, except that what comes into being again here is will-full.

1[49]

What does music do? It dissolves an intuition into will.

It contains the universal forms of all conditions of desire: it is throughout a symbolism of the instincts and as such intelligible, completely and to everybody, in its simplest forms (beat, rhythm).

Music, then, is always more universal than any single action. That is why it is more intelligible to us than any single action. Therefore music is the key to drama.

The demand for unity, unjustified as we have seen, is the source of everything that is wrong about opera and song. Once the impossibility of constructing a unity of the *whole* had been recognised, the next step was to place the unity into the *parts* and to *break up* the whole into separable absolute parts.

---

[6] A form of early poetry sung and danced by choruses of up to 50 men (or boys), devoted to the worship of the god Dionysus.

A parallel step was that taken by Euripides, who placed the unity also into the single drama.[7]

The Greek musical drama is a preliminary stage of absolute music, one form within the whole process. Initially the lyrical-musical parts have a universal, objectively contemplative content, representing the sorrows and joys, desires and farewells of *all*. The *cause* of these was *imagined* by the poet, because he knew no absolute music or lyric. He feigned a past state in which this or that universal mood demanded its lyrical-musical expression. This had to be a condition of cosily kindred beings: and nothing is more kindred than the mythical world, a reflection of our most universal conditions seen in an ideal and idealising past. Thus the poet asserts the universal validity of the musical-lyrical moods for all times, i.e. he takes a step towards absolute music.

This is the limitation of ancient music: it remains occasional music, i.e. it is assumed that there are certain musical conditions on the one hand and certain unmusical states on the other. The state in which a human being *sings* was taken as a yardstick.

In this way two worlds which more or less alternated were kept side by side, so that the world of the eye disappeared when that of the ear began, and vice versa. The action served only to lead to the suffering, and the *outpouring* of the pathos again made a new action necessary. As a consequence, it was not the mediation between the two worlds that was sought, but a diametrical opposition between them: once the realm of emotion had been staked out, it was time for the intellect to come into its own; Euripides introduced dialectics, the tone of the law court, into the dialogue.

Here we see the annoying consequence: if one unnaturally separates emotion and intellect, music and action, the mind and the will, each separate part will waste away. And thus *absolute music* and *family drama* came into being out of the dismembered ancient musical drama.

---

[7] It was the Athenian practice to have competing tragedians present sets of four plays ('tetralo-gies': three tragedies (a 'trilogy') plus a so-called satyr-play) at the major dramatic festivals. As becomes clear from some other fragments (e.g. 1[109], not included in this selection), Nietzsche held that the early tragedians always presented coherent sets of three thematically unified trag-edies, for instance Aeschylus' *Oresteia* which tells the story of the house of Atreus through three plays. Euripides, however, presented 'trilogies' of unconnected dramas, each individual play having its unity only in itself.

1[108]

The ethical philosophy of the tragedians: how does it relate to the recognised philosophers? Externally, not at all (except in Euripides) because poetry and philosophy were regarded as separate things. Ethics belonged with the former: therefore it was part of pedagogics.

II. Plato's philosophical drama is neither tragedy nor comedy: there is no chorus, no musical element, no religious theme. Rather, it is an epic of the Homeric school. It is the ancient novel. Above all, not meant to be put into practice, but read:[8] it is a rhapsody. It is the literary drama.

---

[8] *nicht bestimmt zur Praxis, sondern zum Lesen.* This presumably means both (a) they were to be read, not acted, and (b) they were to be read, but not put into practice, although (b) would be the more natural sense of the phrase taken on its own.

Notebook 2, winter 1869/1870 – spring 1870

2[1]

Christianity, originally a matter of talent, had to be democratised. The slow struggle to become a world religion, whereby everything profound, esoteric, accessible to the talented individual was extirpated. – This also brought back optimism, without which a world religion cannot keep going. Purgatory and κατάστασις[1] are its creations.

2[10]

Music is a language which is capable of infinite explanation.

Language explains only through concepts, so that the shared sensation is created through the medium of thought. This sets a limit for it.

This is valid only for the objective written language; the spoken language resonates, and its intervals, rhythms, tempi, volume and stress are all symbols of the emotional content that is to be represented. All this is contained in music simultaneously. The largest amount of feeling does

---

[1] The basic meaning of this term is the act of putting things in their appropriate place, or the state that results when things have been put in their appropriate place. In the classical period it could also be used to refer specifically to a 'school' of music, the appointment or installation of (duly chosen) magistrates, the presentation of (duly accredited) ambassadors to the assembly, or to the fact that a certain community lived in a settled state. Early Christian writers also use the term in a variety of more specific senses such as 'the way of life of those who follow a monastic rule' (see *A Patristic Greek Lexicon*, ed. G. W. H. Lampe (Oxford University Press, 1961), *s.v.*). It is not possible to know what exactly Nietzsche had in mind by using it here, but two suggestions that immediately present themselves are that Nietzsche thinks that the establishment of monastic rules represents a 'democratisation' of asceticism, or that he is referring to the Christian doctrine that the souls of all the dead are distributed to their appropriate places (heaven, hell, purgatory, limbo) after death, and that this represents a kind of democratisation.

not express itself through words. And the word itself barely hints: it is the surface of the choppy sea, while the storm rages in the depths. This is the limit of spoken drama. The inability to represent things that exist side by side.

The tremendous process of obsolescence in music: anything symbolic can be imitated and thereby killed: the incessant development of the stereotypical 'set phrase'.[2]

In this respect music is one of the most transient arts; it even has something of the art of the mime. Only: the emotional life of the masters is usually a long way ahead. The development of the unintelligible hieroglyphic to the set phrase.

Poetry often finds itself on a road to music: either by seeking out the most delicate concepts in whose ambit the coarse material quality of the *concept* almost vanishes —

2[11]

Word and music in opera. The words are intended to interpret the music for us, but the music expresses the soul of the action. Words are of course the most deficient signs.

By the drama we are stimulated to exercise the *imagination of the will*, a seemingly nonsensical term; by the epic, the imagination of the intellect, in particular the eye.

A drama we read cannot really rouse the imagination of the will to excitement and productivity, because the visual imagination is over-stimulated.

In lyric poetry we do not step outside ourselves; but we are stimulated to produce emotional moods of our own, mostly through ἀνάμνησις.[3]

---

[2] A mere conventional phrase lacking in content.
[3] This is the word generally translated 'recollection'. Plato believed that the things we encounter in the world of experience are mere approximate copies of real originals (which he called 'ideas' or 'forms'). The relation between the two is something like that between a triangle drawn in chalk on a particular blackboard somewhere and the ideal 'triangle' which is the object of investigation in traditional geometry. We can come to know important properties of the triangles we encounter in this world without being explicitly taught about them, but simply by using our powers of reasoning, because before we were born our souls existed outside our bodies and 'saw' the 'ideas' of which the objects in this world are copies. Seeing one of the copies thus can cause us to 'recollect' our ante-natal acquaintance with the original, one of the 'ideas'. See Plato, *Meno*, esp. 81, and *Republic* 514–19.

2[25]

It is nonsense to talk about a union of drama, lyric and epic in the old heroic lay. For here the tragic is taken as the dramatic; while the only thing that is specifically dramatic is the *mimic*.

The shocking outcome, φόβος[4] and ἔλεος[5] have nothing whatsoever to do with drama: and they are inherent in tragedy *not* because it is drama. Any story can have them: but the musical lyric most of all. With the slow but serene unfolding of image after image as its business, the epic is altogether a higher work of art. All art demands a 'being outside oneself', an ἔκστασις;[6] it is from here that we take the step to the drama, by *not* returning within ourselves, but entering into another being, by acting as if we were bewitched, in our ἔκστασις. Hence our profound astonishment when we watch a drama: the ground trembles, the belief in the indissolvability of the individual.

Faced with a lyric we are also astonished to re-experience our most personal feelings, to have them reflected back to us out of other individuals.

2[26]

The origin of the fundamental dramatic laws is to be explained.

The great processions with representations were already *drama*.

The epic wants us to receive pictures before our eyes.

The drama, which directly presents pictures –

what do I want when I look at a picture book? I want to understand it. Conversely, then: I understand the epic narrator who hands me one concept after another; I then help things along by means of the imagination, and adding all together I have a picture. At this point I have achieved my purpose: I understand the picture because I have created it myself.

In drama I start with the picture: if I work out that such and such is supposed to mean such and such, I miss the enjoyment. It should be 'self-evident'.

---

[4] fear; see next footnote.
[5] pity. The production of the two affects of 'fear' and 'pity' was traditionally thought to be the effect of a good performance of a tragedy on the audience. See Aristotle, *Poetics*, chapter 14, esp. 1453b 10–14.
[6] The state of being 'outside oneself'.

Notebook 3, winter 1869/1870 – spring 1870

3[1]

Unfortunately we are used to enjoying the arts separately, a folly that is most glaringly revealed at art galleries and so-called concerts. Because of this sorry modern vice of the absolute arts, there is no organisation that cultivates and develops the arts as one comprehensive art.[1] The last phenomena of this kind were, perhaps, the great Italian *trionfi*;[2] today the musical drama of antiquity has only a pale analogue in the union of the arts within the rite of the Catholic church.

Such an ancient drama is a great work of music. However, the music was never enjoyed as something absolute, but always in connection with divine service, architecture, sculpture and poetry. In short it was occasional music, and the connecting dialogue served only to create occasions for the musical pieces, each of which retained its distinctly occasional character.

At the earliest original stage of art unity is never aimed at. What distinguishes the miracle and morality plays from the Greek dithyrambs? The former are action right from the outset; at first the word plays a supporting part and only gradually comes into its own. The latter are originally groups of costumed singers; visual images are conveyed to the imagination first through words and only later through action. Among the Greeks the enjoyment and the art of hearing had already been highly

---

[1] This topic of the need to integrate the various arts was a central one in Wagner's aesthetics. See GSD III.42–177.

[2] A festive celebration of a triumph, especially one with elaborate costumes and decorations.

17

developed by the epic rhapsodes[3] and the performers of melics.[4] Their reproductive imagination was much more active and lively, and much less in need of graphic action. In contrast, Germanic people were much less in need of an external representation of internal processes because they had an inner abundance of them. The Greeks watched the ancient tragedy in order to collect themselves, Germanic people wanted to be drawn out of themselves in order to be distracted. The mysteries and moralities were much more worldly despite their subject matter. People came and went, there was no question of a beginning and an end, nobody wanted and nobody offered a whole. Conversely, when the Greeks watched they did so in a religious frame of mind: it was high mass, with the glorification of the god at the end, which had to be waited for.

People are tempted and seduced into placing the series of scenes side by side like paintings and examining the composition of that comprehensive picture. This is an actual confusion of artistic principles in that the laws of simultaneity are applied to succession. The demand for unity in drama is the demand of the impatient will that does not want to contemplate in tranquillity, but to storm ahead unimpeded to the end along its chosen path.

3[2]

Action[5] first entered tragedy with the dialogue. This shows that from the start the purpose of this genre was not $\delta\varrho\tilde{\alpha}\nu$[6] but $\pi\acute{\alpha}\vartheta o\varsigma$.[7] Initially it was nothing but objective lyric poetry, i.e. a song arising from the state of certain mythological beings, and therefore sung in their costume. At first the costumed singers themselves indicated the reason for their lyrical mood. Later one person stepped forward to relate the main action, and

---

[3] Professional reciters of poetry, especially the epic poetry of Homer, in ancient Greece.

[4] The ancient Greeks of the classical period did not have a single unitary category of what we would call 'lyric' poetry, but distinguished a variety of genres by reference to a number of different dimensions. Were they intended to be recited or sung; if sung, then by individuals or groups; unaccompanied or accompanied by which instruments? Epic poems were recited, and used the same metrical scheme for each line. 'Melics' were songs with a distinct recurrent strophic form. Within the strophe each line might have a different metrical structure, but one that would be the same as that of the corresponding line in each other strophe.

[5] Or 'plot' (*Handlung*).

[6] 'to do, act'; the verb from which the noun 'drama' is derived. See Aristotle, *Poetics* 1448a19–1448b1.

[7] The state of being affected by something, of 'suffering' something (in the widest sense).

the lyrical outburst came whenever an important event was related. This person was also in costume and regarded as the leader of the chorus, as a god relating his own deeds. In its beginnings, then, Greek drama is a choral song cycle with a connecting narrative. Greek musical drama is a preliminary stage of absolute music. The lyrical-musical parts are ——

3[10]

Perfect knowledge kills action; indeed if it refers to knowledge itself it kills itself. One cannot move a muscle if one first tries to know precisely what it takes to move a muscle. However, perfect knowledge is *impossible* and therefore action is possible. Knowledge is a screw without an end: whenever it is brought into play an infinity begins: that is why there can never be any action. – All this is valid for conscious knowledge only. I die as soon as I try to ascertain the ultimate causes of a breath before I take it.

Any science that claims to have a practical significance is not a science, e.g. economics.

3[11]

The purpose of science is to annihilate the world. Admittedly it happens that the immediate effect is the same as that of small doses of opium: an enhanced affirmation of the world. In politics we are now at that stage.

It can be proved that in Greece the process was already complete in miniature, although this Greek science had little significance.

The task of art is to annihilate the state. This too happened in Greece. Subsequently science also dissolves art. (Accordingly, for a while it seems that the state and science go hand in hand, the age of sophists – our age.)

Wars must not be, so that the ever rekindled sense of state may finally fall asleep.

3[15]

Language came into being from the shout with the accompanying gesture: here the essence of the thing is expressed through the tone, the volume and the rhythm, and the accompanying idea, the image of the essence, the appearance, through the oral gesture.

An infinitely inadequate symbolism, grown in accordance with firm laws of nature: in the choice of the symbol it is not freedom but instinct that reveals itself.

A symbol that has been *noticed* is always a concept: one conceives what one is able to name and distinguish.

3[32]

Tragedy is nature's healing power against the Dionysian. It must be possible to *live*: therefore pure Dionysism is impossible. For pessimism, practically and theoretically, is illogical. Because logic is only the $\mu\eta\chi\alpha\nu\dot{\eta}$[8] of the will.

3[33]

What was the purpose of the will, which ultimately is *one*? The tragic idea, rescue from truth through beauty, absolute submission to the Olympians[9] out of the most terrible knowledge, was now brought into the world. Thus the will gained a new possibility of being: the *conscious* volition of life in the individual, according to the idea of tragedy, of course not directly, but through art.

That is why now a new art arrives: tragedy.

The lyric as far as Dionysus and the road to Apollonian music.[10]

Enchantment: it is the *suffering* that resounds, as opposed to the *acting* of the epic: the 'picture' of Apollonian culture is presented by man through enchantment.

There are no longer any pictures, but transformations. Everything excessive must be given a voice.

Man must shudder before the truth; a *cure* of man must be accomplished: becoming calm by running riot, longing for illusion due to terrible shocks.

---

[8] instrument; see above, 'On Schopenhauer', footnote 15, p. 6.

[9] Major gods and goddesses in the ancient Greek polytheistic pantheon were thought to 'live' on the top of Olympus, a high mountain in Northern Greece.

[10] Apollo is the Greek god of light, prophecy and healing with a special relation to the lyre. See BT §§ 1–4, also Walter Burkert, *Griechische Religion der archaischen und klassischen Epoche* (Stuttgart: Kohlhammer, 1977), vol. III, 2.5.

The world of the Olympian gods is transformed into the *ethical* world order. Poor man prostrates himself before it.

3[51]

Pessimism is the consequence of recognising the absolute illogicality of the world order: the strongest idealism joins battle with the illogical under the flag of an abstract concept, e.g. truth, morality etc. Its triumph the denial of the illogical as something illusory, not essential. The 'real' is only an ἰδέα.[11]

– Goethe's 'demonic'![12] It is the 'real', 'the will', ἀνάγκη.[13]

The will dying away (the *dying god*) crumbles into individualities. Its aspiration is always the lost unity, its τέλος[14] further and further disintegration. Every unity achieved through struggle is its triumph, above all art, religion.

In every appearance the supreme drive to affirm itself, until it finally falls victim to τέλος.[15]

3[54]

Beauty has no share whatsoever in the domain of *music*.

Rhythm and harmony are the main parts, the melody is only an abbreviation of the harmony.

The idealising power of music, in which all things look transfigured.

3[55]

Annihilation of the world through knowledge! New creation through strengthening of the unconscious! The 'stupid Siegfried' and the knowing

---

[11] 'idea' (particularly in Plato's quasi-technical sense; see above, Notebook 2, footnote 3, p. 15).
[12] Johann Wolfgang von Goethe, *Aus meinem Leben: Dichtung und Wahrheit*, Book IV, chapter 20 in his *Sämtliche Werke*, ed. W. Wiehölter and C. Brecht (Frankfurt: Deutscher Klassiker Verlag, 1994), I.14.
[13] necessity.
[14] end, goal, aim, purpose.
[15] end, goal, aim, purpose.

gods![16] – Pessimism as absolute longing for non-being is impossible: only for being better!

Art is something securely positive against the desirable nirvana. The question only exists for idealistic natures: subjugation of the world through positive action: firstly through science as the destroyer of illusion, secondly through art as the only remaining form of existence: because indissolvable through logic.

3[60]

The only possibility of life: in art. Otherwise a turning away from life. The complete annihilation of illusion is the drive of the sciences: it would be followed by quietism – were it not for art.

Germany as the proper seat of the oracle of art. – Aim: a state-managed cultural organisation – art as a means of education – elimination of *specifically* scientific forms of training.

Dissolution of the still living religious emotions into the domain of art – this is the practical aim. Conscious annihilation of art criticism through the increased *consecration* of art.

To demonstrate this as the drive of German Idealism. Thus: liberation from the predominance of ἄνθρωπος θεωρητικός.[17]

3[62]

The Hellene is neither an optimist nor a pessimist. Essentially he is a *man* who really faces the terrible and does not close his eyes to it. *Theodicy*[18] was *no* Hellenic problem because the creation of the world was not the deed of the gods. The great wisdom of Hellenism, which understood the gods as also being subject to ἀνάγκη.[19] The world of the Greek gods is a fluttering veil which masked the most terrible things.

---

[16] One of the central figures of Wagner's cycle of operas *Der Ring des Nibelungen* is Siegfried, who is represented as an extremely energetic but also very naïve young man. An important part of the plot turns on the relation between Siegfried's spontaneous reactions to various situations and the complex and slightly devious plans of the chief god Wotan (who also happens to be Siegfried's grandfather).

[17] The person whose life is centred on the desire for theoretical understanding.

[18] The philosophical attempt to reconcile the manifest evil in the world with the existence of an omnipotent, benevolent God who has created it.

[19] necessity.

The Greeks are the artists of *life*; they have their gods in order to be able to live, not in order to alienate themselves from life.

The important thing is the *idealism of the living for life*.

A cross wrapped in roses, as Goethe puts it in 'The Secrets'.[20]

[20] Johann Wolfgang von Goethe, *Die Geheimnisse: Ein Fragment*, in his *Sämtliche Werke*, 1.8, pp. 647–58.

Notebook 5, September 1870 – January 1871

5[25]

How does instinct reveal itself in the form of the conscious mind?
In delusions.[1]
Their effectiveness is not destroyed even by knowing about their nature. But knowledge produces a painful condition: the only cure for it in the illusion[2] of art.
Playing with these instincts.
Beauty is the form in which a thing appears under a delusion, e.g. the loved one etc.
Art is the form in which the world appears under the delusion that it is necessary.
It is a seductive representation of the will, pushing its way into the knowledge.
The 'ideal' is such a delusion.

5[26]

Delusions: for those who see through them art is the only solace. Penetration is now a necessity for free thinkers: the attitude of the crowd

---

[1] *Wahn.* This, and the verbal form '*wähnen*' was one of Wagner's favourite terms. See the passage from Wagner's music-drama *Die Meistersinger von Nürnberg* cited by Nietzsche in a particularly prominent place at the beginning of BT § 1.

[2] *Schein.* Schiller is responsible for the popularity of the idea that art is connected with the production of a realm of appearances that are neither exactly 'true' nor strict illusions. Thus, when the actor who plays the hero stabs the actor who plays the villain, it should *look* as if someone is killed, and yet the audience is not intended to believe that someone has actually been killed.

to this cannot be guessed. Enough that *we* need art: we want it by hook or by crook, if necessary by fighting for it. A new cultural sect, as the judge and ruler over the nasty, lacklustre culture of the day. One must begin with the real elements of culture, with pure scientific enthusiasm, with strict military subordination, with the profound emotional need of women etc., with what still exists of Christianity etc.

Socratism as the imagined wisdom (in all phenomena, in orthodox Christianity, in today's Judaism) is averse or indifferent to art.

Like Oedipus, we attain peace only in the grove of the Eumenides.[3]

5[33]

Most people occasionally feel that they are living their lives in a net of illusions. But very few realise how far these illusions reach.

Not letting oneself be ruled by illusions is an infinitely naïve belief, but it is the intellectual imperative, the command of science. In uncovering these spider's webs ἄνϑρωπος ϑεωρητικός,[4] and with him the will to existence, celebrate their orgies: he knows that curiosity never ends and he regards the scientific drive as one of the most powerful μηχαναί[5] of existence.

5[38]

Our musical development is the eruption of the Dionysian drive. It gradually coerces the world: in musical drama it coerces art, but also philosophy.

Music is utterly healthy – in contrast to the terrible depravity of epic culture.

---

[3] Sophocles' last play *Oedipus at Colonus* deals with a story about Oedipus (see below, Notebook 19, footnote 65, p. 131) who, after a long life full of catastrophes including murdering his father, marrying his mother, blinding himself, and wandering about as a beggar for years, attains a kind of peace (and quasi-deification) when he stumbles into a grove dedicated to the 'Furies' ('Eumenides', archaic demons who pursue those who transgress against the solidarity of the family) and performs the sacrifices they demand.

[4] See Notebook 3, footnote 17, p. 22.

[5] The plural of μηχανή; see above, 'On Schopenhauer', footnote 15, p. 6. Thus, 'instruments that will allow it to continue to exist'.

5[54]

The Parsees have an inexplicable inhibition about light and fire. They are the only Orientals who do not smoke, they take care not to blow out a fire.[6]

If Darius had not been defeated, the religion of Zoroaster would have dominated Greece.[7]

5[68]

The *supreme sign of the will*:
the belief in illusion and theoretical pessimism bite their own tail.

5[80]

Compassionate action is a correction of the world in acting; in the realm of thinking its counterpart is religion.

Creating in the realm of the beautiful bears the same relation to finding things beautiful.

Is the individual system breached in the good?

The pure snatching of the will for existence is all we need to derive ethics from.

Duty: obedience to representations: an illusion! The true motives of the will are hidden by these representations of duty. Think of the duties to the fatherland etc. Ethically an act of duty is worthless as an act of *duty*; because neither a poem nor an act is made through abstraction. But it is

---

[6] Nietzsche's knowledge of the religion of the Parsees is derived from Max Müller, *Essays*, vol. I *Beiträge zur vergleichenden Religionswissenschaft* (Leipzig, 1869).

[7] Darius (properly 'Daraya-vauš'; see *The Cambridge Encyclopedia of the World's Ancient Languages*, ed. Roget Woodard (Cambridge University Press, 2004), p. 735), Great King of the Persian Empire (522–486 BC), sent a punitive expedition against Athens in response to their burning of the city of Sardis (498 BC). The Athenian defeat of this expedition on the plain of Marathon, just north east of the city of Athens, in September 490 BC continued to have great symbolic significance for the Athenians, and, because of the great cultural prestige of Athens for other speakers of Greek, for centuries thereafter. 'Zoroaster' is the Hellenised form of 'Zaraθuštra', a shadowy figure whose dates are uncertain, but who most likely lived before the sixth century BC. He was a prophet who preached a religion based on a strict distinction between good and evil, and truth and falsity. Humans had to choose. Later in his life Nietzsche used a literary figure whom he called 'Zarathustra' to propound several philosophical doctrines to which he attached particular importance. See *Thus Spoke Zarathustra*. The idea that if Darius' punitive expedition had not been defeated the Hellenes would have become Zoroastrians is, of course, hugely speculative.

valuable precisely because it cannot come into being from an abstraction, from duty, and nevertheless it has happened.

Goodness and love are qualities of *genius*: the supreme power emanates from them; therefore it is instinct, the will, that speaks. It is a drive for unity, the revelation of a higher order, which manifests itself in goodness, love, charity, compassion.

Goodness and love are practical drives to correct the world – alongside religion, which intervenes as a delusion.

They are not related to the intellect, which has no means whatsoever to deal with them. They are pure instinct, emotion mixed with a representation.

The *representation in emotion* with regard to the actual motion of the will has only the significance of a *symbol*. This symbol is the delusion through which a universal drive exerts a subjective individual irritation.

Emotion – with will and unconscious representation.

deed – with will and conscious representation.

Where does the deed begin? Should 'deed' not also be a representation, something indefinable? A *motion of the will* becoming *visible*? But visible? This visibility is something accidental and external. The movement of the rectum is also a motion of the will, which would be visible if we could take our eyes there.

Nor does the *conscious will* characterise the deed; for we can consciously strive for a sensation, which we would certainly not call a deed.

What is meant by becoming conscious of a movement of the will? A symbolising process that becomes clearer and clearer. Language, the word, nothing but symbol. Thinking, i.e. consciously imagining, is nothing but envisioning and linking linguistic symbols. The primal intellect is something quite different in that it is essentially representation of a purpose; thinking is remembering symbols. Thinking relates to experienced reality as do the games of the visual organ, which likewise reproduce experienced reality in a colourful flux when the eyes are closed: it is a piecemeal rumination.

The separation of the will and the representation is really a product of necessity in thinking: it is a retrospective production, an analogy after the experience of seeing something that we want as a goal before our eyes. But this goal is merely a past reproduced: that is how the movement of the will makes itself understood. The goal is not the motive or the agent of the action: even though this *seems* to be the case.

It is nonsense to maintain that there is a necessary connection between the will and the representation: the representation proves to be a falsifying mechanism which we need not assume to exist in the essence of things. As soon as the will is about to become appearance this mechanism sets in.

In the will there is diversity and movement only through the representation: it is through the representation alone that an eternal being turns into a becoming, into the will; i.e. the becoming, the will itself as something effective, is an illusion. There is only eternal repose, pure being. But where does the representation come from? That is the mystery. Naturally also from the beginning, because it can never have come into being. This is not to be confused with the mechanism of representation in the sentient creature.

But if the representation is merely a symbol, then the eternal movement, all the striving of being, is only an *illusion*. Then there is something that imagines: this cannot be being itself.

Then there is, beside the eternal being, another, totally passive power, that of illusion – – Mystery!

On the other hand, if the will contains the diversity, the becoming, is there a goal? *The intellect, the representation, must be independent of becoming and willing*; the purposes of the continuous symbolising process are purely those of the will. But the will itself has no need of any representations, and nor has it a *purpose*, which is nothing but a reproduction, a rumination, of what has been experienced in conscious thought. The *appearance* is a continuous symbolising process of the will.

Because in delusions we recognise the intention of the will, the representation is a product of the will, the diversity is already in the will, the appearance is a μηχανή[8] of the will for itself.

One must be able to draw the *boundaries* and then say: these necessary consequences of thinking are the intention of the will.

5[90]

The concept of 'drama' as 'action'.[9]

---

[8] instrument. See above, 'On Schopenhauer', footnote 15, p. 6.
[9] Or 'plot': *Handlung*; see above, Notebook 3, footnote 5, p. 18.

This concept is very naïve in its roots: the decisive factor here is the world and the habit of the *eye*. But, after all, what – considered more inwardly – is not action? Emotion expressing itself, the process of becoming clear about something – not action? Must there always be executions or murders? – But one thing is necessary: *becoming* as opposed to being and to the art of sculpture. Fossilisations of the moment there – reality here.

The purpose of such a reality is to appear as *such*. We should not waver between illusion and truth. Here the pathological interest is compulsory. We feel as if we were experiencing something. Whoever is strongest at creating this illusion is the best poet: but *whom* he has to deceive is of fundamental importance. Ideally, he should know how to deceive himself. Here, it must be said, the work of art is measured by an external standard. It makes for knowledge and deeds as an 'effective real work of art'.

5[91]

If one construes a delusion as such, the will – *if* it wants us to continue to exist – must create a *new* one. *Culture* is a continuous replacement of delusions with more noble ones; i.e. the 'motives' of our thinking rise higher and higher above the material and assume a greater universality. The goal of 'humanity' is the most that the will can offer us as a phantom. Basically, nothing changes. The will does what it has to do and the representation tries to reach the universally concerned essence of the will. Culture lies in thinking of the good of organisms that are greater than the individual.

5[102]

By foreshadowing a redemption of the world, tragedy offers the most sublime illusion: *freedom* from *existence* itself.

Here suffering is a necessity – but a comfort.

The illusion providing the background of tragedy is that of the Buddhist religion.

Here we are shown *bliss in recognising the supreme grief.* This is the triumph of the will, which regards its most terrible configuration as the *well* of a possibility of existence.

5[105]

Tragic man – as the fitting *teacher* of men.

Culture and education must not take the average endowment with ἦθος[10] and intellect as the norm, but those tragic natures – .

Here lies the solution of the social question. The rich or talented egoist is sick and subject to pity.

I see enormous conglomerates taking the place of individual capitalists. I see the stock exchange falling victim to the curse under which the casinos have *fallen*.

---

[10] character.

Notebook 6, end of 1870

6[3]

How is an education possible if there is no freedom of the will, if there is no freedom of thought, and if we are merely appearance?

Contrary to this, it can be said that there is an education in the same sense as a freedom of the will – that is, as a necessary delusion, as a feigned explanation of a phenomenon that is totally inaccessible to us. If therefore no education occurs it is a proof that that phenomenon does not exist.

An education to tragic knowledge, then, presupposes the determinability of character, freedom of choice etc. for practical purposes, but denies the same theoretically and immediately places this problem at the head of education. We shall always behave as we *are* and never as we ought to be.

Genius has the power to drape the world with a new net of illusions: education for genius means making the net of illusions necessary by assiduously contemplating the contradiction.

Tragic knowledge, even in relation to the primal single being, is indeed only a representation, an image, a delusion. But in so far as the contradiction, the unconciliatory, is seen in this image, we experience, as it were, how the scene of the possessed boy provokes the transfiguration.[1] To be educated – only means – unfolding oneself. One needs only to regard the desert and the torment of the saint as the necessary prerequisite of the ecstasy.

---

[1] A reference to the painting by Raphael (1483–1520), *The Transfiguration*, now in the Vatican; see also BT § 4.

31

The effect of a genius is usually that a mass is swathed in a new net of illusions under which it can live. That is the magic effect of a genius on the inferior ranks. But at the same time there is an ascending line to the genius: this always tears up the existing nets until finally a higher artistic goal is reached in reaching the genius.

Notebook 7, end of 1870 – April 1871

7[3]

The Hellenic world of Apollo is gradually subjugated by the Dionysian forces from within. Christianity *was* already *present*.[1]

7[13]

The *Gospel according to St John* born out of Greek atmosphere, out of the soil of the Dionysian: its influence on Christianity in contrast to Judaism.

7[18]

The glorification of the will through art is the goal of the Hellenic will. Therefore it was necessary to ensure that artistic creations were possible. Art is the free excess strength of a people which is not squandered in the struggle for existence. Hence the *cruel* reality of a *culture* – in so far as it builds its triumphal gates on enslavement and destruction.

7[21]

The boundless, demanding logic of science develops at the same time as the supreme flowering of art. This kills the tragic work of art. The sacred keeper of the instincts, music, disappeared from drama. The scientific

---

[1] Contrary to his later protestations, in the early period Nietzsche construed Christianity as an essentially 'Dionysian' phenomenon.

existence is the last manifestation of the will: the will no longer appears veiled, but being true it acts as a stimulant in its endless diversity. Everything must be explained: the smallest thing becomes attractive and the eye is, as it were, violently distracted from wisdom (of the artist). Religion, art, science – all merely weapons against wisdom.

7[116]

There is no natural beauty. But there is the disruptively ugly and a point of indifference. Think of the reality of dissonance as opposed to the ideality of consonance. What is productive, then, is the pain, which creates the beautiful as a related counter-colour – out of that point of indifference. We have an eccentric example in the tortured saint, who feels a painless, even blissful, ecstasy.[2] How far does this ideality go? It is continually living and growing, a world within the world. But is the reality perhaps only pain, and the *representation* born of that? But then of what type is the *enjoyment*? The enjoyment of something not real but only ideal? And is perhaps all life, as far as it is enjoyment, nothing but such a reality? And what is the point of indifference reached by nature? How is painlessness possible? Intuition is an aesthetic product. What then is real? What is it that intuits? Are diversity of pain and indifference of pain possible as conditions of a being? What *is* the being at those points of indifference? Could *time* as well as *space* perhaps be explained from those points of indifference? And could the diversity of pain be derived from those points of indifference?

What is important here is a comparison of the work of art to that point of indifference from which it comes into being, and a comparison of the world from a point free of pain. That is where representation is generated. – The subjectivity of the world is not an anthropomorphic subjectivity, but a subjectivity of the world itself: we are the characters in the dream of the god who guess how he is dreaming.

7[117]

Artistic pleasure must exist even without human beings. The bright flower or the peacock's tail relates to its origin as harmony does to that

[2] See BT §§ 3–4.

point of indifference, i.e. as the work of art does to its negative origin. That which creates the former, and creates artistically, is also active in the artist. What then *is* the work of art? What *is* the harmony? In any case just as real as the bright flower.

But if the flower, the human being, the peacock's tail have a negative origin, they are as real as the 'harmonies' of a god,[3] i.e. their reality is the reality of a dream. Then we need a being that produces the world as a work of art, as harmony; then the will, as it were, produces out of the void, Πενία,[4] art as Πόρος.[5] Then everything that exists is the image of the will, in the artistic power also. Crystal, the cells etc.

The tendency of art is to overcome dissonance: thus the world of the beautiful originating from the point of indifference strives to draw dissonance as the disruptive element as such into the work of art. Hence the gradual enjoyment of the minor key and dissonance. It is purveyed by *de*lusion,[6] or indeed any kind of *representation*,[7] based on the fact that a pain-free intuition of things is produced.

The will as the supreme pain brings forth from itself an ecstasy which is identical to the pure intuition and production of the work of art. What is the *physiological* process? A condition of painlessness must be created somewhere – but how?

Here the *representation* is created as a purveyor of that supreme ecstasy.

The world is both core and representation at the same time, the core being the one terrible will, and the representation the diffused world of representation, of ecstasy.

Music proves that that whole world in its diversity is no longer felt to be a *dissonance*.

That which suffers, struggles, tears itself apart is always only the *one* will: it is the absolute contradiction as the primal source of existence.

Therefore individuation is the *result* of suffering, not its cause.

---

[3] See the poem 'An Zimmern' by one of Nietzsche's favourite poets, Friedrich Hölderlin, in *Friedrich Hölderlin: Poems and Fragments*, trans. Michael Hamburger (London: Anvil, 1994), pp. 670f.

[4] Poverty, want, need. See Plato, *Symposium* 203b–c for the myth about the birth of Erotic Desire (Ἔρως) from Poverty (Πενία), impregnated by Means (Πόρος). See also next footnote.

[5] Originally 'means for passing over a river' (etymologically related to English 'ford'), then more generally 'means (for getting anything), resources, provisions'. See also previous footnote.

[6] *Wahnvorstellung.*

[7] *Vorstellung.*

The *work of art* and the *individual* is a *repetition* of the *primal process* in which the world came into being, so to speak, a ripple within the wave.

7[121]

The plant that achieves only stunted flowers in the relentless struggle for existence, having been released from this struggle by a stroke of good fortune, suddenly looks at us with the eye of beauty. What nature has to tell us through this will of beauty, which breaks through everywhere and instantly, will be discussed later: here it may suffice for us to have drawn attention to this drive itself, because we can learn something from it about the purpose of the state. Nature labours to attain beauty; once this is reached somewhere, nature makes sure that it is reproduced. For this purpose nature needs a highly artificial mechanism between the world of animals and plants if the single beautiful bloom is to be perpetuated. I recognise a similar, even more artificial, mechanism in the nature of the state which, in its ultimate purpose, also seems to me to be an institution for the protection and nurture of *individuals*, of genius, no matter how little its cruel origin and barbarous behaviour suggest such goals. Here too we have to make a distinction between a delusion that we avidly seek to reach and a real purpose that the will is able to fulfil through us, perhaps even against our consciousness. In the enormous apparatus surrounding humankind, in the wild jumble of selfish goals, what ultimately matters is also the *individual*: but care has been taken to ensure that these individuals cannot enjoy their abnormal position. When all is said and done, they too are nothing but tools of the will and must suffer the nature of the will as it affects them; but *there is something in them* for which the round dance of the stars and the states is performed as a spectacle. In this respect too the Greek world is more sincere and simple than that of other peoples and times: just as the Greeks in general have this in common with geniuses that, like children and as children, they are loyal and truthful. Only, one must be able to talk with them in order to understand them.

The Greek artist addresses his work not to the individual but to the state; and the education of the state, in its turn, was nothing but the education of all to enjoy the work of art. All great creations, in sculpture and architecture as well as in the other fine arts, have their sights on great popular emotions nurtured by the state. Tragedy, in particular, is an annual act prepared solemnly by and for the state and uniting the whole people. The state was a necessary *purveyor* of the reality of art. But if we have to describe those individual beings, those men who perpetuate themselves in artistic and philosophical work, as the true goal of the tendency of the state, then the enormous power of the political drive, the drive of the homeland in the narrowest sense, may also appear as a guarantee that the succession of individual geniuses is a continuous one, that the soil from which alone they can grow is not torn by earthquakes and inhibited in its fertility. For the artist to come into being we need that dronelike estate exempt from slave labour; for the great work of art to come into being we need the concentrated will of that estate, the state. Only the state, as a *magic power*, can force the selfish individuals to take on the sacrifices and preparations required for the realisation of great artistic projects; which involves above almost everything else the education of the people – an education designed to generate an insight into the exemption of those individuals, together with the delusion that the crowd itself has to foster the development of those geniuses through its concern, its judgement, its culture. Here I can only see the effect of *one* will which, in order to achieve the goal of its own glorification in works of art, blinds the eyes of its creatures with numerous tangled delusions which are far more powerful than even the shrewd insight that one is deluded. But the stronger the political drive, the more the continuous succession of geniuses is guaranteed; provided that the greatly *overloaded* drive does not begin to rage against itself and sink its teeth into its own flesh: in which case the troublesome consequences are wars and party conflicts. However, it seems almost as if from time to time the will uses such self-lacerations as an outlet, in which respect it is also true to its terrible nature. At least the political drive, regulated through such events, has a habit of working on the preparation of the birth of the genius with a new and surprising strength. In any case it must be noted that in the overloading of the political drive among the Greeks nature shows how much it demands of that people in the sphere of art. In that sense the terrible spectacle of the parties tearing each other apart is worthy of admiration: for out of this pushing and shoving arises the song of the genius that has never been heard before.

7[123]

Here it is obvious that only a very small band of the chosen can be initiated into the highest levels[8] and that the masses will always stop in the fore-courts; and likewise that without those epopts[9] of the ultimate wisdom the purpose of the venerable institution remains entirely unachieved, while each of the other initiates, striving for a personal happiness or an individual prospect of a beautiful continuing existence, that is, following the urge of *selfishness*, bravely advances through the levels of knowledge until he has to halt at the point where his eye can no longer bear the terrible splendour of the truth. It is at this boundary that those individuals separate themselves out who, with little regard for themselves, are driven ahead by a painful goad into that devouring brightness – to return with a transfigured look in their eyes, as a triumph of the Dionysian will which, through a wonderful delusion, bends back and breaks even the existence-denying last barb of its knowledge, the strongest spear directed against existence itself. To the mass quite different enticements or threats apply: these include the belief that after death the uninitiated will be lying in the mud, while the initiated may look forward to a blissful continuing existence.[10] Other images, in which existence in this life was seen to be a prison[11] and the body as the tomb of the soul,[12] are more profound. But then the Dionysian myths proper arrive with their everlasting content, which we must regard as the subsoil nourishing all Hellenic art: how the future ruler of the world as a child (D[ionysus] Z[agreus]) is dismembered by the Titans and how he must now be venerated in this condition as Zagreus.[13] This expresses the idea that the dismemberment, the

---

[8] It is clear from the wider context that Nietzsche is discussing the so-called 'mysteries' here. These were esoteric religious rites which were performed in various places throughout the ancient Greek world. Because they were secret, little is known about them, but in most cases initiates seem to have been given instruction and allowed to see various 'sights' as they were led through a series of ritual performances that purportedly moved them from one level to the next of religious knowledge. They often seem to have promised some kind of salvation or survival or the improvement of one's condition after death. See Walter Burkert, *Antike Mysterien: Funktionen und Gehalt* (Munich: Beck, 1991).

[9] 'those who have seen': The highest level of initiates into one of the most prestigious of the mysteries, the Eleusinean Mysteries, located in Eleusis, near Athens.

[10] See Plato, *Phaedo* 69c, also Aristophanes, *Frogs* ll. 138–64.

[11] See also Plato, *Cratylus* 400c and *Phaedo* 62b. For further discussion of material that seems related to, if not directly derived from, 'mysteries' see also *Phaedo* 66–71.

[12] See Plato, *Cratylus* 400c and *Gorgias* 493a.

[13] This myth of Dionysus Zagreus is central to Nietzsche's *Birth of Tragedy*, § 10. For the original myth, see *Orphicorum Fragmenta*, collegit Otto Kern (Berlin: Weidmann, 1922), pp. 226–38. See

actual Dionysian *suffering*, is equal to a transformation into air, water, earth and rock, plant and animal; in accordance with which the condition of individuation has been regarded as the primal source of all suffering and as something in itself reprehensible. The Olympian gods were created from the smile of Phanes, the humans from his tears.[14] In that condition Dionysus has the dual nature of a cruel, depraved demon and a benevolent ruler (as ἀγ[ριώνιος][15] and ὠμ[<ηστής][16] and μειλ[ίχιος][17]). This nature manifests itself in such terrible moods as the demand of the soothsayer Euphrantides before the battle of Marathon that the three sons of Xerxes' sister, three beautiful and splendidly decorated youths, be sacrificed to Dionysus ἀ[γριώνιος], which alone would guarantee victory.[18] The epopts hoped for a rebirth of Dionysus, which we must now understand as an end to individuation: it was this future third Dionysus whom the epopts' thunderous song of jubilation celebrated. And only in this hope is there a ray of joy on the face of the world torn and split into individuals: as is symbolised in the myth of Demeter[19] who, sunk into eternal mourning by the dismemberment of Dionysus, is glad again for the first time on being told that she can *once more* give birth to Dionysus. In the images just quoted we already have all the ingredients of the most profound view of the world: the fundamental recognition of the unity of everything that exists, the perception of individuation as the primal source of all evil, beauty and art as the hope that the spell of individuation can be broken, as the premonition of unity restored. Of course, such a circle of representations must not be dragged into the realm of the everyday,

---

Nonnus, *Dionysiaca* VI. 155–205; Plutarch, 'On the E in Delphi' (in Book V of *Moralia*), chapter 9 (but actually the whole of this fascinating essay is of relevance for Nietzsche's views on Apollo and Dionysus). For a modern interpretation, see Walter Burkert, *Homo necans* (Berlin: de Gruyter, 1972), esp. pp. 1–97.

[14] The origin of this claim is a fragment of a poem cited by the Neo-Platonist Proclus in his commentary on Plato's *Republic*. See Kern, *Orphicorum Fragmenta*, p. 341.

[15] savage, wild. For the dual aspect of Dionysus, see Euripides, *Bacchae* 859ff.; also Plutarch, *Life of Anthony* 24.

[16] who eats raw flesh (i.e. to whom human sacrifices are made).

[17] kind, gentle, mild.

[18] As reported in Plutarch, *Life of Themistocles* 13. Actually Plutarch in this passage says Themistocles sacrificed the three Persians to Dionysus 'ὠμηστής' rather than to Dionysus 'ἀγριώνιος', but this probably amounts to much the same thing. Also the battle in question was the battle of Salamis (a naval battle between a large alliance of Greek cities and the Persians under Xerxes in 480 BC), not the battle of Marathon (a land battle between the Athenians and Miltiades against the Persians under Datis and Artaphernes, generals of Darius, in 490 BC).

[19] Demeter, whose name means 'Earth-Mother', was the major deity involved in the Eleusinean Mysteries. See Kern, *Orphicorum Fragmenta*, pp. 226–38.

39

the regular order of divine services, if it is not to be most shamefully distorted and trivialised. The goal of the entire institution of mysteries was to convey this insight in images only to those who were prepared for it, i.e., those who had already been led towards it by a holy need. But in these images we recognise all those eccentric moods and insights which the orgiasm of the Dionysian spring festivals awakened almost at once and side by side: the destruction of individuation, the horror over the broken unity, the hope of a new creation of the world, in short, the sensation of a blissful shudder, in which the *knots* of joy and terror are tied together. When those ecstatic conditions had cocooned themselves into the order of mysteries the greatest threat to the Apollonian world had been eliminated and now the god of states and Dionysus could, without fear of shattering the state, enter into their visible alliance in order to create their common work of art, tragedy, and to glorify their dual character in *tragic man*. This union expresses itself, e.g., in the feelings of the Athenian citizen, who regarded only two things as the supreme crime: the desecration of the mysteries and the destruction of the constitution of his polity. The fact that nature linked the origin of tragedy to those two fundamental drives, the Apollonian and the Dionysian, may be considered as much an abyss of reason as that same nature's device of attaching propagation to the duplicity of the sexes, which always appeared astonishing to the great Kant.[20] The mystery shared by both is how two mutually hostile principles can give rise to something new in which those conflicting drives appear as a unity: in which sense propagation may be regarded no less than the tragic work of art as a guarantee of the rebirth of Dionysus, as a glimmer of hope on the eternally mourning face of Demeter.

7[124]

The goal of that new creation of art which Euripides, spurred on by Socrates, envisaged was very different from the Platonic: if Plato tried to abolish the Socratic concept of art,[21] Euripides strived to make this

[20] See Kant's essay 'Betrachtungen über das Gefühl des Schönen und Erhabenen' (1764)

[21] That is, presumably, that Plato tried to create works of art in his 'dialogues' that would *not* satisfy the conditions for a 'work of art' laid out in the 'Socratic definition' of art, and thus in some sense challenge that definition. As Nietzsche goes on to say in the passage immediately after this, the 'Socratic definition' he has in mind takes 'art' to be 'the image of an illusory image' (see Plato, *Republic* 595–604). Plato's dialogues then, on this view, were intended in some sense as

concept more precise in his creations. The former rejected the art that had existed up to his time because he thought it reprehensible in its Socratic definition; the latter rejected it because he felt that it did not correspond perfectly to that concept. Thus Plato saw the Socratic definition of art – as the image of the illusory image[22] – as a standard; Euripides as a kind of ideal: that is why the former had to seek a new definition for his new art and the latter a new art for the old definition. How heavily the Socratic rejection of all art must have weighed on the soul of Euripides! And what a stern determination it takes to mould art deliberately into precisely that form to which that rejection really and completely applies! Being thus whipped along the racecourse of dramatic creation and holding the reins thus firmly in order to guide the work of art straight towards the abyss – what sombre conflict! Tragedy, as I have said, died by suicide.[23] Now we understand the orgiastic joy of self-laceration in Euripides. Who could look at the picture of the melancholy Euripides without compassion! Here we see the expression of a powerful intellect, which recognises in the Socratic definition of art not only a critique but also the so far unattained goal of tragedy: and next to it a tremendous poetic force which must discharge itself in dramatic poems, no matter how serious the rejecting voice of Socrates may sound. This harsh conflict, coming to light in one nature, drove Euripides into solitude, from which he could dare to despise his audiences when they rejected him as well as when they adored him. At the same time he was not even allowed to present[24] his idea of the tragic work of art naked and unaccommodated, because this would have been impossible in the Athens of the time. A later generation correctly recognised the difference between the core and the shell: it discarded the latter, and the quintessence of dramatic art, as Socrates understood it and as Euripides tried completely to achieve it, turned out to be a chess-like drama, *the new Attic comedy*.[25] Of this it is true in the boldest sense of the word that it is the image of the image.[26] It was played in every family, and

---

[22] giving reality, not a mere image, perhaps by virtue of the fact that they were actual instances of dialectical argumentation.

[22] *Abbild des Scheinbildes.*

[23] See BT § 11.

[24] *veranschaulichen.*

[25] The most important figure of New Comedy is Menander (*c.* 342–292 BC) who, in contrast to the obscene, surreally phantastic, linguistically exuberant and politically pointed Old Comedies of Aristophanes (*c.* 444?–388?), wrote polished, carefully plotted, quasi-realistic plays about private people facing the small problems and difficulties of everyday life in the ancient world.

[26] *Abbild des Abbildes.*

everyman acted in it. The authors of that comedy knew why they revered Euripides as their genius: Euripides, who had placed the spectator on the stage, who had ploughed into the audience the taste for rehashing everyday life. Nobody noticed the pessimistic and penetrating eye with which Euripides looked down on this art. But what was left behind for all times was a new genre of *Socratic art*, which, in alliance with the novel, has commanded the admiration of the entire un-Greek posterity. *Drama* as the reflection of empirical reality, with a change of government as its goal, the *novel* as the reflection of a fantastic and ideal reality with some sort of metaphysical perspective: these are the two basic forms in which almost two millennia have demonstrated their dependence on the Greeks, indeed their natural descent from them – basic forms which found their final fulfilment and utmost saturation in Cervantes[27] and Shakespeare.

After this glimpse into the farthest distance let us look back once more at Socrates, who has meanwhile no doubt turned into something monstrous: 'He looks like a hippopotamus now, With fearsome jaws and fiery eyes.'[28]

7[125]

What kind of genius is produced time and again by the stimulus of Socratism?

We have already realised how Greek art and ethics, which were based on the instincts and had attained no knowledge of themselves, foundered on the theoretical genius: whereby the Greek state, which had existed only on the basis of that ethics and for the purpose of that art, naturally also received its death sentence. As to the new artistic objective indicated by the initially anti-artistic operation of the theoretical genius and the enormous periods of time covered by the production of this new art, I have had an idea which I will articulate in spite of its resemblance to a metaphysical whim and even at the risk of being treated as a dangerous

---

[27] The novel *Don Quixote de la Mancha* by the Spanish novelist Miguel de Cervantes (1547–1616) was an immediate success when it was published, and enjoyed a revival of popularity in Europe at the end of the eighteenth and the beginning of the nineteenth centuries (see Jean Canavaggio, *Don Quichotte du livre au mythe: Quatre siècles d'errance*, Paris: Fayard, 2005). Nietzsche was repelled by the sadism of the work, noting that Cervantes chooses to satirise not the Inquisition, but its victims (KSA vol. 8, 23[140], 1876–7), and called *Don Quixote* 'one of the most harmful books' (KSA vol. 8, 8[7], 1875).

[28] Goethe, *Faust Part I*, trans. David Luke (Oxford University Press, 1987), ll. 1254–5.

heretic. But before I do so I must note that *time* impresses me as little as it does the geologist, my contemporary, and that therefore I undauntedly take the liberty of disposing of millennia, as something totally unreal, for the creation of *one* great work of art.

The theoretical genius pushes for the unleashing of artistic-mystical drives in two ways: on the one hand through its sheer existence, which demands the existence of its immortal twin, like one colour the other, in accordance with a certain allopathy of nature; on the other hand through the abrupt transformation of science into art every time its limits are reached. We must imagine the beginning of the latter process as follows: at some point of the perceptible world theoretical man becomes aware of the existence of an illusion, of the general existence of a naïve deception of the senses and the intellect, from which he frees himself through the careful use of causality and by means of the logical mechanism. At the same time he discovers that the usual mythical representation of that course of events, in comparison with his insight, contains an error and that therefore the people's world view, which is revered as something credible, contains demonstrable errors. That is the beginning of Greek science, which, already in its very first stages, basically while still a mere embryo of science, turns into art and, from the narrow standpoint it has just gained, concocts a new world picture by means of a fanciful analogy, the world as water or air or fire.[29] Here a simple chemical experiment has been turned into the origin of being through an enlargement by a concave mirror; and for the sake of these cosmogonies the diversity and infinity of that which exists must now be explained through a host of physical phantasms, or, if these do not suffice, even through the old folk gods. Thus the scientific world picture initially departs only slowly from popular representations and, after a brief sidestep, returns to them

---

[29] Much of the Pre-Socratic philosophy we can recover was devoted to cosmological speculation. Thus, the figure usually recognised as the earliest 'philosopher' was Thales, who probably lived in the town of Miletus in Asia Minor during the first half of the sixth century BC. He was thought to have claimed that the basic substance from which everything was made was 'water'. Anaximenes (also of Miletus; mid-sixth century) is said to have declared that the basic substance was 'air', and Heraclitus (of Ephesus in Asia Minor; late sixth – early fifth centuries) 'fire'. Presumably in all these cases the 'water', 'air' etc. of which these philosophers spoke referred to some underlying metaphysical principle, not the liquid or gas we use to fill our baths or to breathe. Given the fragmentary nature of our knowledge of their views, however, we cannot be at all sure how the various Pre-Socratics conceived of the relation between their respective basic principles and the normal phenomena after which the principles were named, or indeed whether they did have a very clear conception of that relation. See Nietzsche's *Philosophie im tragischen Zeitalter der Griechen* in KSA vol. 1, pp. 801–72.

again and again as soon as the narrowly circumscribed actual knowledge is to be expanded into a fundamental knowledge of the world. What force is it that causes those inordinate exaggerations and abuses of analogical inference, and that on the other hand drives theoretical man so seductively from the secure ground he has just conquered to the hodge-podge of imagination? Why this leap into the bottomless pit? Here we must remember that the intellect is merely an organ of the will, so that all its operations, with a necessary craving, push for existence, and that its goal can be only various forms of existence but never the question of being or not-being. For the intellect there is no nothingness as a goal, and therefore no absolute knowledge, because absolute knowledge, compared to being, would be a not-being. Accordingly, to support life – to seduce to life – is the intention underlying all knowledge, the illogical element, which, as the father of all knowledge, also determines the limits of knowledge. Thus that mythical world picture, decorated with phantasms, may appear merely as the exaggeration of a small isolated piece of knowledge: in truth, however, it is the driving cause[30] of this knowledge, even though this process cannot be grasped by consciousness, which is always forced to judge empirically, in accordance with purely empirical principles, and which in fact can only present cause[31] and effect in reverse. Therefore that which always goes beyond the limits of science and as it were - - -

7[126]

Modern art was born during the back-and-forth surge of this struggle. As a sign of these struggles it generally has a 'sentimental' character and it achieves its highest goal when it is able to create the 'idyll'. I am unable to apply Schiller's glorious terminology[32] to the entirety of what is the widest field of all art, because I find a considerable number of periods and works of art that I cannot subsume under those terms, even though I think I am right in interpreting 'naïve' as 'purely Apollonian', as 'the illusion of illusion', in contrast to 'sentimental', as something 'born out of the struggle between tragic knowledge and mysticism'. As certainly as the 'naïve' has been recognised to be the eternal mark of a supreme artistic genre, just as certainly the term 'sentimental' does not suffice to sum up

[30] *der treibende Grund.*
[31] *Grund.*
[32] See his 'On naïve and sentimental poetry'.

the characteristics of all non-naïve art. If we try to do this, how con-
founded are we, for example, by Greek tragedy and Shakespeare! Not to
mention music! In my understanding, the complete opposite of the 'naïve'
and 'Apollonian' is the 'Dionysian', i.e. any art that is not 'the illusion
of illusion', but 'the illusion of being', a reflection of the eternal primal
One, in other words, our whole empirical world, which, from the point
of view of the primal One, is a Dionysian work of art, or, from our own
point of view, music. From the highest seat of judgement, I am obliged to
deny recognition to the 'sentimental' even as a pure work of art, because,
rather than arising from the supreme and enduring reconciliation of the
naïve and the Dionysian, it swings restlessly to and fro between them
and achieves their union only spasmodically, without acquiring permanent possession and holding an uncertain position between the different
arts, between poetry and prose, philosophy and art, concept and intuition, desire and capability. It is the work of art born out of that as yet
undecided struggle which it is on the point of deciding. It does not actually reach that goal, but by moving and elevating us, as does e.g. Schiller's
drama, it points us into new directions. Thus it is 'John the Precursor',
coming to 'baptise all nations'.

7[127]

After these premises, imagine what an unnatural, indeed impossible,
enterprise it must be to compose music for a poem, i.e. to try to illustrate
a poem through music, perhaps even with the explicit intention of symbolising the conceptual representations of the poem through the music
and thus helping music to acquire a conceptual language: an enterprise
that appears to me like that of a son trying to beget his father. Music can
project images[33] out of itself: but these are always mere reflections,[34] as it
were, specimens of its essential content; the image, the representation –
let alone the concept or the poetic idea, as has been claimed – will never
be able to produce music out of itself. On the other hand, it is not such a
ridiculous phenomenon as it has seemed to recent aesth[eticians] for a
Beethoven symphony to elicit time and again a language of images from
the individual listeners, however fantastically motley, indeed contradictory,

[33] *Bilder.*
[34] *Abbilder.*

45

a compilation of the different worlds of images produced by a piece of music may appear. Practising their poor wit on such compilations and failing to recognise that the phenomenon is worth explaining is quite typical of those gentlemen. Indeed, even if the composer has spoken about a composition in images, if, for example, he describes a symphony as 'pastoral' and a movement as a 'scene by the brook' or as a 'merry gathering of country folk',[35] these are nothing but allegorical representations born out of the music, which can teach us nothing whatsoever about the Dionysian content of the music and which in fact have no exclusive value in relation to other images. As for pressing the music into the service of a number of images and concepts, using it as a means to an end, that is, to intensify and to clarify them – this strange presumption found in the concept of 'opera' reminds me of a ridiculous man who tries to lift himself into the air by his own arms: what both that fool and opera in that sense try to do are pure impossibilities. That concept of opera demands from music not an improper use, but – as I have said – an impossibility! Music *can* never become a means to an end, however much one may squeeze, wrench and torture it: even in its rawest and simplest stages, as mere sound, as a drum roll, it overcomes poetry and reduces it to a reflection of itself. Therefore opera as a genre in that sense is not so much a confusion of music as a mistaken representation of aesthetics. Incidentally, in thus justifying the nature of opera for aesthetics, I am of course far from wishing to justify bad operatic music or bad operatic poems. In contrast to the best poem, the worst music can still signify the Dionysian foundation of the world; and the worst poem, given the best music, can be a mirror, an image and a reflection of this foundation: as certainly as the individual tone, in contrast to the image, is already Dionysian, and the individual image, together with the concept and the word, in contrast to music, is already Apollonian. Even bad music together with bad poetry can teach us about the nature of music and poetry. The *recitative* is the most obvious expression of the unnatural. If, for example, Schopenhauer perceived both the music and the poetry of Bellini's *Norma* as the fulfilment of tragedy,[36] he was fully entitled to do so by his Dionysian–Apollonian elation and oblivion of self, because he perceived both the music and the poetry in their most universal and, so to speak, philosophical value, as music and

---

[35] Beethoven gave his sixth symphony (F major, Opus 67) the descriptive title *'Pastoral'* and also gave descriptive titles to each movement.
[36] WWR vol. II § 37.

poetry in an absolute sense; even though this judgement revealed an insufficiently educated taste which failed to make historical comparisons. To us, who deliberately avoid any question about the historical value of an artistic phenomenon and who try to consider only the phenomenon itself in its unchanging, as it were, eternal significance and therefore in its *supreme type* – to us the genre of opera is as justified as the folk song, in so far as we find in both the union of the Dionysian and the Apollonian and may therefore assume that the origin of the opera – that is, the supreme type of opera – was analogous to that of the folk song. It is only in so far as the opera known in history had a completely different origin from that of the folk song that we reject this 'opera', which bears the same relation to the genre of opera defended by us as the marionette does to the living human being. Although the music can never become a means in the service of the text and in any case overcomes the text, it certainly becomes bad music if the composer breaks every Dionysian force rising in him by an anxious glance at the words and gestures of his marionettes. If the librettist has offered him nothing more than the usual schematic characters with their Egyptian regularity, then the freer, the more absolute, the more Dionysian the music becomes, and the more it despises all the so-called dramatic requirements, the greater will be the value of the opera. At its best opera in this sense is indeed good music and only music, while the tricks performed at the same time are, as it were, merely a fantastic disguise of the orchestra – particularly of its prime instruments, the singers – from which the discerning turn away laughing. If the mass relishes the *latter* while merely *tolerating* the music, it is in the same position as those who hold the gold frame of a good painting in higher esteem than the painting itself: who would consider such naïve confusions worthy of a serious, not to say solemn, response? But what may opera mean as 'dramatic' music as far removed as possible from pure, exclusively Dionysian music making its impact as music in its own right? Let us imagine a colourful, passionate drama that carries the spectator away and that can rely on its sheer action for its success: what will 'dramatic' music be able to add to this, if it does not in fact take something away from it? But firstly it *will* take a great deal away from it: for at any moment at which the Dionysian force of the music hits the listener, the eye that sees the action and has been engrossed in the individuals appearing in front of it is veiled: now the listener *forgets* the drama and reawakes to it only when the Dionysian magic has let go of him. Actually, in so far as the music makes the listener forget the drama it is not 'dramatic' music: but what kind of music is that which is not *allowed* to exert a Dionysian power over the listener? And how is that music possible? It is possible as a *purely conventional symbolism* from which convention has drained all natural strength: as a music reduced to a mere mnemonic sign with the desired effect of reminding the spectator of something that he must not miss if he is to understand the drama he is watching: just as a trumpet signal is an invitation for the horse to trot. Finally, before the beginning of the drama and in the intervals between scenes, alongside boring passages of doubtful dramatic effectiveness, and even at the climactic moments, a different, no longer purely conventional music of recollection, but a *music of excitement* would be permissible as a stimulant for blunt or exhausted nerves. I can distinguish only these two elements in so-called dramatic music: a conventional rhetoric of a music of recollection and a *music of excitement* which has a primarily physical effect; and so it swings back and forth between the din of drums and signal horns like the mood of a warrior going into battle. But now the sensibility which has been trained through comparison and which delights in pure music demands a *masquerade* for those two abusive tendencies of music: 'reminder' and 'excitement' is demanded, but through good music, which should be enjoyable and even valuable in itself. What despair for the dramatic musician, who must mask the big drum by good music, which, however, must only have an exciting, not 'purely musical', effect! And now along comes the audience of philistines, wagging its thousand heads, and enjoys this 'dramatic music' – which is always ashamed of itself – lock, stock and barrel, without an inkling of its shame and embarrassment. Rather, this audience feels a pleasant tickle all over its hide: after all, homage is being paid to it in every possible way, to the dull-eyed diversion-seeking hedonists who need excitement, to the conceited connoisseurs who have become as accustomed to good drama and good music as to good food, without actually caring for them very much, to the forgetful and absent-minded egoists who must be led back to the work of art by force and by signal horns because their heads are constantly exercised by selfish plans devoted to profit or enjoyment. Wretched dramatic musicians! 'Take a look at our patrons! Half of them have no taste and half no heart.' 'Poor fools, why pester your Muses to toil for this'[37] And that the muses are

---

[37] Goethe, *Faust Part I*, ll. 123–8.

pestered, indeed tormented and maltreated by them – they do not deny it, these sincerely unhappy people!

We had assumed a passionate drama which carries the listener away and which is certain to make an impact even without music. I am afraid that what is 'poetry' and *not* 'action' proper in this drama will bear the same relation to true poetry as dramatic music does to music pure and simple: it will be a poetry of recollection or a poetry of excitement. The poetry will serve as a means to recall, in a conventional manner, feelings and passions whose expression was found by real poets and became famous, or indeed the norm, together with them. Then it will be expected to lend the 'action', be it a crime and horror story or a manic piece of quick-change wizardry, a hand at dangerous moments and to spread a disguising veil over the crudeness of the action itself. Ashamed that the poetry is only a masquerade which cannot bear the light of day, such 'dramatic' scribbles demand 'dramatic' music: while the dramatic musician for his part, with his talent for the drum and signal horn and with his fear of genuine, self-confident and self-sufficient music, meets the scribbler of such dramas three quarters of the way. And now they see and embrace each other, these Apollonian and Dionysian caricatures, this *par nobile fratrum*![38]

After this appraisal of the opera culminating in 'dramatic' music, as we know it from history, let us turn to that ideal of opera which came into being in an analogous way to the lyrical folk song and which, in the form of Greek tragedy, represents the purest and highest union of the Dionysian and the Apollonian, while in 'dramatic' music the same elements, painfully distorted and dependent, walk together like a pair of cripples who feel more secure because each of them on his own would fall over. The gradual artistic *development of the folk song into tragedy*, as a new artistic movement, begins with the Dionysian-Apollonian Archilochus,[39] the first musician we can recognise as such. But this process, which takes place visibly in a series of *artists*, is paralleled by another process which occurs without the intervention of an artist in the omnipotence of nature and in a much shorter period of time. Let us assume, in

---

[38] a noble pair of brothers. Quotation from Horace, *Sermones* 2.3.243. The quotation continues: '*nequitia et nugis, prauorum et amore gemellum*': 'like twins in their ineptitude and silliness, and their love of what is depraved'.

[39] The earliest Greek lyric poet (mid-seventh century BC) of whose work any significant fragments have survived. See BT §§ 5–6.

analogy to similar phenomena, that the Dionysian rapture of the mass, born in those ecstatic spring festivals, expresses itself in the individual; and that from these beginnings the orgiastic frenzy then spreads faster and faster to ever larger circles. Now let us imagine such a mass, merging more and more into *one* immense individual, obsessed by a common dream vision: Dionysus appears, all see him, all prostrate themselves before him. This phenomenon too, the *same vision* becoming visible to *several*, indeed a whole mass of people, will have been seen first of all by one individual, from whom the vision spreads to all the others, the more, as I say, that the mass merges into one individual. This is the process that is analogous to the slow development, over a century, of the folk song into tragedy. For this is where I recognise the fundamental concept of Greek tragedy, whereby a Dionysian *chorus*, through Apollonian influence, has its own condition revealed to itself through a *vision*: just as in the lyrical folk song the individual, simultaneously aroused in both Apollonian and Dionysian fashion, suffers a similar vision. The increasing arousal, spreading from the individual to the chorus, and the greater and more enduring visibility and effectiveness of the vision resulting from this, seem to me to be the primal process of tragedy: therefore the 'drama', i.e. the action, can be explained by regarding the transmission of the arousal from the individual to the whole chorus as the 'action' of the vision, *as a manifestation of the life of the vision as character.* That is why in the beginnings of tragedy only the chorus, situated in the orchestra, was real, while the world of the stage, the characters and events on it, became visible only as living images, as figments of the Apollonian imagination of the chorus. That process of the *gradual manifestation of the vision* progressing from the individual to the chorus in turn appears as the *struggle and victory of Dionysus* and assumes a sensory quality before the eyes of the chorus. Now we see the profound necessity of the traditional fact that in the earliest time the suffering and victory of Dionysus were the sole content of tragedy; indeed we now realise that any other tragic hero must be understood only as a representative of Dionysus or, so to speak, a mask of Dionysus.

7[128]

What we call 'tragic' is precisely the Apollonian clarification of the Dionysian: if the tangle of emotions created simultaneously by the

Dionysian intoxication is broken down into a series of images, that series of images expresses the 'tragic', as is to be explained immediately.

The most common form of *tragic* destiny is the victorious defeat or the victory achieved in defeat. Each time the individual is defeated: and yet we perceive his destruction as a victory. For the tragic hero it is necessary to be destroyed by that which is intended to make him victorious. In this disturbing contrast we surmise something of the highest esteem for individuation, as already suggested: individuation needs the primal One in order to achieve its ultimate goal of joy, so that passing away appears equally dignified and worthy of reverence as coming into being, and what has come into being must solve the task set it as an individual by passing away.

7[130]

Apollonian and Dionysian.
Lyric.
Tragedy. Tragic.
Dithyramb.
The death of tragedy. Socrates: 'What was at issue was finding the tragic idea.'
Shakespeare: 'The poet of tragic knowledge.'
Wagner.

7[131]

Euripides on the path of science seeks the tragic idea, in order to attain the effect of dithyramb through words.

Shakespeare, the poet of fulfilment, he brings Sophocles to perfection, he is the *Socrates who makes music*.[40]

7[134]

Shakespeare: the fulfilment of Sophocles. The Dionysian has been completely absorbed into images. The omission of the chorus was completely

---

[40] See Plato, *Phaedo* 60c8–61c1. See also BT §§ 15, 17.

justified, but at the same time the Dionysian element was allowed to fade away. It breaks forth in Christianity and gives birth to a new music.

The task of our time: to find the culture for our music.

7[145]

The peaks of humanity are, more accurately, the centres of a semi-circle. For there is an ascending and a descending line. World history is no uniform process. *Its goal is continually reached.*

7[148]

Is pain something represented?

There is only *one* life, *one* sensation, *one* pain, *one* joy. We feel through, and in terms of, representations. Therefore we do not know pain, joy, life as such. The will is something metaphysical, the movement of the primal visions as represented by us.

7[149]

The belief in freedom and responsibility produces the delusion of the 'good', i.e. of that which is wanted purely, wanted without selfishness. Now what is selfishness? A sensation of joy at the manifestation of the power of the individual. The opposite: a sensation of joy at the abandonment of the individual. Living in the many, the joy outside *the individual,* among *individuals* as such. Feeling at one with all that appears is the goal. That is love. The god of the saint is usually the most ideal reflection of what appears and in so far the saint and his god are *one.* To make the appearance beautiful is the goal of the artist and the saint: i.e. to raise the appearance to a higher power.

7[156]

My philosophy is an *inverted Platonism*: the further something is from true being, the purer, the more beautiful, the better it is. Living in illusion as the goal.

7[157]

The *visions of the primal One* can only be *adequate* reflections of *being*. In so far as contradiction is the essence of the primal One, it can be the supreme pain and the supreme joy at the same time. The supreme joy is immersion in appearance: when the will has completely become external surface.[41] The will achieves this in the genius. At any moment the will is both supreme ecstasy and supreme pain: think of the ideality of dreams in the brain of a drowning man – an infinite time, and concentrated into a second. Appearance as that which is *becoming*. The *primal One* gazes at the genius, who sees the appearance purely as appearance: this is the peak of the world's ecstasy. But in so far as the genius himself is only appearance, he must *become*: in so far as his task is to perceive, the diversity of appearances must exist. In so far as he is an adequate reflection of the primal One he is the image of contradiction and the image of pain. Now every appearance is at the same time the primal One itself: any suffering felt is *primal suffering*, albeit seen through the appearance, localised, in the net of time. *Our pain is a represented pain*: our representation always stops at the representation. Our life is a *represented* life. We do not make an inch of progress. The freedom of the will, any activity, is only a representation. Therefore the work of the genius is also representation. *These reflections in the genius are reflections of the appearance*, no longer of the primal One: as *images of the image*[42] they are the purest respites of being. The truly non-existent – the work of art. The other reflections are only the *surface of the primal One. Being satisfies itself in the perfect illusion.*

7[161]

The individual, *the intelligible character*, is only a *representation of the primal One*. Character is no reality, but only a representation: it is drawn into the realm of becoming and therefore has a surface, empirical man.

7[162]

In great geniuses and saints the will comes to its redemption.

---

[41] *Außenseite.*
[42] *Abbilder des Abbildes.*

Greece is the image of a people that has attained the highest intentions of the will completely and has always chosen the nearest paths to this.

This happy relation of the Greek development to the will gives Greek art that *smile of satiation* which we call *Greek serenity.*[43]

In unfavourable circumstances the highest that can be attained is the *smile of longing*, e.g. in the works of Wolfram von Eschenbach[44] or Wagner.[45] In contrast, there is also a base form of serenity, that of the *slave* and the *old man*.

That smile of satiation is the gaze of one who is *dying*. It is something parallel to sanctification. This gaze no longer *desires* anything; that is why it seems cool, dismissive and flat to one who is still subject to desire. It no longer shows the distant horizon of the unsatisfied wish.

Homer is not serene; Homer is *true*. Tragedy attains occasionally (e.g. in Oedipus at Colonus)[46] the serenity of satiation.

7[165]

Dissonance and consonance in music – we may say that a chord *suffers* through a false note.

The secret of *pain* must also rest in *becoming*. If every world of the moment is a new world, where do sensation and pain come from?

There is nothing in us that could be traced back to the primal One.

The will is the most universal form of appearance: i.e. the alternation of pain and joy is the prerequisite of the world as the continuous curing of pain through the joy of pure intuition. The *All-One suffers* and projects the will as a cure, as a means of achieving pure intuition. Suffering,

---

[43] The idea that the ancient Greeks were a particularly light-hearted and cheerful people was one that was widespread in Germany during the late eighteenth century and the first two thirds of the nineteenth (see M. Silk and J. Stern, *Nietzsche on Tragedy* (Cambridge University Press, 1981), ch. 1, and J. von Reibnitz, *Ein Kommentar zu Friedrich Nietzsche 'Die Geburt der Tragödie aus dem Geiste der Musik' (Kapitel 1–12)* (Stuttgart: Metzler, 1992), pp. 226–8 with the further literature cited there). It was a conception that the early Nietzsche rejected root and branch. An early projected title for the book that became *The Birth of Tragedy* was *Tragedy and Greek Serenity* (KSA vol. 7, 5[120], September 1970–January 1871). See also below, KSA vol. 7, 11[1] pp. 78–82.

[44] Wolfram von Eschenbach (*c.* 1170–1220) was the author of the epic poem *Parzival* on which Wagner's opera of the same name was (broadly) based, but also of a small number of lyric poems in which lovers lament the coming of dawn (see *Minnesangs Frühling*, ed. H. Moser and H. Tervooren (Stuttgart: Hirtzel, 1977), vol. 1, pp. 436–51).

[45] In Act III, scene 1 of Wagner's *Tristan und Isolde* the dying Tristan has a vision of Isolde crossing the sea and smiling to solace him ('*sie lächelt mir Trost/ und süße Ruh'/ sie führt mir letzte/ Labung zu*').

[46] See above, Notebook 5, footnote 3, p. 25.

longing, need as the primal source of things. That which truly is cannot suffer? Pain is the true being, i.e. the sensation of self.

Pain, contradiction is the *true being. Joy, harmony is illusion.*

7[166]

Euripides and Socrates signify a new beginning in the development of art: *out of tragic knowledge.* This is the task of the future, which so far only Shakespeare and our music have completely appropriated. In this sense Greek tragedy is only a preparation: a yearning serenity. – The Gospel according to St John.

7[167]

The projection of illusion is *the artistic primal process.*

All that lives, lives on illusion.

The will pertains to illusion.

Are we at the same time the one primal being? At least we have no path leading to it. But we must be it: and completely, since it must be indivisible.

Logic accurately fits only the world of appearance: in this sense it must be congruent with the *nature of art.* The will is already a *form of appearance*: that is why *music* is still the *art of illusion.*

Pain as an appearance – a difficult problem! The only means of theodicy. The *outrage* as *becoming.*

The genius is the peak, the enjoyment of the one primal being: illusion enforces the *becoming* of the genius, i.e. the world. Every born world has its peak somewhere: at every moment a world is born, a world of illusion indulging itself in the genius. The succession of these worlds is called causality.

7[169]

If contradiction is the true being and joy is illusion, if becoming pertains to illusion – then to understand the world in its depth is to understand contradiction. Then we are the being – and must create the illusion out of ourselves. Tragic knowledge as the mother of art.

1. Everything exists through joy; the medium of joy is illusion. Illusion makes empirical existence possible. Illusion as the father of empirical being: which therefore is not the true being.
2. Only pain and contradiction are truly being.

3. Our pain and our contradiction are the primal pain and primal contradiction, refracted through representation (which generates joy).
4. The tremendous artistic capability of the world has its analogue in the tremendous primal pain.

7[170]

In man the primal One looks back at itself through the appearance: the appearance reveals the essence. I.e. the primal One looks at man, more precisely, at man looking at the appearance, at man looking through the appearance. There is *no road to the primal One* for man. He is all appearance.

7[172]

The individual, considered empirically, is a step towards genius. There is only one *life*: where this appears it appears as pain and contradiction. Joy is possible only in appearance and intuition. Pure immersion in illusion – the supreme goal of existence: where pain and contradiction appear not to exist. – *We* recognise the primal will only through appearance, i.e. *our knowledge itself is a represented knowledge*, a mirror of the mirror, as it were. Genius is *what is represented as purely intuiting*. What does the genius intuit? The wall of appearances, purely as appearances. Man, the non-genius, intuits appearance as reality or *is represented in that way*: represented reality – that which is represented as being – exercises a similar force as absolute being: pain and contradiction.

7[175]

It is the nature of every man to *rise* as high in intuition as he can. This development is linked to the representation of freedom: as if he could do otherwise!

The fact that man can *rise* means that he is never the same at any one moment, just as his body is also a becoming. Only the *one* will *is*: man is only a representation born at every moment. What is firmness of character? An activity of the intuiting will, and so is the capacity of a character for being formed.

And thus our thinking is only an *image* of the primal intellect, a thinking that came into being through the intuition of the *one* will, which thinks of itself as thinking its own visionary form. We intuit thinking as we do the body – because we are will.

The things we touch in our dreams are also *firm* and *hard*. Likewise, for the intuiting will, our body, and the whole empirical world, is firm and hard. Thus we are this one will and this one intuiter.

But it seems that our intuition is only the image of the one intuition, i.e. nothing but a vision, created at every moment, of the *one* representation.

The unity between the intellect and the empirical world is the pre-established harmony, born at every moment and completely congruent down to the smallest atom. There is nothing internal to which something external would not correspond.

Thus every atom has its corresponding soul. I.e. everything that exists is *representation twice over*: first as an *image*, second as the *image* of the *image*.

Life is the ceaseless production of these twofold representations: the will alone *is* and *lives*. The empirical world only *appears*, and *becomes*.

This perfect congruency of the internal and the external at any moment is *artistic*.

In the *artist* the primal force operates through the images, it is the primal force that creates. These moments are intended at the creation of a world: now there is an image of the image of the image?[47]   (?) The will needs the artist, in whom the primal process repeats itself.

In the artist the will arrives at the ecstasy of intuition. It is only at this point that the primal pain is completely outweighed by the joy of intuiting.

I believe that the will has no understanding. The projections are viable after infinite efforts and countless failed experiments. The artist is achieved only now and then.

7[201]

We are on the one hand *pure intuition* (i.e. projected images of a purely ecstatic being that is most at peace in this intuition), and on the other

---

[47] *Bild des Bildes des Bildes.*

hand the one being itself. As something completely real, we are nothing but suffering, willing, pain: as representations we have no reality, or rather a different kind of reality. When we feel ourselves to be the *one* being we are immediately raised into the sphere of pure intuition, which is quite painless: even though we are then at the same time pure will, pure suffering. But so long as we ourselves are merely 'something represented', we have no share in that painlessness, while that which represents enjoys it pure.

In art, however, we become 'something that represents': hence the ecstasy.

As that which is represented we do not feel the pain (?). Man, for instance, as a sum of innumerable small atoms of pain and will, whose suffering is suffered only by the *one* will, and whose diversity is the consequence of the ecstasy of the *one* will. Thus we are incapable of suffering the true suffering of the will, but suffer it only through the representation and through the isolation of the parts in representation. Therefore:

the individual projection of the will (in the ecstasy) is in reality nothing but the one will; however, it gains a sense of its own nature, which is will, only as projection, i.e. in the fetters of space, time, causality, and therefore cannot carry the suffering and the joy of the *one* will. The projection gains consciousness only as appearance; it feels itself to be only appearance through and through; its suffering is mediated only through representation and is thus broken. The will and its primal source, pain, cannot be grasped directly, but through objectivation.

Let us imagine the visionary figure of the tortured saint. We are this figure. Now how does the visionary figure *suffer* and how does he acquire insight into his own nature? *The pain and suffering must also pass into the vision* from the representation of the tortured saint: and now, as intuiter, he does not perceive their visionary images as suffering.

He *sees* tormented figures and terrible demons. These are only images, and that is our reality. But at the same time the feeling and suffering of these visionary figures always remains a *riddle*.

The artist too includes harmonies and disharmonies in his representation.

We are the will, we are visionary figures: but wherein lies the connection? And what is the life of the nerves, brain, thought, sensation? – We are at the same time the intuiters – there is nothing but the vision to intuit – we are the intuited, only something intuited – we are those in whom the whole process begins anew. But does the will still suffer when it intuits? Yes, because if it ceased to do so, the intuition would cease. But the sense of joy is in surplus.

What is *joy* if only suffering is positive?

7[204]

1. Proof that the world can only be a representation.
2. This representation is an ecstatic world projected by a suffering being. Proof by analogy: we are at the same time will, but completely entangled in the world of appearances. Life as a continuous paroxysm projecting appearances and doing so joyfully. The atom as a point, without any content, pure appearance, at every smallest moment becoming, *never being*. Thus the whole will has become appearance and intuits itself.

The representation created out of pain turns solely to vision. Naturally, it has no self-awareness.

Thus we too are conscious only of the vision, not of the essence.

Do we then *suffer* as *one will*?

How *could* we suffer if we *were* purely *representation*? We suffer as *one will*, but our knowledge is not directed at the will; we see ourselves only as appearances. We suffer only as *represented sufferers* and we *do not know at all what we suffer* as one will. Not that we are *first* to represent ourselves as sufferers. But how can a visionary figure thought to be suffering really *suffer*? Nothing can pass away, because nothing really exists – what is it that actually suffers? Is suffering not just as inexplicable as joy? If two Cortian fibres[48] collide, why do they *suffer*?

Since the actual process of collision is only a representation, are the colliding fibres also representations? Therefore we may say that the pain

---

[48] fibres in the inner ear.

of the smallest atom is at the same time the pain of the *one* will; and that all pain is one and the same. We perceive it through representation in terms of time and space, while in the case of non-representation we do not perceive it at all. The representation is the ecstasy of the pain which breaks the pain. In this sense the *worst pain* is still a broken, represented pain, as opposed to the primal pain of the *one* will.

The delusions as ecstasies in order to break the pain.

Notebook 9, 1871

9[28]

The thought of the tragic hero must be included entirely in the tragic illusion: he must not try to explain the tragedy to us. Hamlet is a model: he is constantly saying the wrong thing, constantly looking for the wrong reasons – tragic knowledge does not enter his reflection. He has *seen* the tragic world – but he does not speak about it. He speaks only about his own weaknesses, in which he discharges the impression of that sight.

The thoughts and reflections of the hero are not an Apollonian *insight* into his real nature, but an illusionary stammer: the hero errs. The dialectic errs. The language of the dramatic hero is a constant error, a self-deception.

9[33]

The limits of ancient tragedy are within the limits of ancient *music*: it is only here that the modern world can show an infinite progress in the domain of art; and even that only through a gradual ossification of the Apollonian talent.

9[104]

Two different starting points of Greek *tragedy*:
    the chorus that sees a vision,
    and the enchanted Dionysian improviser.

The chorus explains only the *living image*: the improviser the *drama*. Comedy teaches us most about that.

The *ecstatic observer*, the chorus, immediately raises the *observed improviser* to an *ideal* height.

The fusion of the vision with the enchanted improvisation – the origin of drama.

Here we learn from the expectant *silence* of the Aeschylean characters, caricatured by Euripides.[1] Initially the stage character is only vision: now he begins to improvise, from the ideal height of the chorus's emotion.

The cothurnus[2] of pathos –

In Greek tragedy, then, we have a *succession* of music and vision – while the modern goal is *simultaneity*.

It is the *chorus* that determines the ideal language of tragedy: as was perceived by Schiller.[3]

The *improvisations* of *Aeschylus* – Aeschylus as *actor*.

Not understanding the *lyrical text* and the *unintelligibility* of Aeschylean *pathos* –

9[105]

What is this ability to *improvise out of the character of another*? There is no question of *imitation*: for the origin of such improvisations is not reflection. What must really be asked: how is it possible to *step into the individuality of another*?

To begin with, this is a liberation from one's own individuality, that is, an immersion of one's self in a representation. Here we see how representation is able to differentiate the manifestations of the will, and how every character is an inner representation. This inner representation is obviously not identical with our conscious thinking about ourselves.

This step into the individuality of another is also an *artistic treat*, i.e. through an *increasingly deep* representation the manifestations of the will eventually turn into something else, i.e. something differentiated, and are finally silenced.

---

[1] Actually this refers to the character 'Euripides' in Aristophanes, *Frogs* (ll. 911ff.)

[2] The high-soled boot worn on stage by actors in tragedy. Thus metonymically the high-flown form of speech used by actors in tragedy.

[3] Schiller's 'Preface' to his drama *The Bride of Messina* (1803).

Dissimulation, in the service of selfishness, also shows the power of representation to differentiate the manifestations of the will.

Character, then, seems to be a representation poured over our drives, under which all the manifestations of those drives come to light. This representation is the illusion and our drives are the truth: our drives are the eternal, illusion is the transitory. The will is the universal, the representation is that which differentiates. *Character* is a typical representation of the primal One, which we only get to know as a diversity of manifestations.

The primal representation that constitutes character is also the mother of all *moral* phenomena. And any temporary sublation of the character (in the enjoyment of art, in improvisation) is an alteration of the moral character. It is the world of the *best*, linked to *illusion*, that gives rise to the moral phenomenon. For the illusory world of representation aims at the redemption and perfection of the world. The perfection of the world would lie in the destruction of the primal pain and primal contradiction, i.e. in the destruction of the nature of things and in illusion alone – thus in non-being.

Everything good comes into being from a temporary *immersion in representation*, i.e. from becoming one with the illusion.

9[106]

If Richard Wagner attributes to music the character of the 'sublime', as opposed to the pleasingly beautiful, this shows the *moral* side of modern art.[4]

The *will* that moves beneath all emotion and knowledge and that is portrayed by music is, in contrast to the empirical world, a *paradisal primal state rich in anticipation* which relates to the world as the idyll does to the present.

We enjoy this *primal state* with the moral sensation of the sublime, of something irrecoverable, the '*mothers*' of existence: it is from there that we have to fetch the true Helen, music.[5]

---

[4] See GSD IX.78, 102 *et passim*.
[5] In Part II of Goethe's *Faust*, Faust is told that in order to summon up Helen of Troy he needs to descend to 'the mothers': Goethe, *Faust Part II*, trans. David Luke (Oxford University Press, 1994), ll. 6182–621.

9[128]

Wagner must be regarded above all as a musician: his texts are 'musical mist'.

9[129]

I believe that unless we are musicians we understand music only by idyllic moods and in an idyllic way. That is our modern destiny: we enjoy as *moral* creatures. The Greek world is gone.

Notebook 10, beginning of 1871

Fragment of an expanded version of *The Birth of Tragedy* written in the first weeks of 1871.

10[1]

Those who have gained an understanding of the contrasting but related worlds of the Apollonian and the Dionysian through the characterisation given so far will now go one step further and, given that point of view, comprehend *Hellenic life* in its most important manifestations as a *preparation* for the supreme expressions of those drives, for *the birth of genius*. While we must think of those drives as *forces of nature* without any connection to social, political or religious orders and customs, there is also a much more artificially and deliberately prepared, as it were, indirect revelation of those drives by the individual *genius*, about whose nature and supreme significance I must now take the liberty of speaking in a semi-mystical figurative language.

Man and *genius* are opposites in so far as the former is a work of art, but does not become conscious of this because the gratification he provides as a work of art belongs to a totally different sphere of knowledge and outlook: in this sense he is part of nature, which is nothing but a visionary reflection of the primal One. In contrast, the genius – in addition to the significance due to him as a man – also has the power, peculiar to that other sphere, to feel the ecstasy of the vision itself. If the gratification provided by dreaming man is only dimly comprehensible to the man himself, the genius is at the same time capable of deriving the highest

65

gratification from that condition; on the other hand he has control over that condition and is able to generate it out of himself alone. Given what we have remarked about the crucial importance of the dream for the primal One, we may regard the entire *waking* life of the individual man as a preparation for his dream; now we must add that *the entire dream life of many men* is in its turn the preparation of the *genius*. In this world of non-being, of illusion, everything must *become*: and so genius too *becomes*. It does so as that pleasure in the dream which is dimly felt by a complex of humanity, a larger individual, steadily intensifies till it reaches the level of the enjoyment peculiar to genius: a phenomenon we can visualise by the gradual rising of the sun, announced by a red dawn and a spearhead of rays. Mankind, with the whole of nature presumed to be its maternal womb, may be described in this widest sense as the continuing birth of the genius: from the immense omnipresent viewpoint of the primal One the genius is reached at every moment and the whole pyramid of illusion is perfect up to its apex. We, confined in the narrowness of our view and within the representational mechanism of time, space and causality, must be satisfied if we recognise the genius as one among many and after many men; indeed we must be happy if we have recognised him at all, which can basically only happen by chance and in many cases has certainly never happened.

The nature of the genius as a man 'not awake and only dreaming', who, as I said, is prepared and comes into being in the simultaneously awake and dreaming man, is *Apollonian* through and through: a self-evident truth, given the earlier characterisation of the Apollonian. This leads us to define the *Dionysian* genius as a man who in total self-oblivion has become one with the primal source[1] of the world, and who now creates out of the primal pain the reflection of that pain in order to redeem it: a process we have to venerate in the *saint* and the great *musician*, both of whom are only repetitions and recasts[2] of the world.

If this artistic reflection of the primal pain brings forth a second reflection, like a mock sun, we have the joint *Dionysian–Apollonian work of art*, the mystery of which we are trying to approach in this figurative language.

For the one eye of the world, before which the empirical world is poured out *together with* its reflection in the dream, that union of the Dionysian

[1] *Urgrund.*
[2] *zweite Abgüsse.*

and Apollonian therefore is an eternal and unchangeable, indeed the only, form of enjoyment: there is no Dionysian illusion without an Apollonian reflection. For our short-sighted, almost blind eye that phenomenon breaks down into isolated, partly Apollonian and partly Dionysian, enjoyments, and it is only in tragedy that we hear the voice of that supreme double art which, in its union of the Apollonian and the Dionysian, is the image of the primal enjoyment of the eye of the world. Just as, to the eye of the world, the genius is the apex of the pyramid of illusion, tragedy may be regarded as the apex of the pyramid of art accessible to our eye.

Forced as we are to understand everything in terms of becoming, i.e. as *will*, we shall now trace the *birth* of the three different kinds of genius in the world of appearance, which is the only world known to us: we shall examine the most important *preparations* the 'will' requires in order to attain them. In so doing we have every reason to conduct our demonstration with reference to the *Greek world*, which speaks to us about that process simply and expressively, as is its way.

If the genius is really the goal and ultimate purpose of nature it must now be possible to demonstrate that the other manifestations of the Hellenic character can be perceived only as necessary auxiliary mechanisms and preparations for that ultimate goal. This point of view compels us to examine the roots of some much-cited conditions of antiquity, which so far have not been discussed by any modern man with sympathy: as a result we shall find that the wonderful tree of life which was Greek art could have grown only from precisely those roots. It may be that this knowledge will make us shudder: since this shudder is one of the necessary effects of almost any deeper knowledge. For nature, even where it strives to create the greatest beauty, is something terrible. It is in accordance with this character of nature that the triumphal processions of *culture* benefit only an incredibly small minority of privileged mortals, while on the other hand the *slave labour* of the mass is necessary if art is to conceive a proper desire to come into being. We moderns have the advantage over the Greeks in two concepts strutting like peacocks, which are given, so to speak, as a comfort to a world that behaves utterly slavishly while anxiously avoiding the word 'slave': we talk about the 'dignity of man' and the 'dignity of labour'.[3] All men struggle miserably to perpetuate a

---

[3] See 'The Greek State', in Friedrich Nietzsche, *On the Genealogy of Morality*, ed. Keith Ansell-Pearson (Cambridge University Press, 1994), pp. 176ff.

miserable life; this terrible need coerces them into exhausting labour, at which, seduced by the 'will', they occasionally gaze in wonder as if it were something dignified. But if labour were to deserve honours and complimentary names, existence itself, for which labour is only a painful expedient, would above all else need to have somewhat more dignity than appears to any philosophies and religions that are meant to be taken seriously. What can we find in the agonising labour of all those millions other than the drive to continue to vegetate at all costs: and who does not see the same all-powerful drive in stunted plants stretching their roots into soilless rock?

From this terrible struggle for existence only those individuals can emerge who are occupied straight away with the delusions of artistic culture in order to avoid practical pessimism, a condition nature abhors to the utmost. In the modern world, which, unlike the Greek, mostly creates abnormities and centaurs, and in which man as an individual, like the fabulous creature at the beginning of Horace's *Art of Poetry*,[4] is composed of a motley collection of pieces, we often see in one and the same man the greed of the struggle for existence and that of the need for art: this unnatural fusion made it necessary to excuse and, as it were, consecrate the greed of the struggle for existence in front of the need for art, which has been accomplished through those excellent representations of the dignity of man and labour. The Greeks need no such pitiful expedients: they state squarely that labour is an indignity – not because existence is an indignity but because they feel that a man struggling for bare survival cannot possibly be an artist. In antiquity man *in need of art* rules by means of his concepts, while in modern times it is the *slave* who determines the representations: the slave who is forced by his nature to describe all his circumstances by deceptively glamorous names in order to be able to live. Phantoms such as the dignity of man or the dignity of labour are the feeble products of slavery hiding from itself. Unfortunate age, in which the slave has been tempted to think about, and beyond, himself! Unfortunate seducers who have destroyed the innocence of the slave through the fruit of the tree of knowledge! Now, merely in order to be able to live, the slaves must fob themselves off with transparent lies such as can be recognised by anybody looking deeper into 'equal rights for all', the 'fundamental rights of man' as a member of a species, or the dignity of labour. For they must

---

[4] Ll. 1–5.

not be allowed to understand at what point, at roughly what level, it first becomes possible to talk about 'dignity' – and the Greeks did not allow it even then – which is where the individual fully transcends himself and is no longer obliged to procreate and labour in the service of his continuing individual existence. Even at this height of 'labour' the Greeks still have the same undeceived naïveté. Even that pale epigone Plutarch[5] has enough Greek instinct in him to tell us that no nobly born youth would have the desire to become himself a Phidias if he saw Zeus in Pisa, or a Polycletus if he saw Hera in Argos: nor would he wish to become Anacreon, Philetas or Archilochus, however greatly he might relish their poems. For the Greeks artistic creation falls as much under the ignoble concept of labour as any philistine trade. But if the compelling force of the artistic drive is active in him he *must* create and submit to that hardship of labour. The Greek felt like a father who admires the beauty and talent of his child, but who thinks of the act of procreation with shame and distaste. His joyous astonishment at the beautiful did not blind him to the process of becoming, which appeared to him, as did all creation in nature, as an enormous need, as a greedy stampede to existence. The same feeling that makes the process of procreation appear as something to be hidden with shame, even though in it man serves a higher purpose than his individual preservation, the same feeling also veiled the production of great works of art, even though these inaugurate a higher form of existence, just as the act of procreation inaugurates a new generation. Thus *shame* seems really to occur where man is no longer anything but an instrument of an infinitely greater manifestation of the will than he may consider himself to be as the isolated figure of an individual that he is.

Now we have the general concept under which we must classify the Greeks' perception of slavery and labour. They regarded both as a necessary indignity, of which one is ashamed: hidden in this feeling is the unconscious knowledge that the true goal *needs* these prerequisites, but that here lies the terrible and predatory quality of nature, the sphinx presenting the torso of a beautiful girl with the intention of glorifying the artistic freedom of cultural life.[6] Culture, which I understand to be

[5] Plutarch, *Life of Pericles*, ch. 2.
[6] The sphinx had the torso of a young woman mounted on the body of a lion. She attracted young men by the beauty of her torso, and then ripped them to death with her claws. The idea here is that similarly 'nature' attracts humans by presenting a beautiful aspect (in individual works of art and the whole 'free' life of culture) but that this hides the savage and destructive reality,

mainly a true need for art, has a terrifying foundation: and it is this that reveals itself in the vague sense of shame. To supply the soil for a greater development of art, the vast majority, in the service of a minority, must be enslaved to the demands of life *beyond* their individual need. The privileged class must be freed from the struggle for existence at the expense of the majority, in order to create a new world of need. Accordingly, we must be prepared to declare that slavery, as the cruel fundamental condition of any culture, is an integral part of the essence of a culture: an insight that can give one a real fright of nature. These are the vultures gnawing at the liver of the Promethean[7] patron of art. The misery of the struggling mass must be made even greater to enable a number of Olympian men to produce the world of art. Here is the source of that badly concealed rage against the arts, but also against classical antiquity, nurtured by the communists and socialists and by their paler descendants, the white race of liberals of all times. If culture really depended on the wishes of a people, if no inescapable forces were at work here as a law and limitation to the individual, then the contempt for culture, the glorification of the poverty of the spirit, the iconoclastic destruction of the claims of art would be more than a revolt of the oppressed mass against dronelike individuals: it would be the cry of *compassion*, which would tear down the walls of culture; and the drive for justice, for an equality of suffering, would drown all other representations. In fact, an overpowering sense of compassion has now and then breached all the dams of cultural life for short periods: a rainbow of compassionate love and peace appeared with the arrival of Christianity, and under it the most beautiful fruit of Christianity, the Gospel according to St John, was born. There are also examples of how powerful religions, as it were, petrify a certain degree of culture for long periods: think of the mummy-like millennia-old culture of Egypt. But one must not forget one thing: the same cruelty that we have found in the nature of every culture is also found in the nature of every powerful religion; so that we shall understand it equally well if a culture tears down an overly high bulwark of religious demands by the call for justice. Anything

---

which is that inherently undignified labour and, in fact, slavery for the vast majority of humans is the precondition for the existence of culture.

[7] A member of the mythical race of 'Titans' who, violating an explicit prohibition from Zeus, stole fire and gave it to mankind. For his transgression, Zeus punished him by having him chained to a rock; each day his liver was gnawed by an eagle. He thus became a symbol of a creative benefactor of humanity, punished by the powers that be.

that wants to, i.e. has to, live in this terrible constellation of things is by its very nature an image of the primal pain and primal contradiction, and must therefore appear to our 'earth-worldly eyes'[8] as will, as an insatiable greed for existence. Therefore we may compare culture in its glory to a victor in his triumphal procession, dripping with blood and dragging behind him his defeated enemies tied to his chariot as slaves; whose eyes have been blinded by a charitable power, so that, almost crushed by the wheels of the chariot, they still cry 'dignity of labour! dignity of man!'

Modern man is used to a very different, pampered way of looking at things. That is why he is eternally dissatisfied, because, rather than ever daring to entrust himself fully to the terrible ice-ridden river of existence, he runs anxiously up and down the bank. The modern age, with its 'rupture', must be understood as an age that shrinks from all consequences: it wants nothing *completely*, completely even with all the natural cruelty of things. The dance of its thoughts and actions is truly ridiculous because, full of longing, it constantly pounces on new shapes in order to embrace them, but is forced suddenly to let them go with a shudder, like Mephistopheles with the seductive lamias.[9] The tremendous social crises of the present are born from the pampering of modern men: as their entirely natural antidote I venture to recommend *slavery*, if necessary under a more moderate name; slavery, which in no way seemed repugnant, let alone reprehensible, either to original Christianity or to the old Germanic world. To say nothing of the Greek slaves: what an uplifting effect observing the medieval serf has on us, in his inwardly strong and delicate legal and moral relationship with the higher orders, in the profound and poetic limitation of his narrow existence. How uplifting – and how reproachful!

Those who cannot think about the configuration of *society* without melancholy, those who have learnt to understand society as the continuous painful birth of those exempt men of culture in whose service everything else must be consumed, will no longer be deceived by the false glamour the moderns have spread over the origin and significance of the *state*. For what can the state signify to us if not the means by which the social process just described can be activated and guaranteed to continue without hindrance? However strong the drive for sociability may be in

[8] Goethe, *Faust Part II*, l. 1907.
[9] Ibid. ll. 7769–84.

the individuals, only the iron clamp of the state forces the mass together, so that the chemical decomposition of society, with its new pyramidal structure, *must* take place. But what is the source of this sudden power of the state, which has a goal far beyond the knowledge, and even the self-ishness, of the individual? How did the slave, the blind mole of culture, come into being? The Greeks have revealed it to us in their instinct for the laws governing the relations between peoples, an instinct whose iron voice, even in the most mature fullness of their morality and humanity, never ceased to utter words such as: 'The vanquished, with his wife and child, his worldly goods and his lifeblood, belongs to the victor. Violence comes first; and there is no right that is not founded on violence.'

So we see the pitiless rigidity with which nature forges for itself the cruel tools of the state it needs to achieve society: those iron-handed conquerors who are nothing but the objectivations of the instincts described above. Faced with their indefinable greatness and power, the beholder feels that they are solely the instruments of a purpose that manifests itself in them and yet hides from them. As if a magic will radiated from them, the weaker forces join them and are miraculously transformed under the sudden swell of that avalanche of violence, the spell of that creative core, and acquire an unprecedented affinity.

If we see how little the subjects worry about the terrifying origin of the state, so that basically there are no events of any kind about which world history gives us worse information than about the way those violent, bloody and almost always inexplicable usurpations come to pass; if, rather, hearts are involuntarily drawn to the magic of the state, sensing an invisibly deep purpose, where the calculating intellect can only see an addition of forces; if the state is even revered as the goal and peak of the individual's sacrifices and duties: then all this proclaims the tremendous necessity of the state, without which nature would not be able to achieve, through society, its redemption in illusion, in the mirror of the genius. What knowledge is not overcome by the instinctive delight in the state! One would think that whoever took a glimpse into the origin of the state would henceforth seek his salvation only at a fearful distance from it: and where does one not see the monuments of that origin, ravaged countries, destroyed cities, brutalised people, consuming hatred of nations! The state, of ignominious birth, for the vast majority a continually gushing source of hardship, in frequently recurring periods the voracious torch of mankind – and yet a sound that makes us forget ourselves, a battle cry that has inspired countless truly heroic deeds, perhaps the supreme and most venerable object for the blind and selfish mass, which has the strange expression of greatness on its face only at the awesome moments of the life of the state!

Because their art represents the unique zenith of human achievement we must construe the Greeks, a priori, as 'political men *par excellence*'; and really history knows no second example of such a terrible unleashing of the political drive, of such an absolute sacrifice of all other interests in the service of this state instinct: we might at most honour the men of the Italian Renaissance with the same title by way of comparison and for similar reasons. The political drive is so overloaded among the Greeks that it continually begins to rage against itself and to sink its teeth into its own flesh. The bloody jealousy of city against city, party against party, the murderous greed of those small wars, the tigerish triumph over the body of the slain enemy, in short, the ceaseless renewal of those Trojan scenes of battle and atrocity that Homer, as a typical Hellene, watches with profound relish[10] – what does this naïve barbarism of the Greek state point to, where does it find its excuse before the tribunal of eternal justice? Proud and composed, the state steps before this tribunal, leading by the hand the gloriously vital woman, Greek *society*. It was for this Helen and her children that it waged those wars: what judge could condemn it?[11]

Given this mysterious connection that we surmise to exist between the state and art, political greed and artistic creation, battlefield and work of art, we understand by the state only the iron clamp that enforces the social process, as has been said before; while without the state, in the natural *bellum omnium contra omnes*,[12] society is totally unable to strike roots on a larger scale and beyond the bounds of the family. Now that states have developed everywhere, the drive of the *bellum omnium contra omnes* is concentrated in the terrible tempest of war between peoples and

---

[10] Toward the end of Homer's *Iliad* (Book XXII) Achilles finally kills the Trojan warrior Hector, stabbing him in the throat with his spear, but Homer adds that the spear did not cut the windpipe, so Hector, although lying on the ground dying could still speak (ll. 324–30) and ask Achilles to give his body back to his parents for proper burial (ll. 338–43). Achilles replies that he intends to leave his body for the dogs and birds to eat, and is only sorry he doesn't have the appetite to cut it up and eat it raw (ll. 346–7). Achilles then pierces Hector's tendons, ties him to the back of his chariot, so that his head drags on the ground, and drives about dragging the body behind him for twelve days (ll. 395–400).

[11] *Iliad*, Book III, ll. 146ff.

[12] war of all against all. A description of the state of nature before the institution of political authority. See Thomas Hobbes, *De Cive* 1.12 and *Leviathan*, ch. xiii.

discharges itself, as it were, in less frequent but all the more violent blows. However, in the intervals society finds time to internalise the condensed effect of that *bellum* and to germinate and sprout everywhere in order to allow the luminous flowers of the genius to spring up as soon as there are a few warmer days.

With the political world of the Hellenes in mind, I do not want to conceal those phenomena of the present in which I recognise some dangerous atrophies of the political sphere that are equally alarming for art and society. If there should be any men who are placed, as it were, by birth outside the instincts of the people and the state, and who therefore need to accept the state only to the extent of their own interest, such men will necessarily imagine that the ultimate goal of the state is, as far as possible, the peaceful coexistence of great political communities in which they would be allowed to pursue their own intentions without restriction and before all others. With this idea in their heads they will promote whatever policy offers the greatest security to these intentions, while it is unthinkable that they would sacrifice themselves to the tendency of the state, against their own intentions, for instance under the guidance of an unconscious instinct: unthinkable because they lack precisely that instinct. All the other citizens of the state are in the dark about what nature with its state instinct intends for them, and they blindly obey. Only those who stand outside that instinct know what *they* want from the state and what the state should grant them. Therefore it is downright unavoidable for such men to gain a great influence over the state, because they are entitled to regard the state as a *means*, while all the others, subject to the power of the unconscious intentions of the state, are themselves only means to the state's ends. If they are to use the state as an instrument to further their selfish goals to the utmost, the state needs above all to be totally freed from the terribly unpredictable convulsions of war, so that it can be used rationally; therefore they strive, as consciously as possible, for a condition in which war is an impossibility. For that purpose they first try, as far as possible, to prune and weaken the drives for independent political action and to make the favourable outcome of a war of aggression, and thus of any war, most improbable through the creation of large, *evenly matched* states and mutual guarantees between them. At the same time they seek to wrest the question of war and peace from the decision of individual rulers, so that they can themselves appeal to the selfishness of the mass or its representatives: for which, in turn, they must slowly dissolve the monarchic instincts of the peoples. They achieve this objective through the most universal dissemination of liberal optimism, an outlook rooted in the teachings of the French Enlightenment and the French Revolution, i.e. in a totally un-Germanic, flat philosophy of a *genuinely Latin* kind. In the currently dominant nationalist movements and the simultaneous spread of universal suffrage I cannot help seeing primarily the effects of the fear of war, and behind these movements those who are most afraid, the truly international, homeless, money hermits who, with their natural lack of the state instinct, have learnt to misuse politics as an instrument of the stock exchange and both the state and society as mechanisms for their own enrichment. The only remedy against the diversion of the tendency towards the state into the tendency towards money, which is to be feared from this quarter, is war and war again: at least the excitements of war show that the state is not an institution founded on fear of the war demon and designed to protect selfish individuals, but that in the love of the fatherland and the prince it brings forth an ethical impulse which indicates a much higher purpose. Therefore, if I describe the use of revolutionary ideas in the service of a selfish, stateless, money aristocracy as a dangerous characteristic of the political present; if I understand the enormous spread of liberal optimism as the result of modern finance fallen into strange hands, and if at the same time I consider all the evils of the social condition, including the unavoidable decay of the arts, as having germinated from that root or grown together with it: then I will have to be excused for occasionally striking up a paean to *war*. His silver bow clangs horribly: and even if he comes like the night, he is still Apollo,[13] the fitting god for consecrating and purifying the state. But first, as we are told at the beginning of the *Iliad*, he aims his arrow at the mules and dogs. Then he hits the men and everywhere the pyres burn with bodies. Let me therefore say clearly that war is just as necessary for the state as the slave is for society: and who could shirk this knowledge if he asks himself honestly about the reasons for the unequalled perfection of Greek art?

If we consider war and its uniformed possibility, the estate of soldiers, in relation to the nature of the state as described so far, we must conclude

---

[13] *Iliad*, Book I, ll. 43–52. Apollo is a god strongly associated with the sun and with various forms of purification and healing (see above Notebook 3, footnote 10, p. 20). It is thus very striking that the first glimpse we have of him is as the cause of a plague, and that Homer, employing the first simile in European literature, describes him as descending 'like night' (l. 47).

that war and the soldier class show us an image, perhaps even the archetype, of the state. We see here, as the most common effect of the tendency towards war, an immediate decomposition and division of the chaotic mass into military castes, from which the structure of 'warlike society' rises in the form of a pyramid with the broadest possible slavish base. The unconscious purpose of the whole movement forces every individual under its yoke, producing, even in heterogeneous natures, so to speak, a chemical transformation of their properties, until they are brought into affinity with this purpose. In the highest castes one has a somewhat stronger sense of what this internal process is basically about, namely the production of the military genius – whom we came to know as the original founder of states. The imprint of that fundamental idea of the state, the production of the military genius, can be seen in many states, e.g. in the Lycurgan constitution of Sparta.[14] If we imagine the military primal state in its liveliest activity, its actual 'labour', and if we visualise the entire technique of war, then we cannot help correcting our concepts of the 'dignity of labour' and the 'dignity of man', soaked up from everywhere, by asking whether the concept of 'dignity' also applies to a labour designed to destroy 'dignified' men or to a man entrusted with that 'dignified labour'; or whether such a self-contradictory concept does not cancel itself out in this warlike task of the state. I would have thought that the warlike man is an instrument of the military genius and his labour likewise only an instrument of that same genius. Therefore he deserves a degree of dignity, not as an absolute man and non-genius, but as an instrument of the genius – who may also choose his destruction as an instrument of the craft of war – that is, the dignity of being recognised as an instrument of the genius. But what is shown here by one example is valid in general: every man, with all his activity, has dignity only in so far as he is a conscious or unconscious tool of the genius. From this we may immediately deduce the ethical consequence that 'man-in-himself', absolute man, has neither dignity nor rights nor duties. Only as a totally determined being serving unconscious purposes can man excuse his existence.

According to these reflections, Plato's perfect state[15] is certainly something greater than even the serious-minded among his followers believe, not to mention the smirking contempt with which our 'historically'

---

[14] For a brief, elementary discussion of the 'Lycurgan constitution' see ch. 5 of W. G. Forrest, *The Emergence of Greek Democracy 800–400 BC* (New York: McGraw Hill, 1966).
[15] See Plato, *Republic*, Books II–V.

educated contemporaries dismiss such a fruit of antiquity. Here the true purpose of the state, the Olympian existence and constantly renewed pro-creation of the genius, in relation to which all other men are merely pre-paratory instruments, is found by a poetic intuition: Plato saw through the terribly devastated herm of the life of the state in his time, and still perceived something divine in its interior.[16] He believed that this divine quality could be taken out and that the grim and barbarously deformed exterior was not part of the essence of the state; the whole fervour of his political passion was fuelled by that desire. That he did not place the genius in the most general sense at the head of his perfect state, but included only the genius of wisdom in the highest rank while excluding the artistic geniuses altogether from his state, was a rigid consequence of the Socratic judgement about art, which Plato made his own in his strug-gle against himself, and which will be examined more closely shortly. This rather external and almost accidental gap must on no account be counted among the main features of the Platonic state.

Just as Plato brought to light the innermost purpose of the state from behind all its disguises and opacities, so he also understood the most profound reason for the attitude of *Hellenic woman* to the state: in both cases he saw in what existed around him an image of the ideas revealed to him, beside which the real was only a picture of mists and and a play of shadows. Those who follow the common habit of regarding the position of Hellenic woman as altogether undignified and distasteful to humanity must level the same reproach against the Platonic conception of this posi-tion: for Plato, as it were, merely describes what exists in a more logically precise manner. Here we must reiterate our question: may there not be a *necessary* connection between the nature and position of Hellenic woman and the goals of the Hellenic will?

The most important thing that Plato as a Greek could say about the position of woman in relation to the state was the highly offensive demand that in the perfect state the *family* must *cease*. If we ignore how, in order to carry out this demand in a pure form, he even abolished marriage, putting in its place some solemn, state-ordained[17] . . .

---

[16] See Thucydides, *The Histories* VI.27ff. and Plato, *Symposium* 221d1–222a6.
[17] Plato, *Republic* 458b–461e.

Notebook 11, February 1871

11[1]

Preface to Richard Wagner

One of the things I know about you, my honoured friend, and about you alone, is that like me you distinguish between a true and a false concept of 'Greek serenity'[1] and that at every step you encounter the latter – the false one – in a condition of safety and comfort; I also know that you think it impossible to arrive at an understanding of the nature of tragedy from that false concept of serenity. That is why you are the rightful addressee of the following discussion of the origin and purpose of the tragic work of art, in which I have made the difficult attempt to conceptualise our wonderfully concordant feelings about this serious problem. Both the well- and the ill-disposed reader will realise to his surprise that we are dealing with a serious problem, when he sees how we must mobilise heaven and hell in explaining it, and how we are finally obliged to place it squarely in the centre of the world, as a 'vortex of being'.[2] Admittedly, taking an aesthetic problem so seriously causes offence on all sides, to our sentimental aesthetes with their repulsive mawkishness as well as to the robust or portly rabble that is unable to see art as anything more than a jolly appendage to the 'serious business of life', a tinkling of bells one can easily do without: as if nobody knew what this confrontation of art with the 'serious

---

[1] See Notebook 7, footnote 42, p. 54.

[2] Several Pre-Socratic philosophers, including Anaxagoras (see below, Notebook 19, footnote 12, p. 97) and Democritus (see below, Notebook 19, footnote 10. p. 97), seem to have given a very prominent place to 'vortex' (δῖνος) as a fundamental factor in explaining the variety and changeability of the world. See KSA vol. 1, pp. 867–8.

business of life' is about. If the phrase 'Greek serenity' resounds from so many different circles the world over, we must at least be glad when it is not meant to be interpreted straight away as a 'comfortable sensualism'; in which sense Heinrich Heine[3] has often used it, and always with longing. However, those whose praise stops at the transparency, clarity, firmness and harmony of Greek art, and who believe that under the protection of the Greek model they can come to terms with all the horrors of existence – the kind of men whose nature you, my honoured friend, have already brought to light in incomparably sharp outlines in your memorable essay 'On Conducting'[4] – must be convinced that the reason why the foundation of Greek art appears so flat to them lies partly with them and partly with the innermost nature of that Greek serenity. In this respect I would suggest to the best among them that they are in the same situation as those who, gazing into the brightest water of a sunlit lake, believe the bottom of the lake to be quite close to them, as if they could reach it with their hand. We have been taught by Greek art that there is no truly beautiful surface without a terrible depth; but those in search of the art of pure surface may once and for all be referred to the present as the true paradise for such treasure-seeking, while in the strange light of Greek antiquity they might mistake diamonds for drops of water or – the greater danger – demolish magnificent works of art by mistake or clumsiness. As the Greek soil is increasingly ransacked I become anxious and would like to take any talented or untalented person in whom I suspect a certain professional leaning towards antiquity by the hand and declaim in front of him: 'Do you know what risks you are running, young man, sent on a journey with your moderate book-learning? Have you heard that, according to Aristotle, being struck dead by a statue is an untragic death?[5] You are threatened precisely with this untragic death. Ah, a beautiful death, you will say, so long as it is a Greek statue! Or don't you even understand this? Know, then, that our philologists have been trying for centuries to right the statue of Greek antiquity that has fallen and sunk into the earth, but so far their strength has always proved inadequate to the task. Time and again, having scarcely been raised from the ground, the

---

[3] The specific phrase 'comfortable sensualism' does not seem to be one Heine uses, but he does often contrast 'Greek serenity' with the Jewish and Christian rejection of the life of the senses. See his *Elementargeister* (Part III) or his *Der Doktor Faust* (Act IV).

[4] GSD VIII. 261–337.

[5] See Aristotle, *Poetics* 1452a 1–10.

statue falls back and crushes the men under it. That may be acceptable; for everything must die of something. But who guarantees that the statue itself is not shattered in the process? The philologists founder on the Greeks: one could get over that. But antiquity disintegrates under the hands of the philologists! Think of that, reckless young man, turn back if you are not an image breaker!'

I have no more fervent wish than to meet a man to whom I would be unable to address this speech, a man of angry majesty, of the proudest gaze, of the boldest will, a fighter, a poet and a philosopher at one and the same time, striding as if he had to stride over snakes and monsters. On the brow of this future hero of tragic knowledge will lie the reflection of that Greek serenity, the halo inaugurating the still awaited rebirth of antiquity, the *German* rebirth of the Hellenic world.

O, my admired friend, I can hardly say how I connect my hopes of this rebirth with the current bloodstained glory of the German name.[6] I too have my hopes. These hopes made it possible for me to contemplate my topic ceaselessly, even in the midst of the terrible immediate effects of the war, while the earth trembled beneath the steps of Ares;[7] I actually remember, as I lay in the lonely night in the supply train together with wounded soldiers,[8] being with my thoughts in the three abysses of tragedy: whose names are 'delusion, will, pain'. And where did I find the comforting certainty that the future hero of tragic knowledge and Greek serenity will not already be strangled at birth by very different kinds of knowledge and serenity?

You know how utterly I abhor the misguided belief that the people, let alone the state, should be an 'end in itself': but I equally balk at seeking the purpose of mankind in the future of mankind. Neither the state nor the people nor mankind exist for their own sake; the goal lies in their peaks, in the great 'individuals', the saints and artists, that is, neither before nor behind us, but outside time. And this goal points entirely beyond mankind. It is not in order to prepare a general education or an ascetic self-destruction, let alone a universal state, that the great geniuses raise their heads here and there against all expectation. But what the existence of

[6] This text was written during the Franco-Prussian war. The armies of the Second (French) Empire had capitulated to Prussia and its allies in September 1870, and the Paris Commune was surrounded and put under siege, capitulating in January 1871.
[7] The Greek god of war.
[8] Nietzsche served as a medical orderly during the Franco-Prussian war for two months.

the genius points to, what most sublime purpose of existence, can be felt
here only with a shudder. Who may be so bold as to say that the saint in
the desert has missed the supreme intention of the world's will? Does
anybody really believe that a statue of Phidias[9] can truly be destroyed if
even the idea of the rock from which it was made does not perish? And
who would doubt that the world of the Greek heroes existed only for the
sake of one Homer? And to end with a profound question of Friedrich
Hebbel:

> If the artist made a picture, knowing that it would last for ever,
> But that a single hidden feature, deeper than any other,
> Would be recognised by no man living either now or in the future,
> To the end of time, do you think he would omit it?[10]

All this clearly shows that the genius does not exist for the sake of mankind; although he is definitely the peak and ultimate goal of it. There
is no higher cultural tendency than the preparation and creation of the
genius. The *state* too, despite its barbarous origin and its domineering
gestures, is only a means to that end.

And now my hopes!

The only productive *political* power in Germany,[11] which we need not
specify to anybody more closely, has now achieved the most momentous
victory and will henceforth dominate the German character down to its
atoms. This fact is of the utmost value, because that power will destroy
something that we hate as the true opponent of any profound philosophy
or contemplation of art, a condition of illness from which the German
character has suffered above all else since the great French Revolution
and which strikes even the finest German personalities with recurrent
gouty convulsions, not to mention the masses, in whose case that illness,
blatantly desecrating a well-meant word, is called 'liberalism'. The whole
of that liberalism, built on an imaginary dignity of man, of man as a generic concept, will bleed to death together with its coarser brothers on
encountering the rigid power indicated above; and we are happy to sacrifice the small attractions and kindnesses pertaining to liberalism, if only

---

[9] A highly regarded Athenian sculptor who flourished about 460–430 BC, and who was responsible
for much of the decoration of the Parthenon.
[10] A German dramatist and poet (1813–63). The title of this poem is 'Gewissensfrage' ('A Question
of Conscience').
[11] Prussia (under the leadership of Bismarck).

this essentially anti-cultural doctrine is cleared out of the genius's way. – And what may be the purpose of that rigid power, born out of violence, conquest and bloodshed through centuries, if not to prepare the way for the genius?

But what a way!

Perhaps our future hero of tragic knowledge and Greek serenity will be an anchorite – perhaps he will induce the deeper German personalities to go to the desert – happy time in which the world, driven inward through terrible suffering, will hear the song of the Apollonian swan!

My noble friend, do you agree with what I have said so far? I almost suspect that you do; and every time I look at your 'Beethoven' I find your words: 'The German is brave; let him also be brave in peace. Let him refuse to seem something that he is not. Nature has denied him the art of pleasing; instead, he is fervent and sublime.'[12]

This courage, together with the last-named qualities, is the other pledge of my hopes. If it is true that all deeper knowledge is terrible, which may be called my credo, then who other than the German will be able to take up that tragic position of knowledge which I demand as the preparation of the genius, as the new cultural goal of a nobly striving young generation? Who other than a German youth will have the fearless gaze and the heroic urge for the tremendous that will make him turn his back on all the feeble comforting doctrines of liberal optimism in every possible form to 'live resolutely' in wholeness and fullness? Thus he, the tragic man who has educated himself to seriousness and terror, will inevitably also desire the Greek serenity that we personify as Helen, and exclaim with Faust:

> And shall I not, by passion's power, draw
> Back into life that unique form I saw?[13]

Friedrich Nietzsche

Lugano on 22 February 1871,

on Schopenhauer's birthday.

---

[12] Not Wagner's exact wording: Nietzsche seems to be quoting GSD IX.125 inexactly from memory.
[13] Goethe, *Faust Part II*, ll. 7438–9.

Notebook 12, spring 1871

12[1]

What we have asserted here about the relationship between language and music must, for the same reasons, also be valid for the relationship between *mime and music*. Measured against the eternal significance of music, mime too, as the heightened symbolism of human gestures, is only a parable, which cannot represent the innermost secret of music but only its rhythmical exterior, and even this only very superficially, by means of the substratum of the human body in passionate motion. But if we include language in the category of bodily symbolism, if, according to the canon established by us, we compare even *drama* with music, then a sentence of Schopenhauer is likely to move into the brightest light (*Parerga*, vol. II, p. 465): 'It is possible that, although a thoroughly musical mind does not desire it, notwithstanding that the pure language of tones is self-sufficient and needs no assistance, it may be associated with and adapted to words or even to an action produced through intuitive perception so that our intuitively perceiving and reflecting intellect, which does not like to be completely idle, may yet obtain an easy and analogous occupation. In this way, even the attention is more firmly fixed on the music and follows it; at the same time, a picture or image of intuitive perception, a model or diagram so to speak, like an example to a universal concept, is adapted to what the tones say in their universal language of the heart, a language that is without picture or image; indeed such things will enhance the impression of the music.'[1] If we disregard the rationalistic

---

[1] *Parerga and Paralipomena*, trans. E. F. J. Payne (Oxford: Clarendon Press, 1974), vol. II, pp. 432–3.

external motivation – according to which our intuitively perceiving and reflecting intellect does not like to be idle while listening to music, and our attention follows better when guided by an intuitively perceptible action – then Schopenhauer was entirely justified in characterising drama in relation to music as a model or example of a universal concept; and if he adds that 'indeed such things will enhance the impression of the music', then the fact that vocal music, the combination of sound with image and concept, is so enormously universal and is everywhere at the origin of music, guarantees the correctness of this statement. The music of every people begins in a close alliance with lyric poetry, and long before there can be any thought of an absolute music it undergoes the most important stages of development in that combination. If, as we must, we understand this primal poetry of a people as an imitation of artistically prefiguring nature,[2] we must regard the *duality in the essence of language* which is prefigured by nature as the original model[3] of that combination of music and poetry: which, having discussed the relationship between music and image, we shall now explore more deeply.

The diversity of languages immediately reveals that the word and the thing are not completely and necessarily congruent, but that the word is a symbol. But what does the word symbolise? Surely nothing but representations, be they conscious or, in the majority of cases, unconscious: for how could a verbal symbol correspond to that deepest essence of which we, together with the world, are images? We know that core only as representations, we are familiar with it only in its expression through images; nor is there anywhere a bridge leading us directly to it. The totality of drives, the play of feelings, sensations, affects, acts of will – as I must insert here contrary to Schopenhauer – are, on closest self-inspection, known to us only as representations, not in their essence; and we may say that even Schopenhauer's 'will' is nothing but the most universal manifestation[4] of something, for us, totally indecipherable. If, then, we must submit to the rigid necessity of staying within the realm of representations, we can nevertheless distinguish two main kinds of representation within that realm. Those of one kind manifest themselves as sensations of pleasure and displeasure, and they accompany all those of the other type as an eternally present ground bass. This most

---

[2] *Nachahmung der künstlerisch vorbildenden Natur.*
[3] *Vorbild.*
[4] *Erscheinungsform.*

universal manifestation, from which and by which alone we understand all becoming and all willing, and for which we shall retain the name 'will', also has its symbolic sphere in language: and this sphere is as fundamental to language as that manifestation is to all other representations. All the degrees of pleasure and displeasure – manifestations of *one*, to us, unfathomable primal source – are symbolised in the *tone of the speaker*; while all the other representations are indicated by the *gestural symbolism* of the speaker. In so far as that primal source is the same in all men, the *tonal foundation* is also universal and comprehensible beyond the diversity of languages. It is here that the gestural symbolism, which is more arbitrary and not entirely adequate to that foundation, develops; and this is the beginning of the diversity of languages, which we may regard, so to speak, as a strophic text set to the primal melody of the language of pleasure and displeasure. We believe that the whole area of consonants and vowels – *both* of which, without the most necessary fundamental tone, are merely *positions* of the speech organs, in short, gestures – may be classed under gestural symbolism; as soon as we imagine the *word* pouring out of man's mouth, what comes into being first of all is the root of the word and the basis of gestural symbolism, the *tonal foundation*, the echo of the sensations of pleasure and displeasure. In the same way as our whole physical being relates to the most primal manifestation, the will, the word, made of consonant and vowel, relates to its tonal foundation.

The original manifestation, the 'will', with its gamut of sensations of pleasure and displeasure, acquires an increasingly adequate symbolic expression in the course of the development of music, and this historical process is paralleled by the continuous striving of lyric poetry to paraphrase the music in images: precisely the way that dual phenomenon was prefigured in language from the very beginning, as has just been explained.

Those who have followed us in these difficult reflections readily, attentively and with some imagination – kindly amplifying the argument where we expressed ourselves too tersely or too absolutely – will now have the advantage, with us, of being able to ask more seriously and answer more profoundly some of the exciting contentious questions of today's aesthetics, and even more those of contemporary artists, than is generally the case. After all these assumptions, let us think of what an enterprise it must be to compose music for a poem, i.e. to try to illustrate a poem by music and thereby help music to acquire a conceptual language: what a topsy-turvy world! An enterprise that seems to me like that of a son trying to beget his father! Music can create out of itself images, which will always be mere models or, in a manner of speaking, examples of its true universal content. But how could the image, the representation, create out of itself music! Not to mention that the concept or, as has been said, the 'poetic idea' is even less able to do this. There is certainly a bridge leading from the mysterious castle of the musician to the free land of images – and the poet crosses this bridge – but it is impossible to make the opposite journey, even though some individuals are said to exist who believe that they have done so. One may people the air with the imagination of a Raphael;[5] one may see, as he does, St Cecilia raptly listening to the harmonies of the choirs of angels – but not one single note issues from this world that seems to be lost in music. Indeed, if we only imagined that harmony really beginning to ring out by some miracle, where would Cecilia, St Paul and Magdalene, where would even the singing choir of angels suddenly have disappeared to! We would immediately cease to be Raphael! And just as the worldly instruments are lying shattered on the ground in that picture, our painter's vision, conquered by something higher, would fade and vanish like a shadow. – But how could the miracle happen! How could the Apollonian world of the eye, totally immersed in intuitive perception, create out of itself the note, which symbolises a sphere that is expressly excluded and overcome by the Apollonian condition of being lost in illusion? The enjoyment of illusion cannot out of itself arouse the enjoyment of non-illusion: the bliss of intuitive perception is bliss only because nothing reminds us of a sphere in which individuation is broken and sublated. If we have defined the Apollonian more or less correctly in contrast to the Dionysian, the idea of attributing to the image, the concept or the illusion the power to create the sound out of itself can only strike us as fantastically wrong. One should not try to refute us by reference to the musician who sets existing lyric poems to music: for after all that has been said we must maintain that the relationship between the lyric poem and its setting must in any event be different from that between a father and his child. But what kind of relationship?

---

[5] A reference to a painting by Raphael entitled *The Ecstasy of St Caecilia* (1514; now in the Pinacoteca Nazionale, Bologna).

Here we shall be confronted with the proposition, based on a popular aesthetic view, that 'it is not the poem, but the *feeling* generated by the poem, which gives birth to the composition'. I do not agree with this: in the realm of productive art feeling, the gentler or stronger excitation of the foundation of pleasure and displeasure, is the inartistic as such, and only its exclusion makes the artist's complete immersion and disinterested intuition possible. Here I may be told that I myself have just said that the 'will' acquires an increasingly adequate symbolic expression in music. My reply, summed up in an aesthetic principle, is this: *the will is the object of music, but not its origin*, that is, the will in its greatest universality, as the most original manifestation by which all becoming must be understood. What we call *emotions*, in relation to this will, is already permeated and saturated by conscious and unconscious representations and therefore no longer directly the object of music; and even less could it generate music out of itself. Take, for example, the emotions of love, fear and hope: music has no direct use for them, since each of these emotions is already so replete with representations. On the other hand, these emotions can serve to symbolise music. This is how the lyric poet uses them when he translates the domain of the 'will', the true content and object of music, which is unapproachable through concepts and images, into the metaphorical world of emotions. All those listeners to music who are aware of *an effect of the music on their affects* resemble the lyric poet: in their case the distant and remote power of the music appeals to an *intermediate realm* which as it were gives them a foretaste, a symbolic preliminary concept, of the music proper, and which is the intermediate realm of the affects. About the affects one could say that the relationship between them and the 'will', the sole object of music, is like the relationship between the analogical morning dream and the dream proper according to Schopenhauer's theory. But all those who can approach music only through their affects must be told that they will always remain in the antechambers and will not be admitted to the sanctum of music: which the affect, as I said, cannot show but can only symbolise.

In contrast, as far as the origin of music is concerned, I have already explained that this can never ever lie in the 'will', but rather rests in the lap of that force which creates out of itself a visionary world in the form of the 'will': *the origin of music is beyond all individuation*, a proposition which, after our discussion of the Dionysian, proves itself. At this point

I would like to take the liberty of repeating in clear outline the decisive assertions we were forced to make by the contrast of the Dionysian and the Apollonian.[6]

The 'will', as the most primal form in which things appear, is the object of music. In this sense music can be called an imitation of nature, but of the most universal form of nature. –

The 'will' itself and the emotions – as manifestations[7] of the will already permeated by representations – are totally incapable of creating music out of themselves; on the other hand, music is totally denied the capacity to represent feelings, to have feelings as its object, whereas its sole object is the will. –

Those who experience emotions as the effects of music have access, as it were, to a symbolic intermediate realm which can give them a foretaste of music, but which at the same time excludes them from music's innermost sanctums. –

The lyric poet interprets music to himself through the symbolic world of affects, while he is himself relieved of those affects in the peace of Apollonian intuition. –

Therefore, if a musician composes a song based on a poem, he is stimulated, as a musician, neither by the images nor by the emotional language of the text; rather, a musical impulse coming from quite different spheres *chooses* the text of that song as a metaphorical expression of itself. Thus there can be no question of a necessary relationship between song and music; for the two worlds of note and image connected here are too distant from each other to form more than a superficial alliance; the song is only a symbol and relates to the music as does the Egyptian hieroglyphic for courage to the courageous soldier himself. In comparison with the supreme revelations of music, we even involuntarily feel the *crudeness* of any use of images and any affect dragged in for the sake of analogy: Beethoven's last quartets,[8] for example, entirely put to shame any intuitive perception and indeed the whole realm of empirical reality. Faced with the supreme god who really manifests himself, the symbol no longer has any meaning: now it actually appears like an offensive superficiality.

We hope that it will not be taken amiss if, from this point of view as well, we include in our reflections the tremendous and inexplicably

---

[6] See also BT §§ 1–6.
[7] *ursprünglichtste Erscheinungsform.*
[8] Between 1823 and 1826 Beethoven wrote six string quartets, the last he ever wrote.

magical *last movement of Beethoven's Ninth Symphony*, in order to talk about it quite openly.[9] That Schiller's poem 'To Joy' is totally incongruent with this music's dithyrambic jubilation over the redemption of the world and is drowned like pale moonlight by that ocean of flames – who would want to rob me of this most certain feeling? Indeed, who could disagree with me that the only reason why this feeling does not cry out when we listen to that music is that we are totally incapacitated by the music to take in either image or word and *no longer hear Schiller's poem at all?* Alongside the truly naïve and innocent folk melody ringing out in joy, the noble sweep, even sublimity, of Schiller's verse seems irritating, disturbing, not to say crude and offensive: except that we do not hear it, because the ever fuller development of the choral singing and the orchestral masses keeps that sense of incongruity away from us. What then are we to think of the monstrous aesthetic superstition that, in the fourth movement of the Ninth, Beethoven himself made a solemn confession about the limits of absolute music and as it were unlocked the gates of a new art in which music is able to represent even the image and the concept, thus becoming accessible to the 'conscious spirit'?[10] And what does Beethoven himself say to us as he introduces the chorale through a recitative: 'Oh friends, not these tones! Let us raise our voices in more pleasing and more joyful sounds!'[11] More pleasing and more joyful! For that purpose he needed the convincing sound of the human voice, he needed the innocent air of the folk song. The sublime master, in his longing for the most soulful collective sonority of his orchestra, reached not for the word but for the 'more pleasing' sound, not for the concept but for the most intimately joyful tone. And how could he be misunderstood! Rather, what Richard Wagner says about the great *Missa Solemnis*, which he calls 'a purely symphonic work of the most genuine Beethovenian spirit', is equally true of this movement. 'Beethoven', p. 47: 'Here the vocal parts are handled entirely in that role of human instruments which alone Schopenhauer very rightly wished to see assigned to them: the text to which these great sacred compositions are set is never grasped by us in their conceptual meaning, but simply serves, in the spirit of the musical

---

[9] The last movement of Beethoven's Ninth Symphony (Op. 125 in D minor) contains a choral setting of Schiller's 'Ode to Joy'.

[10] The 'superstition' to which Nietzsche refers is one of the most central and deeply entrenched components of Wagner's aesthetics of music. See GSD III.310–16, IV.138–55.

[11] Beethoven, Symphony No. 9 in D minor (Op. 125), fourth movement.

work of art, as material for the singing; and the simple reason why it has no disturbing effect on our musical impressions is that it prompts no sequences of representations in us, but affects us solely through well-known symbolic formulae of faith, as is indeed demanded by its sacred character.'[12] Incidentally, I do not doubt that Beethoven, if he had written the projected tenth symphony – of which there are some sketches left – would have written precisely the *tenth* symphony.[13]

After these preparations, let us embark on the discussion of *opera*, so that we may then move on to its counterpart in Greek tragedy. What we observed in the last movement of the Ninth, that is, on the highest peaks of modern musical development – that the verbal content is drowned unheard in the universal ocean of sound – is nothing unique or strange, but the universal and eternally valid norm of the vocal music of all ages, which alone corresponds to the origin of lyrical song. Neither the man in a state of Dionysian arousal nor the orgiastic crowd require a *listener* to whom they have something to communicate. In this they are different from the epic story-teller or the Apollonian artist in general, who does presuppose such a listener. Rather, not knowing any consideration for the listener belongs to the nature of Dionysian art: the ecstatic servant of Dionysus, as I said earlier, is understood only by his own kind. But if we imagined a listener to the endemic outbursts of Dionysian arousal we would have to prophesy for him the same fate as that suffered by Pentheus,[14] the eavesdropper caught in the act, who was torn to pieces by the maenads. The lyric poet sings 'as the bird sings', alone, out of an innermost need, and must fall silent if the listener confronts him with any demands. Therefore it would be entirely unnatural to demand that the words of his songs be intelligible; unnatural because here the demand would be made by the *listener*, who can claim no right whatsoever in the face of a lyrical outpouring. Now one should sincerely ask oneself, with the poems of the great ancient lyric poets in hand, whether these poets could have had any idea of making their images and thoughts clear to the listening crowd around them: and one should answer this serious question

---

[12] GSD IX. 103. Translation adapted from 'Beethoven', trans. William Ashton Ellis in *Richard Wagner's Prose Works* (London: Kegan Paul, 1896), vol. V.

[13] The Ninth Symphony was the last Beethoven completed, but Wagner claimed that if Beethoven had written a tenth symphony it would not have been a traditional symphonic work, but a kind of music-drama.

[14] See Euripides, *Bacchae* ll. 1043–152.

with Pindar[15] and the Aeschylean choral songs in mind. These boldest and darkest knots of thought, this swirl of images tempestuously born and reborn, this oracular tone of the whole, which we are so often unable to penetrate, even with the most concentrated attention and *without* being distracted by music and dancing – should this whole world of miracles have been as transparent as glass to the Greek mass, in fact an interpretation of music through images and concepts? And with such mysteries of thought as are found in Pindar, would the wonderful poet have wanted to make music, so powerfully clear in itself, even clearer? Are we not bound to understand here what the lyric poet is, namely artistic man who must interpret music to *himself* through the symbolism of images and affects, but who has nothing to communicate to the listener; who, in total abstraction, even forgets those standing next to him and greedily listening? And as the lyric poet sings his hymn, so the people sing the folk song, for themselves, out of an inner urge, without caring whether the words are intelligible to anybody who does not join in the singing. Let us think of our own experiences with music of the higher artistic kind: how much would we understand of the text of a mass by Palestrina, of a cantata by Bach, of an oratorio by Handel, if we did not ourselves sing them? Only for *those who join in the singing* is there a lyric, is there vocal music: the listener is faced with absolute music.

But now, according to the clearest testimonies, the *opera* begins with the *listener's demand to understand the word.*

What? The listener *demands*? The word is to be understood?

---

[15] A Theban choral poet, born *c.* 520; died late 440s.

Notebook 16, summer 1871 – spring 1872

16[13]

The *unconscious force that creates forms* manifests itself in *procreation*: here an artistic drive is active after all.

5. It seems to be the same artistic drive that forces the artist to idealise nature and that forces every man to perceive himself and nature pictorially. Ultimately this drive must have induced the construction of the eye. The intellect proves to be a *consequence* of an initially artistic apparatus.

The awakening of the artistic drive differentiates the animal creatures. Seeing nature in this way, this artistic way, is something that we do not share with any animal. But there is also an artistic gradation of animals.

Seeing the forms – is the means of transcending the continuous suffering of the drive. It creates organs for itself.

In contrast, the tone! It does not belong to the world of appearances but, eternally comprehensible, speaks of what never appears. It joins, while the eye separates.

Notebook 19, summer 1872 – beginning of 1873

19[1]

At the right level everything comes together and agrees – the thoughts of the philosopher, the works of the artist and good deeds.

It must be shown how the entire life of a people reflects, in an impure and confused form, the image presented by its supreme geniuses: these are not the product of the mass, but the mass shows their repercussions.

Otherwise what is their relationship?

There is an invisible bridge from genius to genius – that is the truly real 'history' of a people; everything else is nothing but innumerable shadowy variations in worse material, copies by unpractised hands.

The ethical forces of a nation also show themselves in its geniuses.

19[2]

The characteristics of post-Socratic morals – all are eudemonic and individual.

19[3]

To be paraphrased: the world in which the philosopher and the artist are at home.

19[4]

Preface to Schopenhauer – entrance to the underworld – I have sacrificed many a black sheep to you[1] – which the other sheep complain about.

19[5]

In the glorious world of art – how they philosophised! When a certain perfection is reached in life, does philosophy end? No: it is only now that true philosophy begins. Their judgement *on existence says more*, because it has before it that relative perfection and all the veils and illusions of art.

19[9]

Those Greek philosophers *overcame the spirit of the age* in order to be able to empathise with the Hellenic spirit: they expressed the need to solve eternal questions.

19[10]

In the world of art and philosophy man constructs an 'immortality of the intellect'.

The will alone is immortal – compare this with the miserable state of the immortality of the intellect achieved through education, an immortality which requires human brains:

one can see the lineage of this in nature.

– But how can the genius be at the same time the highest goal of nature? *Continuing to live through history* and continuing to live through *procreation*.

Here Plato's procreation in the beautiful[2] – that is, in order for the genius to be born, history must be overcome, bathed in beauty and eternalised.

Against *iconic historiography*! This contains a barbarising element.

---

[1] In Book XI of the *Odyssey* Odysseus sacrifices a black sheep in order to make the spirits of the dead speak to him.
[2] See Plato, *Symposium* 206–10.

History must speak only of the great and unique, of the model to be emulated.

This sums up the task of the new philosophical generation.

None of the great Greeks of the age of tragedy have anything of the historian about them: – – –

19[11]

The drive for knowledge *without choice* is on a par with the indiscriminate sexual drive – a sign *of coarseness*!

19[12]

The task of the philosopher is consciously to fight against all temporalising elements – and therefore to support the unconscious task of art.

In both a people achieves the unity of all its qualities and their supreme beauty.

The present task vis-à-vis the sciences.

19[13]

The philosopher of the tragic age

The philosopher is not an exception quite apart from the people: the will wants something from him too. It wants the same as it does from art – its own transfiguration and redemption. The will *strives for purity and ennoblement*; from one stage to the next.

Education and culture as the form of existence – the will acting on the heads of men.

19[14]

The limited drive for knowledge

The seven wise men[3] – the epic-Apollonian stage of philosophy.

---

[3] Many in antiquity spoke of a group of seven men who had lived in the late seventh and early sixth centuries BC, and to whom various pithy bits of good advice were attributed (e.g., 'Do not revile your neighbours because if you do, you will hear things back that will pain you', and 'honour old age', attributed to Chilon (see DL 1.69–70); 'strike while the iron is hot' ($\kappa\alpha\iota\rho\grave{o}\nu\ \gamma\nu\tilde{\omega}\theta\iota$),

19[15]

Those drives that distinguish the Greeks from other peoples are expressed in their philosophy.

They are precisely their *classical* drives.

Their way of dealing with history is important.

The gradual degeneration of the concept of the historian in antiquity – dissolution into inquisitive knowing-it-all.

19[16]

Task: to recognise the *teleology* of the philosophical genius. Is he really only a wanderer who appears by accident? In any case, if he is a true philosopher, he has no truck with the accidental political situation of a people, but as opposed to his people he is *timeless*. Nevertheless, he is not connected with the people by accident – the specificity of the people here becomes visible in the form of an individual, and the drive of the people is explained as a *universal drive* and used to solve the riddle of the world. For once nature succeeds in intuitively perceiving its own drives through *separation*. The philosopher is a means of finding peace in the restless flux and, with contempt for the infinite multiplicity, becoming conscious of the enduring types.

19[17]

The philosopher is a self-revelation of the workshop of nature – both the philosopher and the artist speak of the trade secrets of nature.

Above the tumult of contemporary history lives the sphere of the philosopher and the artist, remote from necessity.

The philosopher as the *brake on the wheel of time.*

It is in times of great danger that philosophers appear – when the wheel rolls faster and faster – they and art take the place of disappearing myth. But

attributed to Pittacus (DL 1.79)). Although everyone agreed there were seven of these men, and although some figures (e.g. Solon (see below, Notebook 6, footnote 19, p. 216), Thales (see above, Notebook 7, footnote 29, p. 43), Pittacus) are almost invariably cited as members of the Seven Wise Men, there was no agreement in antiquity on the full membership list. A late compiler, Diogenes Laertius, lists a total of seventeen people who had been considered one of the Seven by one previous author or another (see DL 1.40–3).

they are far ahead of the rest because the attention of their contemporaries is slow to turn towards them.

A people that becomes conscious of its dangers produces the genius.

19[18]

Freedom from myth. Thales. *One element as Proteus!*[4]
The tragic quality of existence. Anaximander.[5]
The artistic play of the cosmos. Heraclitus.[6]
The eternal logic. Parmenides.[7] The battle of words.
Pity for all living things. Empedocles.[8] The slave.
Measure and number. Pythagoras.[9] Democritus.[10]
(The contest. Heraclitus.)
(Love and education. Socrates.)
The $νοῦς$[11] the smallest assumption. Anaxagoras.[12]

---

[4] See above, Notebook 7, footnote 29, p. 43. Proteus was a minor sea-god who was capable of changing his shape, just as 'water', considered as a cosmological first principle, would have to remain one and the same while changing its 'shape' into all of the variety of forms we see in the world.

[5] We have only one highly cryptic fragment by Anaximander of Miletus (DK 1, KR p. 117), which seems to speak of the transitoriness of all things which is based on both a physical and a moral-legal necessity: all entities must pass away because they must 'pay the penalty for their injustice'. See also KSA I. 817–22.

[6] See above, Notebook 7, footnote 29, p. 43; DK 52; KSA I.822–35.

[7] Parmenides, who 'flourished' in the early part of fifth century, expressed his views in a long poem in dactylic hexameter. In contrast to the 'Milesians' (i.e., philosophers born in Miletus: Thales, Anaximenes, Anaximander), whose interest in the investigation of nature made them as much ancestors of natural science as of philosophy, Parmenides and his followers (called the 'Eleatics' after Parmenides' birthplace, Elea in Southern Italy) were interested in constructing an ontology based on purely logical principles and thought sense perception inherently deceptive. See KSA I.835–51.

[8] Empedocles of Akragas (today Agrigento), who flourished in the mid-fifth century BC, was a physician, shaman and political figure who also had philosophical views; most notably perhaps he held that human souls could be reincarnated after death in the bodies of animals (DK 117, KR p. 354), and that meat-eating was wrong (DK 136, 137, 139, KR pp. 350–1). He believed in two explanatory principles which he called 'love' (or 'friendship') and 'strife' (DK 17, KR pp. 324, 326–8).

[9] A shadowy fifth-century (BC) figure who seems to have been born on the island of Samos (in the Aegean), but to have moved to Southern Italy where he founded a school that had some of the characteristics of a religious sect, and many of whose members seem to have had a strong interest in mathematics. Transmigration of souls was also a central part of the doctrine. See KR pp. 217–31, 236–62.

[10] An ancient atomist, born about 460 BC, who wrote prolifically on a variety of philosophic topics.

[11] mind, reason.

[12] Anaxagoras was born about 500 BC in Klazomene in Asia Minor, but apparently spent a considerable amount of time in Athens where he became friends with Pericles. He was prosecuted by the

19[20]

After Socrates the common good can no longer be salvaged, hence the individualising ethic that tries to save the *individuals*.

19[21]

The excessive and indiscriminate drive for knowledge, with its historical background, is a sign that life has grown old: there is a great danger that individuals become *bad*, and therefore their interests are forcibly tied to objects of knowledge, regardless of what these may be. The universal drives have become so feeble and no longer keep the individual under control.

Germanic man has transfigured all his limitations through the sciences by transferring them: fidelity, modesty, self-restraint, diligence, cleanliness, orderliness are family virtues; but so are formlessness, all the lifelessness of life, pettiness – his limitless drive for knowledge is the consequence of a miserable life: without this drive he would become petty and malicious, and often is in spite of it.

Now we have been given a higher form of life, a background of art – and now the next consequence is a fastidious drive for knowledge, i.e. *philosophy*.

Terrible danger: a fusion of the American type of political wheeling and dealing with the unstable culture of scholars.

19[22]

With the fastidious drive for knowledge, *beauty* once more emerges as power.

It is most remarkable that Schopenhauer *writes beautifully*! His life too has more style than that of university teachers – but stunted surroundings!

Athenians for 'impiety' (see DL II.13), probably because of some of his cosmological beliefs – e.g., he held that the sun was a molten rock the size of the Peloponnese (and not, that is, a god; KR pp. 391–2) – but escaped conviction by leaving Athens. In Plato's *Phaedo* (97b8–99d2) Socrates expresses his dissatisfaction that, although Anaxagoras announces as a general principle that Mind (νοῦς) was the cause of everything in the universe, he does not actually appeal to Mind as intending to realise some good in giving individual explanations. See KSA I.852–67.

Nowadays nobody knows what a good book looks like: it must be demonstrated by example. People do not understand the meaning of composition. Their feeling for it is more and more ruined by the press.

To be able to capture the sublime!

19[23]

Against iconic historiography and against the natural sciences enormous *artistic* forces are needed.

What must the philosopher do? In the midst of the ant-like teeming of life he must stress the problem of life, indeed all the eternal problems.

The philosopher must *recognise what is necessary*, and the artist must *create* it. The philosopher must empathise with universal suffering most strongly, just as each of the ancient Greek philosophers expresses a need: it is there, in that gap, that he places his system. He builds his world into that gap.

It is necessary to collect all the means by which it is possible to save man for tranquillity: given that the religions are dying!

To make clear the difference between the effect of philosophy and that of science: and likewise the difference between their origins.

19[24]

It is not a question of destroying science, but of *controlling* it. For science in all its goals and methods depends entirely on philosophical views, *although it easily forgets this. But the controlling philosophy must also remember the problem of the degree to which science should be allowed to grow: it has to determine* **value***!*

19[25]

Proof of the *barbarising* effects of the sciences. They easily lose themselves in the service of 'practical interests'.

19[26]

Schopenhauer is valuable because he calls *naïve universal* truths to mind: he dares to utter so-called 'trivialities' beautifully.

We have no noble popular philosophy because we have no noble view of the *peuple* or *publicum*.[13] Our popular philosophy is for the *peuple*, not for the public.

19[27]

If we are ever to achieve a culture, tremendous artistic forces are needed in order to break the boundless drive for knowledge and once more to create a unity. *The supreme dignity of the philosopher manifests itself here, where he concentrates the boundless drive for knowledge and restrains it into a unity.*

This is how the ancient Greek philosophers must be understood: they restrain the drive for knowledge. How did it happen that after Socrates this drive gradually got out of hand? Initially we see the same tendency even in *Socrates and his school*: the drive for knowledge must be limited through the *individual* concern for a *happy life*. This is a last low phase. Once it was not a question of *individuals* but of the *Hellenes*.

19[28]

The great ancient philosophers belong to *Hellenic life in general: after Socrates sects* develop. Gradually the reins of science slip out of the hands of philosophy.

In the Middle Ages theology takes over the reins of science: now a dangerous period of emancipation.

The general welfare again wants *restraint* and thereby at the same time elevation and concentration.

The *laisser-aller*[14] *of all our science* resembles certain *dogmas of political economy*: people believe in an absolutely beneficial outcome.

In a certain sense *Kant* also had a harmful influence: for the belief in metaphysics was lost. Nobody will be able to count on his 'thing-in-itself' as if it were a restraining principle.

---

[13] For conservatives in Germany the French word for 'the people' (*peuple*) still had some of the pejorative associations it had acquired (for them) during the French Revolution, i.e., the *common* people, or, as we might say, 'the revolutionary masses'. Nietzsche seems to be appealing to the more positive connotations of the Latin word *publicum*, as when one speaks of 'the public or common good' (*bonum publicum*).

[14] 'Let them go', i.e., 'leave them alone'. The economic doctrine is usually called *laissez-faire* ('Let them do [what they want]'), i.e., the view that the government ought not to intervene in the economy.

Now we understand the remarkable phenomenon of *Schopenhauer*: he collects all the elements that are still of use in controlling science. He arrives at the most profound primal problems of ethics and art; he raises the question of the value of existence.

The marvellous unity of Wagner and Schopenhauer! They are rooted in the same drive. With them the most profound qualities of the Germanic mind arm themselves for battle: just as it was with the Greeks. The return of *composure*.[15]

19[29]

Description of the enormous danger of secularisation in the 6th and 5th centuries: the luxuriance of the colonies, the wealth, the sensuality.

19[30]

The problem: *finding the culture to go with our music!*

19[31]

It is necessary to designate the method by which philosophical man has to *live.*

19[32]

To characterise the superficiality of our culture: David Strauss,[16] our theatres, our poets, our criticism, our schools.

19[33]

My task: to comprehend *the internal coherence and the necessity of any true culture.* The preservatives and remedies of a culture, and its relation to the genius of the people. The consequence of every great artistic world

---

[15] The German word Nietzsche uses here, *Besonnenheit*, is the one generally used as translation of the Greek σωφροσύνη, the important ancient virtue of 'temperance' or moderation.
[16] A Young Hegelian writer on religion and politics (1808–74) who was the object of Nietzsche's disapproving attention in the first of Nietzsche's *Unzeitgemäße Betrachtungen*.

is a culture: but as a result of hostile counter-currents this resonance of a work of art often fails to occur.

Philosophy must hold on to the *intellectual mountain range* through the centuries: and with it to the eternal fertility of everything great.

For science there is nothing large or small – but for philosophy there is! The value of science is measured by this proposition.

Capturing the sublime!

What an extraordinary *lack* of books exuding a heroic force in our time! – Even Plutarch is no longer read!

19[34]

Kant says (2nd preface to his *Critique*): '*I have found it necessary to deny knowledge, in order to make room for faith.* The dogmatism of metaphysics, that is, the preconception that it is possible to make headway in metaphysics without a critique of pure reason, is the true source of all that unbelief which opposes morality and is always very dogmatic.'[17] Very important! He was driven by a cultural need!

Strange opposition, '*knowledge and faith*'! What would the Greeks have thought of it? Kant *knew no other opposites*! But *we do!*

Kant is driven by a cultural need: he wants to *save* an area from *knowledge*: that is where he places the roots of all the highest and deepest things, art and ethics – Schopenhauer.

On the other hand, he collects all that is *worthy of knowledge for all time* – the ethical wisdom of the people and of mankind (the point of view of the 7 wise men,[18] of the Greek popular philosophers).

He breaks down the elements of that faith and shows how little the Christian faith in particular satisfies the deepest need: inquire into the value of existence!

The struggle of knowledge against knowledge!

Schopenhauer himself draws our attention to our *unconscious* thought and knowledge.

Restraining the drive for knowledge – whether in favour of a religion or of an artistic culture will now be seen. I side with the second.

---

[17] Adapted from *The Critique of Pure Reason*, trans. Norman Kemp Smith, p. 29.
[18] See above, Notebook 19, footnote 3, p. 95.

I add to this the question of the *value* of *historical iconic* knowledge, and also of *nature*.

Among the Greeks it is a restraint in favour of an artistic culture (*and* religion?), a restraint which is intended to *prevent* a complete absence of control: we want to *restrain* the totally unleashed drive *once more*.

19[35]

The philosopher of tragic knowledge. He does not restrain the uncontrolled drive for knowledge through a new metaphysics. He establishes no new faith. He feels that the *removal of the ground of metaphysics* from underfoot is tragic and yet he can never be satisfied by the bright whirligig of the sciences. He is building a new *life*: he restores to art its rights.

The philosopher of *desperate knowledge* will be absorbed by blind science: knowledge at all costs.

For the tragic philosopher the *image of existence* is completed by the fact that the metaphysical only appears in anthropomorphic form. He is not a *sceptic*.

Here a concept must be *created*: for scepticism is not the goal. The drive for knowledge, having arrived at its limits, turns against itself in order to proceed to a *critique of knowledge*. Knowledge in the service of the best life.

One must *want* even *illusion* – that is where the tragic lies.

19[36]

The last philosopher – they can be whole generations. He must only assist *life*. 'The last' is of course relative. For our world. He proves the necessity of illusion, of art and of the art that dominates life. For us it is no longer possible to produce a succession of philosophers such as Greece did in the age of tragedy. Their task is now performed by *art alone*. Such a system is now possible only as *art*. From today's point of view that whole period of Greek philosophy also belongs in the domain of Greek art.

Now science is restrained only by art. It is a question of *value* judgements about knowledge and encyclopedic knowledge.

The tremendous task and dignity of art in this task! Art must create everything anew and *give new birth to life all alone! What it is capable of* is shown *to us by the Greeks*: if we did not have them our faith would be chimeric.

Whether a religion can be built here, into the vacuum, depends on its strength. *We* incline to *culture*: the 'German' element as a *redemptive force*!

In any case a religion that could do this would need to have a tremendous *force of love*: on which knowledge founders, just as it founders on the language of art.

But perhaps art is even able to create a religion for itself, give birth to myth? That was the case among the Greeks.

19[37]

But the philosophies and theologies that have now been *destroyed* continue to be effective in the sciences: even though the roots have died, here, in the branches, there is some life left for a while. The *historical* is so widely developed, in particular as an opposing force against theological myth, but also against philosophy: here and in the mathematical sciences *absolute knowledge* celebrates its Saturnalia;[19] here the smallest thing that can really be *made out* is held in higher esteem than all metaphysical ideas. Here it is the degree of *certainty* that determines the value, not the degree of *indispensability* for man. It is the old struggle between *faith* and *knowledge*.

These are barbarous biases.

Now philosophy can only stress the *relativity* and the *anthropomorphic* character of all knowledge, as well as the power of *illusion* that prevails everywhere. In so doing it can no longer inhibit the uncontrolled drive for knowledge, which *judges* more and more by the degree of certainty and which seeks smaller and smaller objects. While every man is happy when a day is over, the historian later burrows, digs and combines in order to wrest that day from oblivion: the *small* too is supposed to be eternal, *because it is recognisable*.

For us the aesthetic standard alone is valid: the *great* has a right to history, albeit not an iconic, but a *productive, stimulating portrayal of history*. We leave the *graves in peace*: but we seize that which lives eternally.

---

[19] The Roman winter festival during which many of the usual rules of social behaviour were relaxed or suspended.

The favourite topic of our age: the *great effects of the smallest things*. Historical burrowing, e.g., as a whole, has something magnificent about it: it is like the scanty vegetation that gradually breaks up the Alps. We see a great drive which has small tools, but a *magnificently large number* of them.

One could counter this with *the small effects of the great* – if it is represented by individuals. It is difficult to grasp; the tradition often dies away; hatred against it is ubiquitous; its value rests on quality, which is only ever appreciated by the few.

The great only affects the great: just as the torch signals in *Agamemnon*[20] leap only from one peak to another. It is the task of a *culture* to ensure that the great in a people appears neither as a hermit nor as an exile.

Therefore we will say what we feel: it is not our business to wait till the pale reflection of what seems bright to me penetrates into the valleys. Ultimately the great effects of the smallest are the after-effects of the *great*; they have set off an avalanche. Now we are hard put to stop it.

19[38]

History and the natural sciences were necessary against the Middle Ages: knowledge against faith. Now we confront knowledge with *art*: a return to life! Restraint of the drive for knowledge! Reinforcement of the moral and aesthetic instincts!

This seems to us to be the *salvation of the German spirit, so that it may again be the saviour*!

We have grasped the essence of this spirit in *music*. Now we understand how the *Greeks* made their culture dependent on music.

19[39]

A religion would be created if a man *awakened belief* in a mystical edifice that he built in a vacuum, i.e. if the belief met an extraordinary need.

It is *unlikely* that this will ever happen again after the *Critique of Pure Reason*.[21]

---

[20] In Aeschylus' tragedy *Agamemnon*, the news that Troy has fallen is transmitted with exceptional quickness to Agamemnon's palace in Mycenae through a series of torch signals arranged beforehand (see *Agamemnon* ll. 1–39, 281–316).

[21] Because the *Critique of Pure Reason* contained a devastating criticism of any form of natural theology.

On the other hand I can imagine an entirely new kind of *philosopher-artist* who would fill the gap with a *work of art*, with aesthetic value.

Fortunately being good and being compassionate are independent of the failure or success of a religion: on the other hand, *doing good* is very much determined by religious imperatives. By far the greatest amount of dutiful good deeds has no ethical value, but is *enforced*.

Practical morality will suffer greatly from every collapse of a religion. A metaphysics of punishment and reward seems indispensable.

If we could create *custom*,[22] a powerful *custom*! We would then also have morality.[23]

But *custom* is created through the *example of individual powerful personalities*.

I do not count on *goodness* awakening in the mass of the wealthy, but one could lead them to a *custom*, to a duty towards tradition.

If mankind were to assign what it has so far spent on building churches to education and schools, if it were now to apply the intellect spent on theology to education.

19[40]

The *poetic freedom* with which the Greeks treated their gods!

We are too used to the contrast between historical truth and untruth. It is funny that the Christian myths are supposed to be absolutely *historical*!

19[41]

The problem of a *culture* is seldom correctly understood. The goal of a culture is not the greatest possible *happiness* of a people, nor the unimpeded development of *all* their talents: rather, a culture is revealed in the right *proportion* of these developments. Its goal points beyond earthly happiness: the creation of great works is its goal.

In all Greek drives a *restraining unity* manifests itself: let us call it the Hellenic *will*. Each of these drives tries to exist alone to infinity. The ancient philosophers tried to construct the world out of them.

---

[22] *Sitte.*
[23] *Sittlichkeit.*

The *culture* of a people manifests itself in the *unifying restraint of the drives of that people*: philosophy restrains the drive for knowledge, art restrains the drive for form and ecstasy, ἀγάπη restrains ἔρως²⁴ etc.

Knowledge *isolates*: the earlier philosophers represent in isolation what in Greek art is made to appear together.

The contents of art and of ancient philosophy coincide, but in philosophy we see the *isolated* components of art being used in order to *restrain the drive for knowledge*. This must also be demonstrable among the Italians: individualism in life and in art.

19[42]

The Greeks as discoverers and travellers and colonisers. They know how to *learn*: they have a tremendous power of appropriation. Our age should not think that it stands so much higher in its drive for knowledge: only, with the Greeks everything became *life*! With us it remains knowledge!

19[43]

If what matters is the *value* of knowledge, and if on the other hand a beautiful delusion²⁵ – provided that it is believed in – has the same value as something known, then we see that life needs illusions,²⁶ i.e. untruths taken to be truths. It needs the belief in truth, but then illusion is found to be sufficient, i.e. 'truths' prove themselves through their effects, not through logical evidence, but evidence of power.²⁷ The true and the effective are regarded as identical; even here force is bowed to. How then did any logical demonstration of truth ever take place? In the *struggle between 'truth' and 'truth'* the alliance with reflection is sought by both. *All real striving for truth came into the world through the struggle for a holy conviction*, through the πάθος²⁸ of struggle; otherwise man has no interest in a logical origin.

---

²⁴ ἔρως is specifically sexual desire, erotic love; ἀγάπη refers generally to an affection that is not specifically sexual.

²⁵ *Wahn.*

²⁶ *Illusionen.*

²⁷ The doctrine held by certain Christian theologians that the truth of Christianity could be 'proved' by the 'power' it conferred on those who believed.

²⁸ emotional attitude.

19[44]

The purpose is to determine the teleology of the philosopher in the midst of culture.

We ask the Greeks of the period in which there was unity in their culture.

Important: there is philosophy even for the richest culture. Why?

We ask the great philosophers. Ah, they have perished! How carelessly nature behaves!

19[45]

How does the philosophical genius relate to art? There is little we can learn from his direct behaviour. We must ask: what in his philosophy is art? Work of art? What *remains* if his system is destroyed as science? But it must be precisely what remains that *restrains* the drive for knowledge, i.e. the artistic quality. Why is such a restraint necessary? For, scientifically considered, it is an illusion, an untruth, that deceives and only temporarily satisfies the drive for knowledge. The value of philosophy with regard to this restraint lies not in the sphere of knowledge, but in the sphere of life: the *will to existence uses philosophy* for the purpose of a higher form of existence.

It is not possible for art and philosophy to turn *against* the will: but morality too is in its service. Universal domination of the *will*. One of the most delicate forms of existence is relative nirvana.

19[46]

Everything must be said as precisely as possible and any technical term, including 'will', must be left on one side.

19[47]

The beauty and magnificence of a construction of the world (aka philosophy) now determines its value – i.e. it is judged as *art*. Its form will probably change! The rigid mathematical formula (as in Spinoza) – which had such a calming effect on Goethe[29] – now is justified only as a means of aesthetic expression.

19[48]

This proposition must be established: we live only through illusions; our consciousness skims the surface. Many things are hidden from our gaze. Nor need it ever be feared that man will *completely* know himself, that at any moment he will understand all the laws of leverage or mechanics, all the formulae of architecture or chemistry, which are necessary for his life. However, it is possible that everything will become known through a *diagram*. This changes almost nothing for our lives. Moreover those are all mere formulae for absolutely unrecognisable forces.

19[49]

We really live in a continuous illusion as a result of the superficiality of our intellect: i.e. in order to live we need art at every moment. Our eye binds us to *forms*. But if we ourselves have gradually acquired this eye by training, then we see an *artistic force* at work in ourselves. Therefore we see in nature itself mechanisms against absolute *knowledge*: the *philosopher recognises the language of nature* and *says*: 'we need art' and 'we need only a part of knowledge'.

19[50]

Every kind of *culture* begins by *veiling* many things. The progress of man depends on this veiling – life in a pure and noble sphere and the exclusion of the baser stimulations. The struggle against 'sensuality' by means of virtue is of an essentially aesthetic kind. If we use the *great* individuals as our lodestars we veil a great deal about them; indeed we veil all the circumstances and accidents that made it possible for them to come into being; we *isolate* them in order to venerate them. Every religion contains such

---

[29] Perhaps a reference to a conversation Goethe had with Sulpiz Boisserée on 3 August 1815. See *Goethe's Gespräche*, ed. Flodoard Frh. von Biedermann (Leipzig: Biedermann, 1909), vol. IV, p. 318.

an element: men are seen as being in divine care, as something infinitely important. Indeed, all ethics begins when we regard the single individual as *infinitely important* – unlike nature, which behaves cruelly and playfully. If we are better and nobler it is due to the isolating illusions!

Natural science contrasts this with the absolute truth of nature, although higher physiology will recognise artistic forces already in our evolution, and not only in that of man, but also of animals: it will say that the *artistic* too begins with the *organic*.

19[51]

The consequences of Kant's theory. The end of metaphysics as a science.

The barbarising effect of knowledge.
The restraint of knowledge as the drive of art.
We *live* only by means of the illusions of art.
Every higher culture is one as a result of this restraint.
The philosophical systems of the early Greeks.
The same world as that which created tragedy manifests itself.

Here we comprehend the unity of philosophy and art for the purpose of culture.

The aesthetic concept of the great and sublime: the task is to educate for this. Culture depends on how one defines 'the great'.

19[52]

Absolute knowledge leads to *pessimism*; art is the remedy against it.

Philosophy is indispensable for *culture* because it *draws knowledge into* an artistic conception of the world and thereby ennobles it.

19[53]

Schopenhauer was entirely motivated by the concern that his eternal work should not be withheld from mankind and perish: he knew the fate of Heraclitus,[30] and his first edition was pulped! He had the forethought of a

---

[30] Heraclitus was said to have become increasingly misanthropic as he grew older and finally to have buried himself in a dung heap inside a cowshed in a vain attempt to cure himself of 'dropsy' (see DL IX.3–5).

father: all his unpleasant characteristics, his contact with literary figures such as Frauenstädt,[31] can be explained by this. His obsession with fame was a precautionary instinct for the benefit of mankind: he knew the ways of the world.

It is possible to imagine an even greater superiority to mankind: but then he would not have written! He longed for continuing procreation in the beautiful![32]

19[54]

The chemical transformations in inorganic nature may perhaps also be called artistic processes, mimetic roles, played by a force: but there are *several* that it can play!

19[60]

The emergence of philosophical sects in Greek antiquity.

Out of the most profound transformation of the Hellenic spirit.

Beginning with the Pythagoreans, from whom *Plato* learns it.

The academy sets the *type*. They are institutes of opposition to Hellenic life.

The earlier philosophers are isolations of individual drives of the Hellenic character.

We are experiencing the transition of the philosophical sectarian spirit to cultural consciousness, the *transition of philosophy to culture*. There the *separation* of philosophy and culture.

The superficiality of all post-Socratic ethics! The profound early Hellenic ethic could not be represented in words and concepts.

19[61]

Heraclitus with his hatred against the Dionysian element,[33] also against Pythagoras, also against excessive knowledge. He is an Apollonian product and he speaks oracles, the nature of which one must interpret

---

[31] Julius Frauenstädt was the editor of Schopenhauer's collected works. The point of this reference seems to be that Frauenstädt was a *literary* agent and popularizer rather than a philosopher.

[32] See above, Notebook 19, footnote 2, p. 94.

[33] Against Dionysus, see DK 15, KR p. 211; against Pythagoras, see DK 40, 81.

for oneself and for him. He does not feel suffering, but he does feel stupidity.

19[62]

Great uncertainty as to whether philosophy is an art or a science.

It is an art in its purposes and its production. But the means, i.e. representation in concepts, it has in common with science. It is a form of poetry. – It cannot be accommodated in any existing category: therefore we must invent and characterise a species for it.

The description of the philosopher's nature. He knows through creating poetry, and he creates poetry through knowing.

He does not grow, I mean, philosophy does not take the same course as the other sciences, even though some of the philosopher's domains are gradually transferred into the hands of science. Heraclitus can never become obsolete. It is a poetic creation beyond the limits of experience, the continuation of the *mythical drive*; also essentially in images. Mathematical representation is not part of the nature of the philosopher.

Overcoming knowledge through *mythopoeic forces. Kant* remarkable – knowledge and faith! Most intimate relationship between *philosophers* and the *founders of religion*!

19[63]

Strange problem: the self-consumption of philosophical systems! Unheard-of in either science or art! The situation is *similar* in the religions: this is remarkable and significant.

19[64]

Illusion necessary for the sentient being to live.

Illusion necessary for progress in culture.

What does the insatiable drive for knowledge want?

– In any case it is hostile to culture.

Philosophy tries to restrain it; it is a means of culture.

The early philosophers.

19[66]

Our intellect is a surface force, it is *superficial*. This is also called 'subjective'. The intellect knows through *concepts*: i.e. our thinking is a process of categorisation, of naming. Thus it is something that boils down to an arbitrary decision by man and does not reach the thing itself. Man has absolute knowledge only when he *calculates* and only in the forms of space, i.e. the ultimate limits of everything knowable are *quantities*; he does not *understand* quality, but only quantity.

What may be the purpose of such a surface force?

The image first corresponds to the concept; images are primal thought, i.e. the surfaces of things are collected in the mirror of the eye.

The *image* is one thing, the *mathematical example*[34] is another.

Images in human eyes! This dominates all human nature: from the *eye*! The subject! The *ear* hears sounds! A completely different, wonderful conception of the same world.

Art is based on the *inaccuracy* of *sight*. For the ear too there is inaccuracy in rhythm, tempering[35] etc., on which again *art* is based.

19[67]

There is a force in us that allows us to perceive the *great* features of the mirror image more intensely, and again a force that stresses the same rhythm even above the real inaccuracy. This must be an *artistic* force. For it *creates*. Its main resource is *omitting* and *overlooking* and *ignoring*. Therefore it is anti-scientific: for it has not the same interest in everything perceived.

The word contains only an image, from which the concept derives. Thinking therefore calculates with artistic quantities.

All classification is an attempt to arrive at an image.

---

[34] That is, a particular mathematical example is an *instance*, not an image, of a general principle.

[35] For a number of complex reasons having to do with a perceived need to transpose or modulate from one key to another, traditional Western music is based not on 'pure' (i.e., physically defined) intervals, but on a set of artificially created or notional intervals. 'Tempering' is the process of modifying the pitches of an instrument so as to allow it to play in a number of different keys in one musical piece. The 'tempered' intervals are thus *not* identical with the intervals as they would be *physically* defined (e.g., by the number of cycles per second of a tuning fork), but yet for the purposes of the musical composition they must be perceived *as if* they were these intervals. The crucial point for Nietzsche seems to be this discrepancy ('*inaccuracy*') between the physical reality and the perception necessary for aesthetic experience.

We relate to every true *being* superficially; we speak the language of the symbol, of the image: then we add something that has artistic power, by strengthening the main features and forgetting the secondary ones.

19[68]

The apology of art

Thales has long since gone – but an artist, standing near a waterfall, will nevertheless agree with him.

19[69]

Our public political and social life boils down to a balance of egoisms: solution of the question how to achieve a bearable existence without any power of love, purely out of the prudence of the egoisms involved.

Our time hates art, as it hates religion. It will not be satisfied either by reference to the beyond or by reference to the transfiguration of the world of art. It regards these as useless 'poetry', fun etc. Our 'poets' *follow suit*. But art as a terrible seriousness! The new metaphysics as a terrible seriousness! We will surround your world with images till you shudder. We have the power to do that! You may block your ears, but your eyes will see our myth. Our curses will be upon you!

Now science must show its utility! It has become the provider, in the service of egoism: the state and society have forced it into their service in order to exploit it for *their* purposes.

The normal condition is *war*; we make *peace* only for specific periods.

19[70]

It is important for me to know how the Greeks philosophised at the time of their art. The *Socratic* schools sat in the middle of an ocean of beauty – what does one see of that in them? Enormous efforts were made on behalf of art. The attitude of the Socratics towards it was either hostile or theoretical.

In contrast, in the early philosophers a drive similar to that which created tragedy was partly at work.

19[71]

The concept of the philosopher and the types. – What is common to all?
He has either sprung from his culture or is hostile to it.

He is contemplative like the visual artist, compassionate like the
religious man, causally oriented like the man of science: he tries to let all
the sounds of the world reverberate in him and to place this comprehensive sound outside himself into concepts. *Swelling to the macrocosm* and
at the same time *composed contemplation*[36]– like the actor or the dramatic
poet who changes and at the same time keeps his composure[37] in order to
project himself outwards.

Dialectical thinking is like a shower discharged over this.

Plato remarkable: an enthusiast of dialectics, i.e. of that composure.

19[72]

Philosophers. Description of the philosopher's nature.

The philosopher alongside the man of science and the artist.
Restraining the drive for knowledge by means of art, the religious drive
    for oneness by means of the concept.
The strange juxtaposition of conception and abstraction.
Significance for culture.
Metaphysics as vacuum.

19[73]

The philosopher of the future?[38] He must become the supreme tribunal of an artistic culture, as it were, the security agency against all
excesses.

---

[36] *besonnenes Betrachten.*
[37] *Besonnenheit.*
[38] Hegel claimed that philosophy was always retrospective. Many of the philosophers of the next
generation, however, were influenced by Feuerbach's reversal of this orientation, and proclama-
tion of a 'philosophy of the future', e.g. in his *Grundsätze der Philosophie der Zukunft* (1843). As a
young political (and artistic) revolutionary Richard Wagner was deeply influenced by Feuerbach's
conception, and identified himself with the project of creating an 'artwork of the future' or com-
posing the 'music of the future', GSD 7.87–138, 3.42–178.

19[74]

We will certainly not describe all classification, all general concepts, as 'philosophical'. Nor everything unconscious and intuitive:[39] even in philological conjecture there is a process of production that cannot be completely dissolved into conscious thinking.

19[75]

Philosophical thinking can be sensed in the midst of all scientific thinking: even in conjectures. It runs ahead on light supports; the intellect pants clumsily behind and seeks better supports, once the alluring magical image has appeared to it. An infinitely fast flight through vast spaces! Is it only the greater speed? No. It is the wingbeat of the imagination, i.e. a leaping from one possibility to the next, which are temporarily taken for certainties. Here and there from a possibility to a certainty and again to a possibility. –

But what is such a 'possibility'? A sudden idea, e.g. 'it might perhaps'. But how does the idea *come about*? Sometimes accidentally and externally: a comparison, a discovery of some analogy, occurs. Then *expansion* follows. Imagination consists in the *rapid perception of similarities*. Subsequently reflection measures and examines one concept against another. The aim is to replace *similarity* with *causality*.

Are 'scientific' and 'philosophical' thinking distinguished only by their *dosage*? Or perhaps by their *areas*?

19[76]

There is *no philosophy apart, separate from science: in both, thinking occurs in the same way.* The reason why *unprovable* philosophising still has a value, indeed usually a greater value than a scientific proposition, lies in the aesthetic *value* of such philosophising, i.e. in its beauty and sublimity. Even if it cannot prove itself as a scientific edifice, it is still present as a *work of art*. But is it not the same in scientific matters? –

In other words: it is not the pure *drive for knowledge* that decides, but the *aesthetic drive*: the poorly supported philosophy of Heraclitus has greater artistic value than all the propositions of Aristotle.

[39] *alles Intuitive.*

The drive for knowledge, then, is restrained by the imagination in the culture of a people. In this process the philosopher is replete with the supreme *pathos of truth*: for him the *value* of his knowledge guarantees its *truth*. All *fruitfulness*, and all driving force, lies in these glimpses *ahead*.

19[77]

The production of the imagination can be observed in the eye. Similarity leads to the boldest continuing creation: but so do quite different conditions – e.g. contrast to contrast – and incessantly. Here one *sees* the extraordinary productivity of the intellect. It is a life in images.

19[78]

When one is thinking one must already have what one seeks,[40] through the imagination – only then can reflection judge it. Reflection does this by measuring it against customary sequences that have often stood the test of time.

What is actually 'logical' about thinking in images? –

A sober man needs and *has* little imagination.

In any case, this production of forms, which then bring something to the memory, is *artistic*: the memory *highlights this form* and reinforces it in the process. Thinking is highlighting.

There are far more sequences of images in the brain than are used up in thinking; the intellect quickly selects similar images; the selected images again produce an abundance of images; the intellect again quickly selects one of these etc.

Conscious thinking is only a selection of representations. It is a long way from there to abstraction.

1) The force that creates the abundance of images 2) the force that selects and emphasises similarities.

Patients suffering from fever treat walls and wallpaper in this way, while the healthy also project the wallpaper.

---

[40] See Plato, *Meno* 80.

19[79]

There is a double artistic force, that which produces images and that which selects them.

The correctness of this is proved by the world of dreams: in dreams man does not proceed to abstraction, or he is not guided and modified by the images that flood in through the eye.

If one looks at this force more closely, here too there is no entirely free artistic invention, which would be something arbitrary and therefore impossible. Rather, the most subtle radiations of nervous activity, seen on a level surface, behave in the same way as Chladni's sound patterns in relation to the sound itself:[41] that is how these images relate to the nervous activity beneath them. The most delicate oscillation and vibration! The artistic process, physiologically, is absolutely determined and necessary. On the surface all thinking appears to us as voluntary and subject to our choice: we do not notice the endless activity.

To imagine an *artistic process without a brain* is highly anthropopathic: but the same applies to the will, to morality etc.

Desire is only a physiological abundance that tries to erupt and exerts pressure all the way to the brain.

19[80]

Result: it is only a question of *degrees* and *quantities*: all men are artistic, philosophical, scientific etc.

We esteem quantities, not qualities. We admire the *great*. That, of course, is also the *abnormal*.

Admiration of the magnificent effects of small things is only astonishment at the disproportion between the result and the smallest cause. Only by adding very many effects together and regarding them as a *unity* do we obtain the impression of greatness: i.e. *we produce* greatness by means of this unity.

But mankind grows only through admiration of the *rare and great*. Even something that is only imagined to be rare and great, e.g. a *miracle*, has this effect. Fright is the best part of mankind.

---

[41] Ernst Chladni (1756–1827) showed that the vibration of string can produce visual patterns in an appropriately constructed sand-box. The visual patterns thus correspond to what the human ear hears as sound.

19[81]

Dreaming as the selective continuation of the images in the eye.

In the realm of the intellect everything qualitative is merely *quantitative*. We are led to the qualities by the concept, the word.

19[82]

Perhaps man can *forget* nothing. The operation of seeing and knowing is far too complicated to be totally obliterated, i.e. all the forms once produced by the brain and the nervous system are then reproduced many times by it. The same nervous activity produces the same image again.

19[83]

Philosophical thinking belongs to the same species as scientific thinking, but it relates to *great* things and concerns. But the concept of greatness is variable, part aesthetic, part moral. It *restrains* the drive for knowledge. That is its cultural significance.

When metaphysics is eliminated, gradually many other things will once more appear *great* to mankind. I believe that philosophers will prefer different areas: I hope those in which they will have a salutary effect on the new culture.

A *jurisdiction of greatness*, a 'naming', is connected with philosophy: 'this is great', the philosopher says, elevating man. It begins with the legislation of morality: 'this is great', the standpoint of the seven wise men, which the Romans never abandoned in good times.

19[84]

The true raw material of all knowledge consists of the most delicate sensations of pleasure and displeasure: the true secret lies on that surface on which nervous activity inscribes forms in joy and pain: that which is sensation projects *forms*, and these in turn produce new sensations.

It is the nature of the sensation of pleasure and displeasure to express itself in adequate movements; these adequate movements, by inducing sensations in other nerves, bring about the sensation of the *image*.

19[85]

Wisdom and science.
On philosophers
Dedicated to Arthur Schopenhauer, the immortal.

19[86]

σοφία[42] and ἐπιστήμη.[43] σοφία contains within it that which selects, that which has taste: while science, lacking such a refined taste, pounces on everything worth knowing.

19[87]

Even if applied to thinking in images, Darwinism is right: the stronger image consumes the lesser ones.

19[89]

What is the philosopher? To be answered with reference to the ancient Greeks?[44]

Thales. Mythologist and philosopher.
Anaximander. Tragic world view. Tragedy.
Heraclitus. Illusion. Artistic elements in the philosopher. Art.
Pythagoras. Mysticism and philosophy. Religion.
Anaxagoras. Purposes. Mind and matter.
Parmenides. Zeno. The logical. Logic.
Empedocles. Love, hate. Justice and the morality of love. Morality.
Democritus. Number and measure, prospect of all physics. Natural philosophy.
Pythagoreans. Sectarianism.
Socrates. The philosopher and culture. Culture.
The origin of philosophers and – the tribunal of philosophers for the culture of the future.

---

[42] wisdom.   [43] knowledge.
[44] See above, Notebook 19, 19[18], p. 97.

19[90]

Whether thinking occurs with pleasure or displeasure is quite essential. Those who find thinking really troublesome have less aptitude for it and will probably also achieve less: they *force* themselves, which is useless in this area.

19[92]

Sometimes a result achieved by leaps immediately proves true and fruitful, as seen from its consequences.

Is a researcher of genius guided by a correct *hunch?* Yes, for he sees *possibilities* without adequate support: and the fact that he regards such a thing as possible shows his genius. He makes a quick calculation of what he is roughly able to prove.

The misuse of knowledge through the eternal repetition of experiments and the collecting of material, when the conclusion can be reached from a few data. The same applies to philology: in many cases the completeness of the material is pointless.

19[93]

What is moral also has no other source than the intellect, but here the connecting chain of images has a different effect than in the case of the artist and the thinker: it stimulates a *deed.* Quite certainly the sensation of similarity, *identification*, is a necessary prerequisite. Then the recollection of one's own pain. Being good would then mean: identifying *very easily* and very *quickly.* Therefore it is a transformation, similar to that of the actor.

In contrast, all rectitude and all justice results from a balance of egoisms: a mutual agreement not to harm one another. That is, from prudence. But in the form of firm principles it looks different: it appears as *firmness* of character. Love and justice are opposites: the point of culmination is self-sacrifice for the world.

The anticipation of possible sensations of displeasure determines the action of a just man: he empirically knows the consequences of hurting his neighbour, but also of hurting himself.

The Christian ethic is the opposite of this: it is founded on the identification of oneself with one's neighbour; here doing good to others is doing good to oneself; here suffering with others is identical to one's own suffering. Love is connected with a desire for unity.

19[96]

Philosophy in Greece began with a great *mathematician*.[45] That was where his sense of the abstract, the unmythical, came from. Nevertheless, despite his anti-mythical mentality, he was regarded as the 'sage' in Delphi:[46] – Orphics[47] show abstract thoughts in allegories.

The Greeks adopted *science* from the Orientals. *Mathematics and astronomy are older than philosophy.*

19[97]

Man demands truth and achieves it in moral contacts with others; all social existence is based on this. One anticipates the bad consequences of reciprocal lies. This is the origin of *the duty of truth*. The epic storyteller is allowed to *lie*,[48] because in that area no harmful effects are to be expected. – Thus, where the lie is regarded as pleasant it is allowed: the beauty and grace of the lie, provided it does no harm. Similarly, the priest invents the myths of his gods: the lie justifies their sublimity. It is extraordinarily difficult to reawaken the mythical sense of the free lie. The great Greek philosophers still live entirely in this entitlement to lie.

Where it is not possible to know anything true, lying is allowed.

Every man allows himself to be lied to constantly at night in his dreams.

The *striving for truth* is an infinitely slow acquisition of mankind. Our historical sense is something quite new in the world. It could be possible that it will suppress art entirely.

---

[45] Thales (see above, Notebook 7, footnote 29, p. 43), the first person now generally recognised as having been a philosopher, was said to have been a keen student of geometry and astronomy.

[46] See above, Notebook 19, 19[14], p. 95.

[47] Extremely obscure religious groups in the sixth and fifth centuries BC which claimed to be followers of the mythical 'Orpheus' and produced a very large body of cosmological writing, much of it in verse and some intended to be read allegorically. The extant fragments are collected in Kern, *Orphicorum Fragmenta*.

[48] A fragment of a poem by Solon (Athenian statesman, late seventh – early sixth century BC) runs: 'bards lie a lot' (πολλὰ ψεύδονται ἀοιδοί), and this apparently became a kind of proverbial saying in Greece. See also Hesiod, *Theogony* ll. 24–8.

Telling the *truth at all costs* is *Socratic*.

19[98]

The philosopher.

Reflections about the struggle of art and knowledge.

19[99]

The 'ochlocracy[49] of scholars' instead of the republic of scholars.

19[100]

Very instructive when Heraclitus compares his language with Apollo and the sibyl.[50]

19[101]

The senses fool us.[51]

19[102]

Truth and lie physiologically.
   Truth as moral law – two sources of morality.
   The nature of truth judged by its *effects*.
   The effects seduce us into assuming unproven 'truths'.
   In the *struggle* of such 'truths' that live by force the need to find a different way to them manifests itself. Either explaining everything by them or ascending to them from examples and appearances.
   The wonderful invention of logic.
   The gradual predominance of the logical forces and restriction of what it is *possible* to know.
   The continuous reaction of the artistic forces and restriction to what is *worth* knowing (judged by the *effects*).

[49] 'rule of the crowd', a derogatory term for democracy.
[50] DK 92, 93; KR pp. 211–12.
[51] DK 46

19[103]

Struggle within the *philosopher*.

His universal drive forces him into bad thinking; the tremendous pathos of truth, created by the far-sightedness of his outlook, forces him into *communication* and the communication in turn into logic.

On the one hand an *optimistic metaphysics of logic* comes into being – gradually poisoning and lying to everything. Logic, as sole ruler, leads to the lie: for it *is* not the sole ruler.

The other sense of truth stems from *love*, the proof of power.[52]

Pronouncing the *blissful truth* out of *love*: this concerns a knowledge of the individual which he is not obliged to communicate, but which forces him to communicate by its own overflowing blissfulness.

19[104]

To be completely truthful – glorious, heroic joy of man, in a mendacious nature. *But possible only in a very relative sense!* That is tragic. That is the *tragic problem of Kant!*[53] Now art acquires an entirely *new* dignity. The sciences, on the other hand, are *degraded* by one degree.

19[105]

The *truthfulness* of art: now it alone is honest.

Thus, by an enormous detour, we return to *natural* behaviour (among the Greeks). It has proved impossible to build a culture on knowledge.

19[106]

Fighting for *one truth* and fighting *over the* truth are quite different things.

---

[52] See above, Notebook 19, footnote 27, p. 107.
[53] Probably this refers to Kant's views about the strict limits to possible human knowledge.

19[107]

Unconscious *conclusions* arouse my doubts: it is probably that transition from *image* to *image* that I mentioned before: the image reached last then operates as a stimulus and motive.

Unconscious thinking must take place without concepts: that is, in *intuitions*.

But this is the inferential method of the contemplative philosopher and the artist. They do the same as everybody does on physiological and personal impulses, transferred to an impersonal world.

This thinking in images is not of a strictly *logical* kind from the outset, but is still more or less logical. The philosopher then tries to replace thinking in images with a conceptual mode of thinking. The instincts too seem to be such a thinking in images, which finally becomes a stimulus and motive.

19[108]

The great ethical strength of the Stoics[54] manifests itself in the fact that they break their own principles for the sake of free will.

19[109]

On the theory of morality: in politics a statesman often anticipates the action of his adversary and does the deed beforehand: 'if I do not do it, he will'. A kind of *self-defence* as a political principle. The point of view of war.

19[110]

The ancient Greeks have no normative theology: everybody has the right to invent one and he may believe what he likes.

The enormous *mass* of philosophical thinking among the Greeks (with its continuation as theology through the centuries).

---

[54] A philosophical school that arose about 300 BC. Nietzsche seems to think that, like the Epicureans (see below, Notebook 19, footnote 58, p. 127), the Stoics betrayed their basic philosophical position which required them to embrace universal determinism in order to allow for the possibility of human freedom.

The great logical forces manifest themselves, e.g., in the organisation of the cultic spheres of the individual cities.[55]

19[112]

The gods of the Stoics are only interested in what is *great*, neglecting the small and the individual.

19[113]

Schopenhauer denies the effect of moral philosophy on moralities: just as the artist, he claims, does not create according to concepts. Strange! It is true that every man is already an intelligible being[56] (determined by innumerable generations?). But nevertheless the stronger stimulation of certain sensations by means of concepts *strengthens* these moral forces. Nothing new is formed, but the creative energy is concentrated towards one side. E.g. the categorical imperative[57] has greatly reinforced the disinterested sense of virtue.

Here too we see that the single outstanding moral man exercises a magic that causes others to imitate him. The philosopher must spread this magic. What is law for the highest specimens must gradually become the law as such: if only as a barrier for the others.

---

[55] The idea presumably is that various originally distinct local 'gods' or 'goddesses' gradually came to be identified with recognised Olympian gods or goddesses by virtue of some similarity in their attributes, myth, or cult, so a local female goddess who was associated with the hunt, and who might not even have any proper local name apart from 'The Goddess' or 'The Mistress', would come to be identified as Artemis; once this was done elements of the panhellenic worship of Artemis could be incorporated into the local cult (and, perhaps, vice versa). This process requires the deployment of certain logical capacities.

[56] Kant thought that in addition to having a certain 'empirical' character (i.e., certain empirical dispositions, preferences, passions) any human individual could also be viewed as an 'intelligible being' outside space and time. This 'intelligible being' had in some sense to 'choose' for itself an 'intelligible character', the choice taking place outside time. In the final analysis a human being was 'free' and also a potential subject of moral evaluation only as such an 'intelligible being'. This doctrine is found most explicitly in Kant's *Critique of Practical Reason* and in his *Religion within the bounds of reason alone*, and was taken over by Schopenhauer.

[57] Kant believed that reason alone could be the source of moral demands on us that bind us absolutely and unconditionally. These he called 'categorical imperatives'. See his *Groundwork of the Metaphysics of Morals*.

19[114]

The Stoics reinterpeted Heraclitus in a shallow fashion and misunderstood him. The Epicureans too inked weak elements into the strict principles of Democritus (possibilities).[58]

The supreme regularity of the world, but no optimism in Heraclitus.

19[115]

The case argued by all religion and philosophy and science in relation to the world: it begins with the crudest anthropomorphisms and *never ceases to refine itself.*

Individual man regards even the stellar system as serving him or in connection with him.

The Greeks in their mythology dissolved the whole of nature into Greeks. They saw nature, as it were, only as a masquerade and disguise of human gods. In that they were the opposite of all realists. The contrast of truth and appearance was deeply embedded in them. What is specific here are the metamorphoses.

That is what Thales expressed in his statement that everything is water.

19[116]

Does intuition refer to generic concepts or to the perfect *types?* But the generic concept always lags far behind a good specimen, and the type of perfection goes beyond reality.

Ethical anthropomorphisms: Anaximander: tribunal.[59]
Heraclitus: law.[60]
Empedocles: love and hate.[61]

---

[58] Epicurus, who in general followed Democritus' physics, seems to have thought that his specific form of atomism was too deterministic because for Democritus everything happened 'by necessity'. This, Epicurus believed, was a threat to human freedom. Unfortunately, Epicurus tried to deal with this difficulty by introducing into atomism the additional assumption that the atoms at some point 'swerve' from the paths they were following. This addition seems completely *ad hoc*, and also does not seem to solve the problem. Why should a blind (and 'causeless', as reported by Cicero, *De Fato* 21–5) 'swerve' by itself ensure the possibility of human freedom? See ancient texts collected by D. Sedley and A. Long in their *The Hellenistic Philosophers* (Cambridge University Press, 1987), vol. II, pp. 104–13. The relation between the philosophies of Democritus and of Epicurus was the topic of Karl Marx's doctoral dissertation (*Differenz der demokritischen und der epikureischen Naturphilosophie* (1841) in *Marx–Engels Werke* (Berlin: Dietz, 1968), vol. I, pp. 259–305.

[59] The idea of a 'tribunal' is implicit in the legal language used in Anaximander's physics. See above, Notebook 19, 19[18], p. 97 and Notebook 19, 19[89], p. 120.

[60] DK 94; KR 203.

[61] DK 17; KR pp. 324, 326–8.

Logical anthropomorphisms: Parmenides: only being.

Anaxagoras: νοῦς.[62]

Pythagoras: everything is number.

19[117]

World history is shortest if one measures it by the significant philosophical insights attained in any given period, leaving those periods hostile to them on one side. Among the *Greeks* we see a dynamism and creative force found nowhere else: the Greeks cover the longest period and they actually produced all the types.

They are the discoverers of *logic*.

Did not language already reveal man's ability to produce logic?

Certainly, in language we find the most admirable logical operations and distinctions. But this did not happen all of a sudden; rather, it is the *logical* outcome of infinitely long periods. Here we must think of the origin of the instincts: they grew quite gradually.

The intellectual activity of millennia is set down in language.

19[118]

Man discovers only quite slowly how infinitely complicated the world is. Initially he imagines it to be quite simple, i.e. as superficial as he is himself.

He starts with himself, the very latest product of nature, and he thinks of the forces, the primal forces, as if they resembled those things that reach his consciousness.

He accepts the *effects of the most complicated mechanisms*, of the brain, as if the effects had been identical from the very beginning. Because this complicated mechanism produces something sensible within a short period of time he takes the world to be very young: it cannot have cost the creator a great deal of time, he thinks.

Thus he believes that he has explained something by the word 'instinct' and he probably even transfers his own unconscious purposive actions to the primal origin of things.

[62] reason, mind.

Time, space and the sense of causality seem to have been given with the first *sensation*.

Man knows the world in the degree that he knows himself: i.e. its depth unveils itself to him in the same degree that he is astonished by himself and his own complexity.

19[119]

It must certainly be possible to show that at one time everything that is and exists *was not* and therefore one day *will not be*. Heraclitus' becoming.

19[120]

To posit the moral, artistic and religious needs of man as the foundation of the world is as rational as the mechanical: i.e. we know neither thrust nor gravity. (?)

19[121]

We do not know the true nature of *a single causality*.
Absolute scepticism: the necessity of art and illusion.

19[122]

Gravity may perhaps be explained by the moving ether, which rotates with the whole solar system round an enormous star.

19[123]

It is not possible to *prove* either the metaphysical or the ethical or the aesthetic significance of existence.

19[124]

Order in the world, the most laborious and slowest result of terrible evolutions, understood as the essence of the world – Heraclitus![63]

---

[63] DK 30, 94; KR 199, 203.

19[125]

It is to be *proved* that all constructions of the world are anthropomorphisms; indeed all sciences, if Kant is right.[64] But there is a vicious circle here – if the sciences are right, Kant's foundation is not ours; if Kant is right, the sciences are wrong.

We must then say against Kant that, even if we agree with all his propositions, it still remains perfectly *possible* that the world is as it appears to us. Incidentally, at a personal level this whole position is useless. Nobody can live with this kind of scepticism.

We must transcend this scepticism, we must *forget* it! How many things do we have to forget in this world! Art, the ideal form, temperature.

Our salvation lies not in *knowledge* but in *creation*. Our greatness lies in the supreme illusion, the most noble passion. If the cosmos is none of our business we want the right to despise it.

19[126]

The terrible loneliness of the last philosopher! Unyielding nature all round him, vultures hovering above him. And thus he calls out into nature: give me oblivion! Oblivion! – *No, he bears the suffering like a Titan – until he is offered reconciliation in the* highest tragic art.

19[127]

To regard – indeed deify – the 'spirit', the product of the brain, as supernatural: what madness!

19[128]

Among millions of perishing worlds for once a possible one! It too perishes! It was not the first!

---

[64] Kantians would, of course, deny that the 'transcendental conditions of the possibility of experience' are in any significant sense 'anthropological', and would thus reject the charge of anthropomorphism. Heidegger's presentation of a similar account of Kant (in *Kant und das Problem der Metaphysik*, 1929) is almost certainly completely independent of Nietzsche.

19[131]

Oedipus[65]
Conversations
of the last philosopher with himself.
A fragment
from the history of posterity.

I call myself the last philosopher because I am the last man. Nobody speaks to me but myself, and my voice comes to me like that of a dying man. Let me spend just one more hour with you, beloved voice, with you, the last faint memory of all human happiness. With you I deceive myself about my loneliness and lie myself into diversity and love. For my heart refuses to believe that love is dead; it cannot bear the horror of the loneliest loneliness, and forces me to speak as if I were two.

Do I still hear you, my voice? You whisper as you curse? And yet your curse should make the entrails of this world burst apart! But the world still lives and gazes at me even more brilliantly and coldly with its pitiless stars. It lives, as stupid and blind as ever, and only one thing dies – man. – And yet! I still hear you, beloved voice! Something else apart from me, the last man, is dying in this universe: the last sigh, *your* sigh, is dying with me, the long drawn-out Woe! Woe! sighed for me, the last of the men of woe, Oedipus.

19[132]

The terrible consistency of Darwinism, which, incidentally, I regard as true. All our admiration refers to qualities we take to be eternal: moral, artistic, religious etc.

---

[65] The city of Thebes was plagued by a sphinx (see above, Notebook 10, footnote 6, p.69) who posed a riddle ('What walks on four legs at morning, two legs at noon, and three legs at evening?'). It killed those unable to give the correct answer. No one gave the right answer ('Man': on four legs as an infant, upright at noon, and with a stick in old age) until Oedipus, who thereby – the exact mechanism is unclear – killed the sphinx, established himself as king in Thebes and married the former king's wife. Unfortunately, he turned out to be the former king's own son (who had been abandoned by his parents in infancy), to have murdered his (unknown) father in a fit of irritation about who had the right of way on a road, and to have married his own mother. His exploits and travails formed the subject matter of a large number of ancient tragedies of which only two treatments of different parts of the myth, written at different times by Sophocles (*Oedipus Rex* and *Oedipus at Colonus*), have survived.

With the instincts we do not advance one step in explaining purposiveness. For these instincts are the product of processes that have already lasted an infinitely long time.

The will does not objectivise itself *adequately*, as Schopenhauer says:[66] that is how it seems if one starts with the most perfect forms.

This will, further, is something final and highly complicated in nature. It requires *nerves*.

And even gravity is not a simple phenomenon but in turn the effect of a movement of the solar system, of the ether etc.

And the mechanical thrust is also something complicated.

The world ether as primal matter.

19[133]

All knowledge is a reflection in quite specific forms which do not exist from the outset. Nature knows no *form* or *size*: things appear so large and so small only to a being that knows. The *infinite* in nature: nature has no limits, anywhere. Only for us do finite things exist. Time is *infinitely* divisible.

19[134]

From Thales[67] to Socrates – nothing but transferences[68] from man to nature – immense shadow-plays of man on nature, as on mountain ranges!

Socrates and Plato. Knowledge and the good universal. The *beautiful* in the beginning. *Ideas* of the artist.

Pythagoreans	number.
Democritus	matter.
Pythagoras	man not a product of the past, but recurrence. The unity of all living things.
Empedocles	the world of animals and plants morally understood, the universal sexual drive and hatred. 'Will' universal.

---

[66] Schopenhauer believed that the things we experience were mere appearances of a more deep-seated reality which he called 'will'. This underlying 'will' was said to 'objectivise' or 'objectivate' itself when it produced the appearances that constitute our world, and it could do this more or less adequately. It is not completely clear, however, what 'adequate' could mean here. See WWR, Book II.

[67] See above, Notebook 19, 19[18], p. 97; 19 [89], p. 120; and 19[116], p. 127.

[68] *Übertragungen*, see Note on the translation.

Anaxagoras	Spirit as primal.
Eleatics	
Heraclitus	the creative force of the artist primal.
Anaximander	judgement and punishment universal.
Thales.	

Previously the gods and nature. The religions are only more open expressions. Astrology. Man as purpose. '*World* history'.

Kant's thing-in-itself as a category.

The philosopher is the continuation of the drive through which we continually interact with nature by means of anthropomorphic illusions. The eye. Time.

19[135]

The philosopher caught in the nets of *language.*

19[136]

I want to describe and empathise with the *tremendous development* of the one *philosopher* who wants knowledge, the philosopher of mankind.

Most men are guided by drives to such an extent that they do not notice what is happening. I want to tell and to show what is happening.

The *one* philosopher is here identical to all scientific striving. For all the sciences rest on nothing but the general foundation of the philosopher.

To demonstrate the tremendous *unity* of all drives for knowledge: the shattered scholar.

19[138]

The Apology of Art

Introduction.
White lie and Descartes's *véracité du dieu.*[69]
Plato *against* art.[70]

1. Language and concept.
2. Forms as surfaces.

---

[69] truthfulness of God. At a crucial point in his argument Descartes appeals to the claim that since God is truthful he would not allow us to be deceived about what we perceive clearly and distinctly. See *Meditationes de prima philosophia* I. 9 (although there Descartes actually speaks of the '*bonitas dei*', the 'goodness of God', as incompatible with certain systematic forms of error). On 'white lie' (*Nothlüge*), see Note on the translation.
[70] See Plato, *Republic* Books II, III and X.

3. The pathos of truth.

4. – – –

19[139]

Infinity is the primal fact: one would only need to explain where the finite comes from. But the point of view of the finite is purely sensual, i.e. a deception.

How can one dare to speak of a purpose of the earth!

In infinite time and infinite space there are no goals: *what exists exists for ever* in some form. What kind of metaphysical world there should be cannot be made out at all.

Mankind must be able to *stand* without any such support – the immense task of artists!

19[140]

Time-in-itself is nonsense: time exists only for a sentient being. Likewise space.

All *forms* belong to the subject. It is the grasping of *surfaces* through mirrors. We must subtract all qualities.

We cannot think things as they are, because we are not really allowed to think them at all.

Everything remains as it is: i.e. all qualities reveal an indefinable absolute facticity. – Roughly the same relationship as that between Chladni's sound patterns and vibrations.[71]

19[141]

All knowledge is produced by separation, delimitation, restriction; there is no absolute knowledge of a whole!

19[142]

Pleasure and displeasure as universal sensations? I think not.

---

[71] See above, Notebook 19, footnote 41, p. 118.

But where do the artistic forces appear? Certainly in the crystal. The production of *form*: but does this not presuppose a being that perceives?[72]

19[143]

Music as *supplement to language*: music reproduces many *stimuli*, and whole stimulatory conditions, that language cannot represent.[73]

19[144]

In nature there is no *form*, because there is no internal or external.
   All art is based on the *mirror* of the eye.

19[145]

Human *knowledge through the senses* certainly seeks *beauty*; it transfigures the world. Why do we grab for any other knowledge? Why do we try to transcend our senses? Restless knowledge leads to the bleak and ugly. –
To be contented with the world as seen through art!

19[146]

As soon as one wants to *know* the thing-in-itself *it is precisely this world –* knowledge is possible only as a reflection and a measuring of oneself by *one* gauge (sensation).
   We *know* what the world is: absolute and unconditional knowledge is wanting to know without knowing.

19[147]

The so-called *unconscious conclusions* must be traced back to the *all-preserving memory* that offers experiences of a parallel kind and thus already *knows* the consequences of an action. It is not an anticipation of the effect, but the feeling, produced by the memory image, that the same causes have the same effects.

[72] *ein anschauendes Wesen.*
[73] *darstellen.*

19[148]

We all too easily confuse *Kant's* thing-in-itself and the *Buddhists'* true essence of things: i.e. reality shows either a complete *illusion*[74] or an *appearance*[75] *that is quite adequate* to the *truth*.

Illusion as non-being is confused with the appearance of being.

The vacuum is filled by all possible kinds of superstitions.

19[149]

The course of philosophy: first, men are thought to be the originators of all things – gradually, things are explained by analogy to single human qualities – finally, one arrives at *sensation*. Great question: is sensation a primal fact of all matter?

Attraction and repulsion?

19[150]

The drive for historical knowledge – its goal is to understand man in the process of becoming, to eliminate the miracle here as elsewhere.

This drive deprives the cultural drive of most of its force: knowledge is pure luxuriance, it does not raise contemporary culture any higher.

19[151]

Philosophy must be considered in the same way as astrology: that is, combining the fate of the world with that of man: i.e. regarding the highest evolution of *man* as the highest evolution of the *world*. All the sciences receive their nourishment from this philosophical drive. Mankind destroys first the religions, then science.

19[152]

The sense of *beauty* is related to procreation.

---

[74] *Schein.*
[75] *Erscheinung.*

19[153]

Man has used even Kant's theory of knowledge for the glorification of man: the world has reality in man alone. It is thrown to and fro in his head like a ball. In truth this only means: imagine that a work of art exists and that there is a stupid man who contemplates it. Of course it exists for that stupid man as a cerebral phenomenon only to the extent that he is an artist and brings the forms with him. He could boldly claim: outside my brain it has no reality at all.

The *forms* of the intellect evolved from matter, very gradually. It is inherently probable that they are strictly adequate to the truth. Where should an apparatus that invents something new have come from?

The main faculty seems to me to be that of perceiving *form*, i.e. based on the mirror. Space and time are only things *measured*, measured by a rhythm.

19[154]

You must not flee into a metaphysic but actively sacrifice yourselves to the *evolving culture*! That is why I am strictly against the idealism of dreams.

19[155]

All knowledge is the process of measuring by a standard. Without a standard, i.e. without any limitation, there is no knowledge. Thus in the area of intellectual forms the situation is exactly as it is if I ask about the value of knowledge as such: I must take up some position that is *higher* or at least *firm*, in order to serve as a standard.

19[156]

If we trace the whole intellectual world back to *stimulus* and *sensation* this very feeble perception explains the least.

The proposition that there is no knowledge without something that knows, or no subject without an object and no object without a subject, is quite true, but trivial in the extreme.

We cannot predicate anything about the thing-in-itself because we have pulled the standpoint of the knower, i.e. the measurer, away from under our own feet. A quality exists *for us*, i.e. as measured against us. If we pull the measure away, what is left as quality?

But what things *are* can be proved only by placing a measuring subject next to them. Their qualities as such do not concern us, except in so far as they affect us.

Now it must be asked: how did such a measuring being come into existence?

The plant is also a *measuring being.*

19[157]

The formidable consensus of men about things proves the total uniformity of their perceptive apparatus.

19[158]

To the plant the world is such and such – to us such and such. If we compare the two forces of perception, we regard our conception of the world as more correct, i.e. as more corresponding to the truth. Man has evolved slowly and knowledge is still evolving: therefore our image of the world is becoming increasingly true and complete. Of course it is only a *reflection*, albeit a clearer and clearer one. But the mirror itself is not something completely alien and unrelated to the essence of things: it also evolved slowly as the essence of things. We see a striving to make the mirror more and more adequate: the natural process is continued by science. – Thus things are reflected more and more purely: a gradual emancipation from the all too anthropomorphic. *To the plant the whole world is plant,* to us man.

19[159]

The thrust, the impact of one atom on another, likewise presupposes *sensation*. Something in itself alien can have no effect on something else.

The difficult thing is not the awakening of sensation, but that of consciousness in the world. However, it is still explicable if everything has sensation.

If everything has sensation we have a medley of the smallest, larger, and largest centres of sensation. These complexes of sensation, larger or smaller, could be called 'will'.

We free ourselves of *qualities* with difficulty.

19[160]

I think it wrong to speak of an unconscious goal of mankind. Mankind is not a whole like an anthill. Perhaps one can speak of the unconscious goal of a town or of a people: but what does it mean if we speak of the unconscious goal of *all the anthills* on earth?

19[161]

Sensation, reflex movements, which occur very frequently and with the speed of lightning, once they have gradually become quite habitual, produce the concluding operation, i.e. the sense of causality. Space and time depend on the sensation of causality.

The memory preserves the reflex movements that have taken place.

Consciousness commences with the sensation of causality, i.e. memory is older than consciousness. E.g. in the mimosa we find memory, but no consciousness. Memory of course involves no *image* in the plant.

But *memory* must then belong to the nature of *sensation*, that is, it must be a primal quality of things. But then so must reflex movements.

The inviolability of natural laws means surely that sensation and memory belong to the essence of things. That one substance, touching another, makes precisely this decision is a matter of memory and sensation. At some time it *learnt* this, i.e. the activities of substances are *laws that have evolved*. But then the decision must be given through pleasure and displeasure.

But if pleasure, displeasure, sensation, memory and reflex movements belong to the essence of matter, then *man's knowledge reaches much more deeply into the essence of things.*

All *logic* in nature then dissolves into a *system of pleasure and displeasure*. Everything clutches at pleasure and flees displeasure: these are the eternal laws of nature.

19[162]

Memory has nothing to do with nerves or brain. It is a primal quality. For man carries the memory of all previous generations with him.

The memory *image* is something very artificial and *rare*.

19[163]

One can talk as little about an unerring memory as about an absolutely purposive action on the part of the natural laws.

19[164]

Is this an unconscious conclusion? Does matter *conclude?* It feels and fights for its individual being. The 'will' manifests itself first in *change*, i.e. there is a kind of *free will* that modifies the essence of a thing as a result of pleasure or flight from displeasure. – Matter has a number of *protean* qualities, which it emphasises, reinforces or deploys for the whole, depending on the attack.

Qualities seem to be only certain modified activities of *one* matter. They occur according to the proportions of measures and numbers.

19[165]

We know only *one* reality – that of *thoughts*. As if that were the essence of things!

If memory and sensation were the *material* of things!

19[166]

Thought gives us the conception of a whole new form of *reality*: it is composed of sensation and memory.

19[167]

Man in the world could really comprehend himself as somebody **out of one** *dream* who is being dreamt together with that dream.

19[168]

Among the Greeks the philosopher, in bright light and visible, continues the activity through which the Greeks acquired their culture.

19[170]

Philosophers are the most distinguished class of those who are spiritually great. They have no public, they need *fame*. In order to communicate their supreme joys, they need *proof*: this makes them unhappier than artists.

19[171]

We see in present-day Germany that it is possible for the sciences to flourish in a barbarised culture; likewise utility has nothing to do with the sciences (even though it seems so, given the preferential treatment of chemical and scientific institutions, and that pure chemists can even become famous 'experts').

The flourishing of sciences has a life ether of its own. A declining culture (such as the Alexandrian)[76] or a non-culture (such as ours) does not make it impossible.

Knowledge is perhaps even a substitute for culture.

19[172]

It is probably only because of the fragmentation of knowledge as a result of the separation of the sciences that knowledge and culture can remain strangers to each other. In the *philosopher* knowledge meets culture again.

The philosopher embraces knowledge and raises the question of the value of knowledge. This is a cultural problem: knowledge and life.

19[173]

Are dark periods, e.g. in the Middle Ages, really periods of health, perhaps times of sleep for the intellectual genius of men?

---

[76] The post-classical culture that flourished in the Greek–speaking city of Alexandria, Egypt from the third century BC.

Or are *dark periods* also the result of higher purposes? If books have their *fata*,[77] then the destruction of a book is probably also a *fatum* with some purpose.

The *purposes* make us *confused*.

19[174]

In the philosopher activities proceed through metaphors. The striving for *united* control. Every thing reaches for the immeasurable; individual character in nature is rarely solid, but stretches further and further. Whether *slowly* or *fast*, is an eminently human question. If one looks on the side of the infinitely small every development is always an *infinitely fast one*.

19[175]

What the truth means to men!

The highest and purest life is possible in the belief that one has the truth. The *belief in truth* is necessary for man.

Truth appears as a social need: through a metastasis it is then applied to everything that does not need it.

All virtues have their origin in needs. The need for truthfulness begins with society. Otherwise man lives in eternal obfuscations. The founding of states awakens truthfulness. –

The drive for knowledge has a *moral* source.

19[176]

How much the world is worth must also be revealed by its smallest fraction – if you look at man you will know what to think of the world.

19[177]

Necessity, in some cases, produces truthfulness as a society's means of existence.

---

[77] A Latin proverb: *habent sua fata libelli*, that is, books [too, i.e., not just people] have their own fates. One cannot, that is, always predict what effect a book will have, whether it will be taken up, how it will be understood, etc. What happens to them seems beyond our control.

Through frequent practice the drive becomes stronger and is, unjustifiably, transferred through metastasis. It becomes an inclination-in-itself. A practice for specific cases becomes a quality. – Now we have the drive for knowledge.

The generalisation occurs through the intervention of the *concept*. This quality begins with a *false* judgement – that to be true means to be *always* true. This results in the inclination not to live in a lie: the elimination of all illusions.

But man is chased from one net into another.

The good man now also wants to be true and believes in the truth of all things. Not only of society, but of the world. Therefore also in the possibility of understanding. Why should the world deceive him?

Thus he projects[78] his inclinations on to the world, believing that the world *must* also be true towards him.

19[178]

I am not asking about the purpose of knowledge: it came into being by chance, i.e. not with a rational intention and purpose. As an extension or a hardening and solidification of a way of thinking and acting which was necessary in certain cases.

By nature man does not exist in order to know.

Two qualities which were necessary for different purposes – *truthfulness* and *metaphor*[79] – produced the inclination to truth. Thus a moral phenomenon, aesthetically generalised, produces the intellectual drive.

Here instinct is the habit of often inferring in a certain way and out of this, $\kappa\alpha\tau\grave{\alpha}$ $\dot{\alpha}\nu\acute{\alpha}\lambda o\gamma o\nu$,[80] arises the duty of having always to infer in that way.

19[179]

Nature has wrapped man in nothing but illusions. – That is his proper element. He sees forms and feels stimuli instead of truths. He dreams, and imagines divine men as nature.

---

[78] *überträgt.*
[79] A 'metaphor' is a kind of 'transfer'. See Notebook 19, footnote 91, p. 157.
[80] by analogy.

Man has become a knowing being by accident, as a result of the unintentional coupling of two qualities. One day he will cease and nothing will have happened.

Men were not men for a long time and when they cease to exist nothing will have occurred. They have no further mission and no purpose.

Man is an extremely solemn animal and he takes all his qualities as seriously as if the hinges of the world revolved in them.

Like recalls like and compares itself with it: that is knowledge, the rapid subsumption of the similar. Only like perceives like: a physiological process. What is memory is also a perception of the new. Not idea upon idea – – –

19[180]

About the lie.

Heraclitus. Belief in the eternity of truth.

Destruction of his work – once destruction of all knowledge.

And what is truth about Heraclitus!

Description of his teaching as anthropomorphism.

Likewise Anaximander. Anaxagoras.

Heraclitus' relationship with the character of the Greek people. It is the Hellenic cosmos.

Origin of the pathos of truth. The accidental origin of knowledge.

The untruthfulness and illusion in which man lives.

The lie and telling the truth – myth, poetry.

The foundations of everything great and living rest on illusion. The pathos of truth leads to destruction. (There lies the 'great'.) Above all to the destruction of *culture*.

Empedocles and the sacrifices. Eleatics. Plato needs the lie for the state.[81]

Separation from culture through *sectarianism* among the Greeks.

We, on the other hand, return to culture in the fashion of *sects*; we try to roll back the immeasurable knowledge in the philosopher and to convince him again of the anthropomorphic nature of all knowledge.

[81] See Plato, *Republic* 414b–415d, 459c–d.

19[181]

The objective value of knowledge – it does not make *better*. It has no ultimate universal goals. Its origin is accidental. The value of truthfulness. – Yes, it does make better! Its goal is downfall. It sacrifices. Our *art* is the portrayal of desperate knowledge.

19[182]

In knowledge mankind has a beautiful means of downfall.

19[183]

That man has become as he is and no different is surely his own work: that he is so immersed in illusion (dream) and dependent on the surface (eye) is his *nature*. Is it a miracle if the drives for truth ultimately also lead back to his fundamental nature? –

19[184]

We feel that we are great when we hear about a man whose life hung by a lie and who still did not lie – even more when a statesman, out of truthfulness, destroys an empire.

19[185]

Our habits become virtues by being freely translated into the realm of duty, i.e. if we include steadfastness in the concept; i.e. our habits become virtues if we regard our own welfare as less important than their steadfastness – thus through the sacrifice of the individual or at least the *imagined possibility of such a sacrifice*. – The realm of the virtues and the arts – our metaphysical world – starts where the individual begins to set little store by himself. *Duty* would be particularly pure if in the nature of things there were *nothing that corresponded to the moral*.

19[186]

It is not the case that thought affects memory, but that thought undergoes countless subtle metamorphoses, i.e. there is a *thing-in-itself* which corresponds to *thought* and which now grasps the analogous thing-in-itself in memory.

19[187]

The individuals are the bridges on which becoming is based. All qualities are originally only *actions performed once*, which are then frequently repeated in similar cases, and finally become habits. The whole nature of the individual takes part in every action, and a specific transformation of the individual corresponds to a habit. In an individual everything, down to the smallest cell, is individual, i.e. it shares all the experiences and pasts concerned. Hence the possibility of *procreation*.

19[192]

The *political* meaning of the early Greek philosophers must be demonstrated as well as their power of *metaphor*.

19[193]

Just as our *theatrical* disposition now only proves itself in the lowest forms, so our sociability only proves itself on the ale bench.

19[194]

Mankind procreates through the impossible, those are its *virtues* – the categorical imperative, and the demand 'little children, love one another',[82] are such demands of the impossible.

Thus *pure logic* is the impossibility whereby science maintains itself.

19[195]

The philosopher is the rarest among the great things, because knowledge came to man only incidentally, not as an original talent. Therefore also the highest type of the great.

---

[82] I.e., the demands of Christianity.

19[196]

We must learn as the Greeks did from their pasts and their neighbours – for *life* and therefore with the greatest selectivity and immediately using everything they learnt as a support to raise themselves high – and higher than all their neighbours. That is, not in a scholarly fashion! What is not fit for life is no true history. Naturally, what matters is how high or how base you consider this *life* to be. Those who bring Roman history to life by repugnantly relating it to pathetic modern party politics and ephemeral *culture* commit an even greater sin against the past than the mere scholar who leaves everything dead and mummified. (As does a historian often cited in our age, Mommsen.[83])

19[197]

The *behaviour of Socrates* at the *trial of the generals*[84] is very remarkable because it shows his truthfulness in political matters.[85]

19[198]

Our natural science, with its goal of knowledge, drives towards *downfall*.

Our historical education drives towards the death of every culture. It fights the religions – and incidentally destroys the cultures.

It is an unnatural reaction against terrible religious pressure – now taking refuge in extremes. Without any moderation whatsoever.

---

[83] Theodor Mommsen (1817–1903) was a historian of ancient Rome.

[84] During the Peleponnesian war a group of Athenian generals was accused of failing in their duty to save the crews of some ships under their command who drowned during a storm. Feeling ran so high in the Assembly that it was proposed that they be tried *en masse* rather than as individuals. This was contrary to Athenian law which stated that every citizen was to be tried individually for any accusation made against him. As luck would have it, the philosopher Socrates was part of the group chosen by lot to initiate the trial, but he refused to vote in favour of beginning, citing the illegality of the proposed procedure, and incurring thereby a significant amount of opprobrium from the incensed citizens in the Assembly. Plato suggests (*Apology* 32) that on this occasion Socrates was close to being lynched. (He was in any case outvoted, and the generals were condemned and executed.) See Xenophon, *Hellenica* I.24–35.

[85] The German term *Wahrhaftigkeit* refers both to the specific property of telling the truth, and to the more general virtue of integrity. Socrates here exhibits the general virtue of integrity by refusing to depart from what he thinks is the right way to act despite attempted intimidation, but it is more difficult to see how this has anything to do with truth-telling in the narrower sense. Perhaps the point is the general connection often made between these two virtues in the philosophical and moral tradition.

19[204]

Abstractions are *metonymies*, i.e. inversions of cause and effect. But every concept is a metonymy and knowledge takes place in concepts. 'Truth' becomes a *power* once we have isolated it as an abstraction.

19[205]

A *negative* morality is most magnificent because wonderfully impossible. What does it mean if a man says 'No!' in full consciousness, while all his senses and nerves say 'Yes!' and every fibre, every cell takes the opposite side?

19[206]

If I speak of the terrible possibility of knowledge driving towards downfall, I by no means intend to pay a compliment to the present generation, which shows no sign of such tendencies. But if one sees the course of science since the 15th century such a power and possibility indeed manifest themselves.

19[207]

A man who does not believe in the truthfulness of nature, but who everywhere sees metamorphoses, disguises and masquerades, in bulls gods, in horses wise explorers of nature, in trees nymphs – now that he is setting up the law of truthfulness for himself, he also believes in the truthfulness of nature towards him.

19[209]

Man has learnt more and more to adapt things to himself and to know them. Through more perfect knowledge he has not moved further away from things; in this respect man is still closer to the truth than a plant.

A perceived stimulus and a glimpse of a movement, combined, result in causality, at first as an empirical statement: two things, i.e. a certain sensation and a certain visual image, always appear together: that one is the cause of the other is *a metaphor, borrowed from the will and the deed*: a conclusion by analogy.

The only causality of which we are conscious is that between willing and doing[86] – we transfer this to all things and we construe a relationship between two changes which are always found together. The intention or the volition results in nouns, the doing in verbs. The animal as something that wills – such is its nature.

From *quality and deed*: a *property* of ours seems to lead to acting. Actually it is the case that we infer properties from actions: we assume properties because we see actions of a certain kind.

Thus: the first thing is the *action*, which we link to a property.

First the word for the action comes into being, and from there the word for the property. This relationship, transferred to all things, is *causality*.

First 'seeing', then 'sight'. That which 'sees' is regarded as the cause of 'seeing'. Between the sense and its function we perceive a regular relationship: causality is the transference of this relationship (from the sense to the function of the sense) to all things.

A primal phenomenon is relating a stimulus perceived by the eye to the eye, i.e. relating an excitation of a sense to the sense itself. The only thing given as such is a stimulus: perceiving this as an action of the eye and calling it seeing is a causal inference. *Perceiving a stimulus as an activity*, actively perceiving something passive, is the first perception of causality, i.e. the first perception already produces this perception of causality. The internal connection between *stimulus* and *activity* is transferred to all things. A word such as 'to see' is a word for that fusion of stimulus and activity. *The eye acts in response to a stimulus*: i.e. it sees. We interpret the world for ourselves through the functions of our senses: i.e. we assume a causality everywhere because we ourselves *continually experience* such changes.

19[210]

Time, space and causality are only *metaphors* of knowledge by which we interpret things for ourselves. We do not know how a stimulus and an activity are connected. We do not understand a single causality, but we have an immediate experience of them. Every suffering provokes an action, every action a suffering – this most general feeling is already a

---

[86] See WWR I. §§ 18–23.

metaphor. The perceived diversity already presupposes time and space, succession and coexistence. Coexistence in time generates the sensation of space.

The perception of time is given together with the sense of cause and effect in reply to the question about the speed of different causalities.

Is the perception of space first derived by means of metaphors from the perception of time – or vice versa?

Two *causalities located next* to each other –

19[215]

The only way of defeating diversity is by establishing categories, e.g. by calling many different ways of acting 'bold'. We explain them to ourselves by subsuming them under the heading 'bold'. All explaining and knowing is really only categorising. – Now, with a bold sweep, the diversity of things is brought under one roof if we regard it, so to speak, as countless actions of *one* quality, e.g. as actions of *water*, as in Thales. Here we have a transference: an abstraction encompasses countless actions and is regarded as their cause. What is the abstraction (quality) that encompasses the diversity of all things? The quality 'watery', 'humid'. The whole world is humid, *therefore humidity is the whole world.* Metonymy! A false conclusion. One predicate is confused with a sum of predicates (definition).

Logical thinking, little practised among the Ionians, develops quite slowly. But we shall more correctly understand their false inferences as metonymies, i.e. rhetorically and poetically.

All *rhetorical figures* (i.e. the essence of language) are *logical fallacies.* That is where reason begins!

19[216]

We see how *philosophising* continues initially, in the same way as *language came into being*, i.e. illogically.

Now the pathos of *truth* and *truthfulness* is added. At first this has nothing to do with logic. It means only that *no conscious deception* is perpetrated. The deceptions in language and in philosophy are at first unconscious and it is very difficult to bring them to consciousness. But owing to the coexistence of different philosophies (or religious systems), established with the same pathos, a strange struggle developed. Each of the hostile religions existing side by side resorted to declaring the other untrue: likewise with the systems.

This instilled scepticism in some: the truth lies in the well! they sighed.

In Socrates truthfulness gains possession of logic: it notices the infinite difficulty of correct categorisation.

19[217]

Our sensory perceptions are based on tropes, not on unconscious conclusions. Identifying like with like – discovering some similarity in one thing and another – is the primal process. *Memory* lives by this activity and practises it continually. *Confusing things* is a primal phenomenon. – This presupposes *seeing forms*. The image in the eye is decisive for our knowledge, followed by the rhythm of our hearing. The eye would *never* lead us to the idea of time, the ear never to the idea of space. The perception of causality corresponds to the sense of touch.

From the beginning we see visual images only *in us*, we hear sounds only *in us* – from there to the assumption of an external world is a long step. A plant, e.g., perceives no external world. The sense of touch and at the same time the visual image provide two empirical perceptions side by side; these, because they always appear together, suggest the idea of a connection (by means of *metaphor* – for not all things that appear together are connected).

Abstraction is an extremely important product. It is a lasting impression, captured and solidified in the memory, which fits very many phenomena and which therefore is very rough and inadequate if applied to any individual case.

19[218]

The pathos of truth in a world of lies.
The world of lies again in the highest peaks of philosophy.
The purpose of these supreme lies is to restrain the unlimited drive for
 knowledge.
Origin of the drive for knowledge in morality.

19[219]

Where does the pathos of truth in the world of lies come from? From morality.

The pathos of truth and logic.

Culture and truth.

19[220]

Every little bit of knowledge carries a great satisfaction within it; albeit not as truth, but as the belief that one has discovered the truth. What kind of satisfaction is this?

19[221]

Culture is a unity. Only the philosopher seems to stand outside. He addresses the most distant posterity – fame.

It is remarkable that the Greeks philosophised. The beautiful lie.

But even more remarkable that *man* has arrived at the pathos of truth at all.

For the images in him are much more powerful than nature around him: as with the German painters of the 15th century, who, in spite of being surrounded by nature, created such spidery limbs – under the influence of the old pious tradition.

Plato wants a new state in which *dialectics* rule; he denies the *culture* of the beautiful lie.

19[222]

In Germany today there is no philosophy and therefore the question what the philosopher really is is unintelligible to Germans. Hence also their continuous surprise, finally turning into malice, that anybody, without caring for them and yet appealing to them, could have lived among them as a philosopher. The Germans today cannot bear to be challenged, any more than ghosts.

The desperate inconvenience of being born as a philosopher among the Germans!

19[223]

The instincts of morality: maternal love – becoming love in general. Likewise sexual love. Everywhere I recognise *transferences.*

19[224]

Many things in nature are humid: everything in nature is humid. Humidity is part of the essence of nature: humidity is the essence of nature. So says Thales.

19[225]

The untruthfulness of man towards himself and others: the prerequisite is ignorance – necessary in order to exist (oneself – and in society). The deception of representations steps into the vacuum. The dream. The traditional concepts (which dominate the old German painters despite nature) are different in all times. Metonymies. Stimuli, not complete knowledge. The eye gives shapes. We cling to the surface. The inclination to the beautiful. Lack of logic, but metaphors. Religions. Philosophies. *Imitation.*

19[226]

Imitation is the medium of all culture; it gradually produces instinct. *All comparison (primal thinking) is an imitation. Species* develop as a result of the first specimens' preference for imitating only similar specimens, i.e. copying the largest and strongest specimen. The instillation[87] of a *second nature* by way of imitation. In procreation the most remarkable thing is the unconscious imitation and at the same time the education of a second nature.

Our senses imitate nature by mimicking it more and more.

Imitation presupposes reception, followed by the continuous transference of the received image into a thousand metaphors, all active.

The analogous – – –

[87] *Anerziehung.*

19[227]

What is the power that enforces imitation? The appropriation of an alien impression through metaphors.

Stimulus – memory image

linked by metaphor (inference by analogy).

Result: similarities are discovered and given new life. In response to a memory image the *repeated* stimulus occurs once more.

Stimulus perceived – now *repeated*, in many metaphors, with related images, from different categories, flooding in. Every perception achieves a multiple imitation of the stimulus, but transferred[88] to different areas.

Stimulus perceived

transferred to related nerves

there, in transference, repeated etc.

A translation[89] of one sense perception into another takes place: some people see or taste something when they hear certain tones. This is quite a common phenomenon.

19[228]

Imitation is the opposite of *knowledge* in that knowledge does not want to accept any transference, but wants to grasp the impression without a metaphor and without any consequences. For that purpose the impression is petrified: it is caught and delimited by means of concepts, then killed, skinned and mummified, and preserved as a concept.

There are no 'literal' expressions and *no knowing the literal sense without metaphor*. But the deception about this exists, i.e. the *belief* in the *truth* of sensory impressions. The most common metaphors, the usual ones, are now regarded as truths and as the standard by which to measure the rarer ones. Actually what prevails here is only the difference between habituation and novelty, frequency and rarity.

Knowledge is merely working with the most popular metaphors, i.e. an imitation that is no longer perceived as imitation. Therefore it naturally cannot penetrate to the realm of truth.

[88] *Übertragung.*   [89] *Übersetzen.*

The pathos of the drive for truth presupposes the observation that the different worlds of metaphor are divided and fight each other, e.g. the dream, the lie etc. and the ordinary, usual view. The first of these are the rarer, the second the more frequent. Thus the usual fights against the exception, the regular against the unusual. Hence the higher esteem for the reality of the day than for the world of dreams.

But the rare and unusual is the *more attractive* – the lie is perceived as a stimulus. Poetry.

19[229]

In political society a firm agreement is necessary; it is based on the usual employment of metaphors. Any unusual employment upsets society, indeed destroys it. Thus employing every word as the mass does is a political convention and morality. Being *true* simply means not departing from the usual meaning of things. The true is that which *is*, in contrast to the non-real. The first convention concerns what is to be regarded as 'being'.

But the drive to be true, transferred to *nature*, generates the belief that nature must also be true towards us. The drive for knowledge is based on this transference.

What is first understood by 'true' is only what is usually the accustomed metaphor – that is, only an illusion which has become habitual through frequent use and is no longer perceived as illusion: a forgotten metaphor, i.e. a metaphor which is no longer remembered as a metaphor.

19[230]

The *drive for truth* begins with the strong observation of how hostile the real world and that of the lie are to each other, and how uncertain all human life is when the conventional truth is not absolutely valid: there is a moral conviction of the necessity of a firm convention if a human society is to exist. If the *state of war* is to cease anywhere it must begin with fixing the truth, i.e. with a valid and binding *designation* of things.

The liar uses words in order to make the unreal appear as real, i.e. he misuses the firm foundation.

On the other hand, there is the constant drive for new metaphors, which discharges itself in the poet, in the actor etc., and above all in religion.

The philosopher, aware of the eternal mythical game of lies, also seeks the 'real', the *enduring*, in the area in which the religions once ruled. He wants a truth that *endures*. Thus he extends the need for firm conventions concerning truth to new areas.

19[231]

The *oldest monotheism* means the *one* resplendent vault of heaven and calls it *dewas*.[90] Very limited and rigid. What progress the polytheistic religions represent.

19[234]

I would like to treat the question of the value of knowledge like a cold angel, who has seen through the whole dirty trick. Without being angry, but also without cosiness.

19[236]

Knowledge, quite strictly speaking, has merely the form of tautology and is *empty*. Any knowledge that advances us is an *identification of the non-identical*, the similar, i.e. it is essentially illogical.

We gain a concept in this way alone and then we pretend that the concept 'man' is something real, whereas it is only created by us through the abandonment of all individual features. We assume that nature proceeds in accordance with such a concept; but here both nature and concept are anthropomorphic. We obtain the concept by *ignoring* the individual characteristics, and it is with this that our knowledge begins: with *classifying*, with establishing *species*. But the nature of things does not correspond to this: it is a process of acquiring knowledge which does not match the nature of things. A thing is determined for us by many individual features, not by all: the equality of these features induces us to collect many things under a concept.

As *bearers of properties* we produce beings and abstractions as causes of these properties.

---

[90] Nietzsche probably takes this to be the origin of the Greek and Latin names of the sky-god: 'Zeus' ('Djeus') and 'Jupiter' (i.e., 'Djus+piter': 'sky-father').

That a unity, e.g. a tree, appears to us as a multiplicity of properties and relations is anthropomorphic in two ways: firstly this circumscribed unity 'tree' does not exist; it is arbitrary to isolate a thing in this way (according to the eye, according to the form); every relation, rather than being the true absolute relation, is tinted with anthropomorphism.

19[237]

The philosopher seeks not the truth but the metamorphosis of the world into man: he struggles for an understanding of the world with self-awareness. He struggles for an *assimilation*: he is satisfied when he has set out something in anthropomorphic fashion. Just as the astrologer sees the world in the service of single individuals, so the philosopher sees the world as man.

Man as the measure of things is also the idea of science. Ultimately, every natural law is a sum of anthropomorphic relations. In particular number: the dissolution of all laws into diversities, their expression in numerical formulae, is a $\mu\varepsilon\tau\alpha\varphi o\varrho\dot{\alpha}$,[91] as somebody who cannot hear judges music and tone by Chladni's sound patterns.[92]

19[238]

It is the sense of *certainty* that develops with the greatest difficulty. At first an *explanation* is sought; and if a hypothesis explains a *great deal* the conclusion is that it explains everything.

19[239]

Anaximander discovered the contradictory character of our world: it is destroyed by its properties.[93]

19[240]

The world is appearance – but *we* are not the only cause why it appears. It is also unreal from another side.

[91] metaphor, which is a linguistic formation parallel to 'trans+fer' or 'trans+late' (both meaning 'carry over [from one place to another]').
[92] See above, Notebook 19, footnote 41, p. 118.
[93] A highly speculative interpretation of Anaximander, DK 1.

19[241]

Our experiences determine our individuality, so that after every sense impression our individuality is determined down to the last cell.

19[242]

The nature of definition: the pencil is an elongated etc. body. A is B. Here that which is elongated is at the same time coloured. The properties contain only relations.

A certain body equals so and so many relations. Relations can never be the essence, but only consequences of the essence. Synthetic judgement[94] describes a thing by its consequences, i.e. *essence* and *consequences* are *identified*, i.e. a *metonymy*.

Thus in the essence of synthetic judgement lies a *metonymy*, i.e. it is a *false equation*.

I.e. synthetic inferences are illogical. In applying them we assume popular metaphysics, i.e. the one that regards effects as causes.

The concept 'pencil' is mistaken for the 'thing' pencil. The 'is' in the synthetic judgement is false: it contains a transference; two different spheres between which there can never be an equation are juxtaposed.

We live and think entirely under the effects of the *illogical*, in not-knowing and wrongly-knowing.

19[243]

The world of untruth:

The dream and waking.
Brief self-awareness.
Narrow memory.
Synthetic judgements.
Language.
Illusions and goals.

---

[94] Kant distinguished between 'analytic' judgements, that is, judgements in which the 'concept of the predicate was contained in the concept of the subject' (as in 'all bachelors are unmarried'), and 'synthetic judgements' in which the concept of the predicate was not contained within that of the subject (as in 'all bachelors have rabies'). See *Critique of Pure Reason* B10–12.

The untruthful[95] standpoint of society.
Time and space.

19[244]

Where on earth does the *pathos of truth* come from?
It does not want truth, but faith, confidence in something.

19[245]

Question about the *teleology of the philosopher* – who sees things not historically and not cosily.

For him the question expands into the question of the value of knowledge.

Description of the philosopher – he needs fame, he does not think of the *benefits* that derive from knowledge, but of the benefits that lie in knowledge itself.

If he were to find a word that, if uttered, would destroy the world, do you think he would not utter it?

What does it mean that he thinks mankind needs truth?

19[246]

What is really the value of knowledge?
The world of the lie – truth gradually comes into its own[96] – all virtues originate in vices.

19[248]

Main part: systems as anthropomorphisms.
Living in lie.
The pathos of truth, mediated through love and self-preservation.
Imitating and knowing.
Restraint of the unlimited drive for knowledge by means of deception.

---

[95] *verlogen.*   [96] *zum Rechte.*

Against iconic historiography.

The religions.

Art.

Impossibility and progress.

An evil demon's reflections about the value of knowledge, scorn. Astrology.

The tragic, indeed resigned, nature of knowledge after Kant.

Culture and science.

Science and philosophy.

The legislation of greatness.

Procreation in the beautiful.

The logician.

Result: came into being without purpose, accidentally, striving for the impossible, moral and historical, despising life. The phantom venerated as truth has the same effects, is also regarded as something metaphysical.

19[249]

Metaphor means treating as *equal* something that one has recognised to be *similar* in one point.

19[250]

Fame is deceived in this: nobody will ever again feel the sense of creation in the same way as the creator himself did. Therefore neither is complete appreciation ever possible.

19[251]

Confidence in a discovered *truth* manifests itself in that one wants to communicate it. It can be communicated in two ways: in its effects, so that it convinces the others of the value of its foundation in reverse; or by demonstrating the origin and logical interconnection of quite certain and already recognised truths. The interconnection consists in the correct subordination of special cases to general propositions – it is pure classification.

19[252]

The relation of art to nature resembles the relation of a mathematical circle to a natural circle.

19[253]

Why do we not want to be deceived?

– We do, in art. At least we desire ignorance about many things, i.e. deception.

As far as is necessary for *living*, man does not want to be deceived, i.e. he must be able to preserve himself; in this area of need he wants to be allowed to have confidence.

He despises only the hostile kind of deception, not the pleasant. He flees from *being cheated*, the bad deception. Thus basically not from the deception itself, but from the consequences of the deception, that is, the bad consequences. Thus he rejects deception where he can be deceived in his confidence with bad consequences. There he wants the truth, i.e. he again wants the pleasant consequences. Truth can be considered only as a remedy against hostile deceptions. The *demand for truth* means: do not do anything evil to men through deception. Man is *indifferent* to the *pure knowledge of truth without any consequences.*

Nor has nature equipped him for this. Belief in truth is a belief in certain happy effects. – Where does all the morality of the demand for truth come from? So far everything is selfish. Or: where does the demand for truth become heroic and pernicious for the individual?

19[254]

Does the philosopher seek the truth?

No, because then he would care more for certainty.

Truth is cold, the belief in truth is powerful.

19[256]

At the natural preliminary stage a people is a unity only to the extent that it has a common primitive art.

19[257]

As a result of isolation some sequences of concepts can become so vehement that they attract the force of other drives to themselves. Thus, e.g., the drive for knowledge.

A nature prepared in this way, determined right down to the cell, procreates and is inherited: intensifying until its absorption in this direction destroys its general strength.

19[258]

Truth does not matter to man: this is shown by tautology, the only accessible form of truth.

Then seeking the truth means correctly classifying, i.e. correctly subordinating the individual cases to an existing concept. But here the concept is our deed, as are also the times past. Subsuming the whole world under the right concepts means nothing other than grouping the individual things under the original human, most universal, forms of relation: that is, only *proving* the concepts, seeking what we have put into them again in them – that is, basically also a tautology.

19[310]

Culture – the rule of *art* over *life*. The degrees of the goodness of a culture depend firstly on the *degree of this rule* and secondly on the *value* of the *art* itself.

Notebook 23, winter 1872/1873

23[7]

What is the philosopher?

1. Beyond the sciences: dematerialise.
2. This side of the religions: undeify – disenchant
3. Types: the cult of the intellect.
4. Anthropomorphic transferences.

What is philosophy to do now?

1. The impossibility of metaphysics.
2. The possibility of the thing-in-itself. Beyond the sciences.
3. Science as rescue from miracle.
4. Philosophy against the dogmatism of the sciences.
5. But only in the service of a culture.
6. The simplification of Schopenhauer.
7. His popular and artistically possible metaphysics. The results to be expected from philosophy are the reverse.
8. Against general education.

23[8]

Philosophy has no commmon characteristics, it is now science, now art.[1]

---

[1] See above, Notebook 19, 19[18], p. 97; 19[89], p. 120; 19[116], p. 127; 19 [134], p. 132.

Empedocles and Anaxagoras: the former wants magic, the latter enlightenment, the former is against secularisation, the latter for.
The Pythagoreans and Democritus: strict natural science.
Socrates and the scepticism that is now necessary.
Heraclitus: Apollonian ideal, everything is illusion and play.
Parmenides: the road to dialectics and scientific organon.
The only one in repose is Heraclitus.
Thales wants to move towards science   Anaxim[ander] away from it.
   Likewise Anaxaroras, Democritus   Empedocles
   Parmenides organon[2]   Pythagoras.
   Socrates.

23[9]

1. The essential *imperfection* of things:
   of the consequences of a religion
      whether optimistic or pessimistic
   [of the] consequences of culture
   [of the consequences] of the sciences.
2. The existence of preservatives, which fight for a while.
   These include philosophy, which in itself does not exist at all.
   Coloured and filled in accordance with the time.
3. The early Greek philosophy against myth and for science, partly against secularisation.
   In the age of tragedy: in agreement Pythagoras, Empedocles, Anaximander,
      hostile in an Apollonian manner: Heraclitus
      dissolving of all art Parmenides.

23[10]

The pure truth unrecognisable: intuitions
                        concepts

---

[2] 'tool, instrument'; in a special philosophical usage: a set of methodological and logical principles or writings.

stimuli, divided according to pleasure
and displeasure, whether by numbers, or
whether purely intellectual phenomena?
stimulus, the prerequisite of all
intuitions.

The value of philosophy: purifying confused and superst[itious] ideas
against the dogmatism of the sciences
in so far as it is science, it is purifying and enlightening
in so far as it is anti-scientific: it is religious and obscurantist.
Elimination of the theory of soul and rational theology.
Proof of the absolutely anthropomorphic.
Against the rigid validity of ethical concepts.
Against the hatred of the body.

Damage done by philosophy: dissolution of the instincts
of cultures
of forms of ethical life.

Special operation of philosophy for now.
Lack of popular ethics.
Lack of a sense of the importance of knowledge and selectivity.
Superficial view of church and state and society.
Anger at history.
Talk about art and the lack of a culture.

23[11]

The concept comes into being through the equation of the non-identical:
i.e. through the illusion that there is something identical, through the
assumption of *identities*: therefore, through false intuitions.

One sees a man walking: and calls it 'walk'. Now a monkey or a dog:
and one also says 'walk'.

23[12]

Three things must not be confused with the ontology of Parm[enides]:

1) the question can we find any content in thinking that is in being?
2) the primary qualities, as opposed to the secondary ones

3) the constitution of matter. Schopenhauer.

4) no dream philosophy of the Buddha kind.

He seeks *certainty*. It is true that non-being cannot be thought.

If he declares the senses invalid he cannot prove being by the sensations of pleasure and displeasure: then these are also illusions.

Thinking and being must be the same: otherwise thinking would not come to know being.

In thinking, then, there is no movement: a rigid intuition of being. In so far as thinking moves and is filled with other things it is no longer being but illusion. –

But the dialectics of thinking – is it not movement?

23[13]

Concepts can arise only from intuition. 'Being' is the transference of breath and life to all things: addition of the human awareness of life.

The only question is whether the origin of all intuitions leads us to a being: no.

The form of thinking, as well as intuition, assumes that we believe in being: we believe in being because we believe in ourselves. If the latter is a category, the former is certain.

23[14]

Philosophy and the people. None of the great Greek philosophers carries the people with him: Empedocles (after Pythagoras) tries hardest, though not with pure philosophy, but with a mythical vehicle of it. Others reject the people from the outset (Heraclitus). Others have a very distinguished circle of educated individuals as their audience (Anaxagoras). Socrates has the most democratic and demagogic tendency: the outcome is the foundation of sects, that is, a counter-proof. Where such philosophers failed, how should lesser ones succeed? It is not possible to found a popular culture on philosophy. Therefore philosophy in relation to a culture can never have a fundamental significance but only a secondary one. What is this?

Restraint of the mythical. – Strengthening of the sense of truth as opposed to free poetic creation. *Vis veritatis*[3] or strengthening of pure knowledge (Thales, Democritus, Parmenides).

---

[3] the power of truth.

Restraint of the drive for knowledge – or strengthening of the mythical and mystical, the artistic (Heraclitus, Empedocles, Anaximander). Legislation of *greatness*.

Demolition of the rigidly dogmatic: a) in religion b) customary morality[4] c) science. *A sceptical streak.*

Every excessive force (religion, myth, drive for knowledge), as a rigid regime, has barbarising, immoral[5] and stultifying effects. (Socrates.)

Demolition of blind secularisation (substitute for religion). (Anaxagoras, Pericles.) A *mystical streak.*

Result: philosophy cannot create a culture
    but can prepare it
    or preserve it
    or moderate it.

For us: the philosopher therefore is the supreme tribunal of schools: preparation of the genius: for we have no culture. The following tasks for schools arise from the symptomatology of our age:

1) demolishing secularisation (lack of popular philosophy)
2) restraining the barbarising effects of the drive for knowledge (at the same time abstention from fanciful philosophy itself).
    Against 'iconic' history.
    against 'working' scholars.

Culture can issue only from the centralising significance of an art or a work of art. Philosophy will involuntarily prepare the world view of that work of art.

23[15]

The philosopher as the physician of culture.

23[42]

The artist does not see 'ideas', he feels pleasure in numerical relations. All pleasure derives from proportion, displeasure from disproportion.

---

[4] *Sitte.*
[5] *unsittliche.*

Concepts are built in accordance with numbers.
Those intuitions which represent good numbers are beautiful.
The man of science calculates the numbers of natural laws
the artist sees them: in the former case regularity,
in the latter case beauty.
What the artist sees is quite superficial, no 'idea'!
The lightest veil around beautiful numbers.

23[43]

Our intuition is already modified by concepts.
Concepts are relations, not abstractions.

23[44]

1. Metaphors refer to activities.
2. They form a system among themselves: A firm basic structure – they form *numbers*.
3. The core of things, the essential, is expressed in the language of number.
4. What is the arbitrary element in metaphors?

23[45]

Philosophy is *not for the people*
    therefore *not the foundation of a culture,*
    therefore only the *tool of a culture.*
    a) Against the dogmatism of the sciences
    b) against the confusion of images produced by mythical religions in nature
    c) against ethical confusion through religions.

In accordance with its purpose, the nature of philosophy
a) 1. is convinced of the anthropomorphic, is sceptical

2. has selectivity and greatness
3. flies beyond the representation of unity

b) is a healthy and simple exegesis of nature, is proof.
c) destroys the belief in the inviolability of such laws.

Its helplessness without culture, described with reference to the present.

Notebook 28, spring – autumn 1873

28[2]

I. *Introduction.* What can the philosopher achieve with regard to the culture of his people?
– He seems to be a) an indifferent hermit
                b) the teacher of the hundred most brilliant and most abstract minds
                c) or the hostile destroyer of popular culture.

– As far as b) is concerned, his effect is only indirect, but present, as with c).
– As far as a) is concerned, it can happen that he remains a hermit as a result of the lack of an effective teleological orientation[1] in nature. Nevertheless, his work remains for later ages. But the question is whether he was necessary for his own age.
– Does he have a *necessary* relationship with the people, and is there a teleology of the philosopher?
– In answering one must know what is called his 'age': it can be a small age or a very great one.
– Main proposition: he *cannot create a culture*

but he can prepare it, remove impediments,	always
or moderate and thereby preserve it,	exclusively
or destroy it.	by negation.

---

[1] *Unzweckmäßigkeit.*

A philosopher has *never* carried the people with him by means of his positive aspects. For he lives in the cult of the intellect.

In relation to every positive aspect of a culture or a religion he is *disruptive and destructive* (even when he tries to *lay foundations*). He is most useful when *there is a great deal to destroy*, at times of chaos or degeneration.

Every flourishing culture strives to make the philosopher *unnecessary* (or to isolate him completely). The isolation or atrophy can be explained in two ways:

by the lack of an effective teleological orientation in nature (when he is necessary), by the practical circumspection of nature (when he is unnecessary).

II. His destructive and curtailing effects – on what?

III. Now – since there is no culture, he has to prepare (destroy) – what?

IV. The attacks on philosophy.

V. The philosophers have atrophied.

Both are the consequence of the lack of an effective teleological orientation in nature, which ruins innumerable germs, but nevertheless achieves a few great men: Kant and Schopenhauer.

VI. Kant and Schopenhauer. The step to a freer culture from the first to the second.

Schopenhauer's teleology with regard to a future culture.

His double positive philosophy (the living central germ is missing) – a conflict only for those who no longer hope.

How the future culture will overcome this conflict. Olympians. Mysteries. Everyday festivals.

28[6]

On *Schopenhauer*. It is ridiculous to imagine him at a university today!

His eudemonological teaching,[2] like that of Horace,[3] is for experienced men; his other, pessimistic, teaching is nothing for the men of today: the latter will at most project their own dissatisfactions into it and, extracting them again, believe that they have refuted Schopenhauer. The whole 'culture' looks so unutterably childish, as does the jubilation after the

---

[2] The doctrine of how to attain happiness as the goal of life.

[3] This aspect of Horace (Roman poet, born 65 BC) is perhaps clearest in his *Sermones* (*Satires*) I.1, and in Odes such as I. 11, 18, 27, 31, etc.

war.[4] He is simple and honest: he seeks no catchphrases. Note the force of all his concepts: the will, negation, the portrayal of the genius of the race. In his portrayal there is no unrest, but the clear depth of a lake which is calm or ruffled by the slightest of waves. He is as coarse as Luther. He is the strictest ideal of a writer that the Germans have: no other writer has been so rigorous. How dignified he is can be seen in comparison with his imitator, Hartmann.[5] The infinite greatness of having once more fathomed existence, without donnish abstractions, without lingering in scholasticism. The study of others is interesting because they immediately arrive at the point where donnish knowledge is allowed, but nothing more. He shatters secularisation and likewise the barbarising force of the sciences. He awakens the most tremendous need: just as Socrates awakened a need. But Socrates summoned science, Schopenhauer religion and art. It had been forgotten what religion was, and the relation of art to life likewise. It took pessimism to make both understood again. But how profound the new religion must be is shown by 1) the fact that the element of immortality lapses with the fear of death, 2) the complete separation of soul and body, 3) the insight that the misery of existence cannot be overcome through corrections of a palliative kind: much more radical, 4) the relationship with a god is over, 5) compassion (not love of self but the unity of all living and suffering things). The counter-image of culture if religion should no longer be possible. Tragic resignation.

Schopenhauer contradicts everything that is now *considered* culture; Plato contradicts everything that *was* culture then. Schopenhauer forges ahead; we already have a premonition of his mission. He is the destroyer of forces hostile to culture; he reopens the depths of existence. Thanks to him the serenity of art becomes possible once more.

---

[4] The Franco-Prussian war.
[5] Eduard von Hartmann, German philosopher (1842–1906), wrote a highly influential *Philosophie des Unbewußten* (1869), which by his own admission was an eclectic combination of elements from various of the previous German Idealists.

Notebook 29, summer – autumn 1873

29[1]

To tell the truth without a eudemonological *purpose*; purely out of duty. Here the peculiar *pleasure* that comes with telling the t[ruth] is often forgotten. In the purest instance the truth brings a *much greater displeasure*, even destruction – and yet the truth is told. A statesman can decide the existence of a state by one word: he tells the truth and destroys the state. Kant's address to duty.[1] A great man is worth more than an empire because he is more beneficial to the whole of posterity. The purpose of a great deed – to produce great deeds.

29[2]

Analysis of the sense of truth common among scholars. Lying as self-defence, the self-protective lie,[2] contains a eudemonological character: it tries to save the individual.

29[3]

The concept of *impossibility* in all those *virtues* that make man great.

29[4]

1. Truth as duty – pernicious truth. Analysis of the drive for *truth – pathos*.
2. The impossible in the virtues.

[1] *Critique of Practical Reason* Ak. p. 154
[2] *Nothlüge.* See Note on the translation.

3. Man did not evolve from these highest drives; his entire nature shows a laxer morality; he leaps beyond his nature with the purest morality.
4. The lie in human nature – dream e.g. self-awareness (veiling of the truth).
5. Language, sensation, concepts.
6. Matter.
7. Art. Self-protective lie and gratuitous lie. But the latter, like the former, can be traced back to a necessity.

All lies are self-protective lies. The pleasure of lying is artistic. Otherwise only the truth holds pleasure in itself. The artistic pleasure is the greatest because it tells the general truth in the form of a lie.

The concept of personality, and indeed that of moral freedom, are necessary illusions, so that even our drives for the truth are founded on lies.

Truth in the system of *pessimism*. Thinking is something that would be better if it did not exist.

29[6]

Benjamin Constant: 'The moral principle that it is one's duty to speak the truth, if it were taken singly and unconditionally, would make all society impossible.'[3]

The Hungarian and the Hegelian professor in Berlin.[4]

Rameau's Nephew: 'One swallows the lie that flatters, but sips the bitter truth drop by drop.'[5]

---

[3] Benjamin Constant (1767–1830) was one of the most important early theoreticians of European liberalism. In 1797 he published a criticism of Kant's claim that we have an absolute duty to tell the truth even to a murderer in hot pursuit of an innocent victim. In reply Kant, who was an opponent both of democracy as a form of government and of liberalism as a political doctrine, wrote a short article entitled 'Über ein vermeintliches Recht aus Menschenliebe zu lügen' (also 1797), in which he reiterated his rigoristic claim. For the context see Stephen Holmes, *Benjamin Constant and the Making of Modern Liberalism* (New Haven: Yale University Press, 1984), pp. 106–9 and Biancamaria Fontana, *Benjamin Constant and the Post-revolutionary Mind* (New Haven: Yale University Press, 1991), pp. 98–117.

[4] It is unclear to what Nietzsche is referring here.

[5] Denis Diderot (1713–84) was a leading figure of the French Enlightenment. His short novel *Rameau's Nephew* gives a picture of the life of a highly gifted, but tormented and socially marginal, proto-intellectual in Paris during the last part of the *ancien régime*. The novel first appeared in print in 1805 in a translation into German which Goethe made from the unpublished manuscript, and was extremely influential in Germany in the nineteenth century.

29[7]

'Truth'

1. Truth as an absolute duty is hostile and destructive towards the world.
2. Analysis of the common sense of truth (inconsistency).
3. The pathos of truth.
4. The impossible as the corrective of man.
5. The foundation of man is a lie because it is optimistic.
6. The world of bodies.
7. Individuals.
8. Forms.
9. Art. Hostility towards it.
10. Without untruth there can be neither society nor culture. The tragic conflict. All good and beautiful things cling to deception: truth kills – in fact it kills itself (in so far as it discovers that it is founded on error).

29[8]

1. What corresponds to *asceticism* in relation to truth? – Truthfulness, as the foundation of all contracts and as the prerequisite of the survival of mankind, is a eudemonistic demand; it is opposed by the knowledge that the supreme welfare of human beings lies in *illusions* and that therefore, according to the eudemonistic principle, both truth *and lie* should be used – as is indeed the case. The concept of a *forbidden truth*, i.e. of a truth that actually *hides* and *masks* the eudemonistic principle. The opposite: the *forbidden lie*, which enters the territory of the permitted truth.

2. Symbol of the forbidden truth: *fiat veritas, pereat mundus.*[6]
   Symbol of the forbidden lie: *fiat mendacium! pereat mundus.*[7]
   The first thing to perish through the forbidden truths is the individual who utters them. The last thing to perish through the forbidden

---

[6] Let there be truth, and let the world perish. Truth, that is, must be told even if this brings about the destruction of the world.
[7] Let there be lying! Let the world perish.

lie is the individual. The former sacrifices himself together with the world, the latter sacrifices the world to himself and his existence.

Casuistry: is it permitted to sacrifice humanity to truth? – 1) It is not really possible! I wish to God humanity could die of truth. 2) If this were possible it would be a good death and a release from life. 3) Nobody can believe so firmly that he is in possession of the truth without some *delusion*: scepticism will not fail to appear. The question whether it is permitted to sacrifice humanity to a *delusion* would have to be answered in the negative. But in practice this happens because the belief in truth is a delusion.

3. Belief in truth – or delusion. Elimination of all *eudemonistic* components (1. as my own belief, 2. as found by me, 3. as the source of good opinions on the part of others, of fame, of being loved, 4. as an overbearing pleasure in resistance).

Once all these components are deducted, is it still possible to tell the truth purely as a *duty*? Analysis of the *belief in truth*: for all possession of the truth is basically only a belief that one possesses the truth. The pathos, the sense of duty, emanates from *this belief*, not from the alleged truth. Belief presupposes, in the individual, an *absolute ability to know* and the conviction that in this respect *no knowing being* will advance any further: that is, a binding force for all knowing beings. *Relation* suspends the pathos of belief, for example by restricting it to the human sphere, with the sceptical assumption that perhaps we are all mistaken.

But how is *scepticism* possible? It appears as the truly *ascetic* standpoint of the thinker. For it does not believe in belief and thus destroys all the beneficial effects of belief.

But even scepticism contains a belief: the belief in logic. Thus the extreme is the abandonment of logic, the *credo quia absurdum est*,[8] doubts about reason and the denial of reason. This is what asceticism brings in its wake. Nobody can *live* in such a denial, any more than in pure asceticism. Which proves that the belief in logic, and indeed

---

[8] 'I believe because it is absurd.' Proposition attributed to the Church Father Tertullian (born in Carthage in the middle of the second century AD), although it does not occur in this form in his work. What one does find is the explicit claim that the resurrection of Jesus from the dead is 'certain because impossible' (Tertullian, *De Carne Christi* 5). The idea is that it is precisely the absurdity of Christian beliefs (e.g., in resurrection from the dead) which shows that they are not of human, but divine origin: a human who wanted to deceive us would have come up with something marginally more plausible.

belief as such, is necessary for life, i.e. that the territory of thinking is eudemonistic. But then the demand for the lie arises: that is, when life and εὐδαιμονία⁹ are an issue. Scepticism turns against the forbidden truths. Then there is no foundation for pure truth-in-itself and the drive towards it is only a masked eudemonic drive.

4. Every natural process is basically inexplicable: in each case we can only establish the setting in which the true drama takes place. We then speak of causalities, while in fact we only see a succession of events. That this succession must always occur, given a particular setting, is a belief that is refuted infinitely often.

5. Logic is merely slavery in the bonds of language. But language contains an illogical element, such as metaphor etc. The initial force causes unequal things to be equated and is thus an effect of the imagination. This is the foundation of concepts, forms, etc.

6. Forms.

7. 'Natural laws'. Nothing but relations to one another and to man.

8. Man as the finished and solidified *measure of things*. As soon as we imagine him as fluid and volatile the rigour of the laws of nature ceases. The laws of sensation – as the core of the laws of nature. The mechanics of movement. The belief of natural science in the external world and the past.

9. The truest things in this world – love, religion and art. The former gazes through all pretences and masquerades at the core, the suffering individual, and shares the suffering; the latter, as practical love, comforts the individual in his suffering by telling him about another world order and teaching him to despise this one. These are the three illogical powers that confess themselves as such.

'in the parched stone desert of the crumbling globe'¹⁰

29[14]

There is no drive for knowledge and truth, but only a drive for the belief in truth. Pure knowledge has no drive.

---

⁹ happiness.
¹⁰ Source unidentified.

29[15]

Drives that are easily confused with a drive for truth:

1. *Curiosity*, in a more intensive form *an obsessive craving for the adventures* of knowledge. The new and rare, in contrast to the boring and old.
2. *The dialectical drive for pursuit* and play, the pleasure in crafty stratagems: what is sought is not the truth, but sly prowling, encircling etc.
3. *The drive for contradiction*, the personality wants to assert itself against another. Pugilism, the pleasure is the struggle, the aim is personal victory.
4. *The drive* to find *certain* 'truths', out of *subservience* to persons, religions, governments.
5. *The drive* to find a saving and comforting truth, out of *love*, pity etc. for a man, a class or humanity – the drive of the founders of religions.

29[16]

All drives are connected with pleasure and displeasure – there can be no drive for truth, i.e. for a pure truth entirely without any consequences or affects, because at that point pleasure and displeasure would cease, and there is no drive that has no premonition of pleasure in its own satisfaction. *The pleasure of thinking* does not indicate a desire for truth. The pleasure of all sensory perceptions derives from the fact that they are brought into being through *inferences*. To that extent man is always swimming in a sea of pleasure. But to what extent can *inference*, a *logical operation, give pleasure?*

29[17]

How is art possible only as a lie?
My eye, closed, sees innumerable changing images within itself – these are produced by the imagination and I know that they do not correspond to reality. Therefore I believe them only as images, not as realities.
Surfaces, forms.
Art contains the pleasure of awakening a belief through surfaces: but are we not deceived? Because then art would come to an end!
Art intends to deceive – but we are not deceived?

What makes us enjoy an attempted deception, an illusion that we always recognise as being an illusion?

Art treats *illusion as illusion*, that is, it does *not* try to deceive, it *is* true.

Pure contemplation without desire is possible only in relation to an illusion that is recognised as being an illusion, that does not try to seduce us into belief and to that extent does not stimulate our will at all.

Only those who could consider the whole world *as an illusion* would be able to look on it without any desire or drive – the artist and the philosopher. The drive ends here.

So long as one seeks truth in the world one is always subject to a drive: but the drive wants *pleasure* and not truth, it wants the belief in truth, that is, the pleasurable effects of that belief.

The world as illusion – saint, artist, philosopher.

29[18]

All eudemonistic drives awaken a belief in the truth of things, of the world – as does the whole of science – directed to becoming, not to being.

29[61]

If a Stoic and an Epicurean unite they conspire to murder Caesar.[11]

29[69]

Inwardness – dishonesty towards the outside. *Philosophy*.

29[87]

To enlighten somebody about the meaning of life on earth is one goal; to place somebody, and with him numerous future generations, firmly in life on earth (for which it is necessary to withhold the first reflection from him) is the other goal. The first seeks a sedative for the will, and so does

[11] Brutus and Cassius, two of the assassins of Julius Caesar, were traditionally considered to be respectively followers of the philosophical schools of Stoicism and Epicureanism, i.e., members of opposing schools of philosophy. See, however, D. Sedley, 'The Ethics of Brutus and Cassius', *Journal of Roman Studies* 87 (1997), 41–53.

the second; but the first finds it in the closest vicinity and is soon satisfied by existence, while the second is insatiable and roams as far afield as possible.

Where the second type prevails, the past should always be contemplated with nothing but pessimism – in order to find the present relatively bearable – but not with so much pessimism as to convey that first doctrine of complete worthlessness. It should be seen as worse than the present, so that those living in the present should not wish to change places with it, but still as containing a certain *progress* towards the present, in order to confirm the belief that happiness can be reached by advancing further. Therefore, the more an age recognises its own misery, the darker it will paint the past, and the smaller the recognition, the brighter the picture. The happy, i.e. the comfortable, will see everything past in a cheerful light, and the present in the most cheerful. In any case the drive to look back will be the stronger, the greater the need of the present becomes: cheerful and active ages have little need for history, which, for the placid, becomes even a luxury.

In our age the historical drive is exceptionally strong, as never before: but the conviction of the happiness of the present is just as strong. A contradiction! Here the natural relationship seems to be missing.

Think of the goal of Livy, of Tacitus, of Machiavelli[12] – escape from the present and comfort – often it is enough to think that once things were *different*, or that they were *just the same*, or that they were *better*.

In contrast, our own time has the whim of writing *objective* history, that is, history as a luxury; and thus it reveals the greatest contentment with itself.

Writing history has become a luxuriant *drive*: therefore it is necessary to become aware of needs and thereby produce a natural relationship between history and current need.

What has made the sense of need so *weak*? The *weak personality*.

---

[12] Livy (born *c.* 59 BC in Padua, died 17 AD) wrote a very extensive history of Rome, only parts of which are preserved. Because of the assumption that he would have had no access to any documents from the earliest period of Roman history, and also because of what seems to be a tendency to idealise the Roman past, the reliability of his history has been seriously questioned since the nineteenth century. Tacitus, born 55–6 AD, wrote histories of the early Imperial period which are shot through with a form of pessimistic moralising. Machiavelli (1469–1527) was a Florentine historian and political thinker; his most influential work, *The Prince* (1532), was the object of significant disapproval for its apparent advocacy of the claim that political success required indifference to the principles of Christian ethics.

But the luxuriant historical drive makes the weak personality still *weaker and weaker.*

29[192]

To take possession of oneself, to organise the chaos, to throw away all fear of 'education' and to be honest: an invitation to γνῶθι σαυτόν,[13] not in the sense of brooding, but in order really to know what our genuine needs are. From that point boldly to throw to one side what is alien, and to grow from within ourselves, rather than fitting into something outside us.

Art and religion are suited to organise the chaos: the latter supplies love of human beings, the former love of existence

at the same time contempt – – –

29[197]

The afflictions of philosophy

From outside: science, history (Example instinct. Has become concept). From within: the courage to live a philosophy has been broken.

The other sciences (natural, historical) can only explain, not command. And if they command they can only refer to *utility.* But somewhere every religion, every philosophy contains something sublimely *contrary to nature,* a conspicuous uselessness. Would this then be the end? – As with poetry, which is a kind of nonsense.

Man's happiness is based on the fact that somewhere there is an *indisputable* truth for him, a coarser truth (e.g. the welfare of his family as his highest motivation) and a more refined truth, such as the belief in the church etc. If anything is said against these, he does not even listen.

In the immense turbulence the philosopher should be a *brake shoe:* can he still be that?

The *distrust* of rigorous researchers against any *deductive* system, see Bagehot.[14]

---

[13] know yourself.
[14] Walter Bagehot (1826–77), best known now for his writings on the British constitution, also wrote a work of sociology entitled *Physics and Society.*

29[199]

To turn *philosophy* into pure science (as Trendelenburg[15] does) is to throw in the towel.

29[205]

The philosopher is a philosopher first for himself, then for others. It is not possible to be a philosopher for oneself alone. As a man the philosopher has a relationship with other men: and if he is a philosopher he must also be a philosopher in these relationships. I believe that even if he strictly isolates himself, as a hermit, he provides a lesson, an example, and is a philosopher for others. He may behave as he likes: being a philosopher, he has a side which is turned towards humanity.

The philosopher's product is his *life* (first of all, before his *works*). That is his work of art. Every work of art is turned first towards the artist, then towards other people. – What are the effects of the philosopher on non-philosophers and other philosophers?

The state, society, religion etc. may all ask: what has philosophy done for us? What can it do for us now? The same holds for culture.

The question about the cultural effects of philosophy in general.

Definition of culture – as a tuning and tempering of many originally hostile forces which now allow a melody to be played.

29[206]

The hostile forces in the Middle Ages were more or less held together by religion: when this bond broke one force rose against another. The Reformation declared many things to be ἀδιάφορα [16] – from this point the division spread more and more. Finally it was the coarsest forces alone that determined almost everything; first and foremost the military state. The attempt of the state to organise everything out of itself and to tie all the hostile forces together. The concepts of a state culture, as opposed to a culture of religion. Now power is evil and wants usefulness more than anything else.

---

[15] A Neo-Aristotelean German philosopher (1802–72).
[16] (morally) indifferent (esp. used as a technical term in Stoic ethics).

We find ourselves in the ice-covered river of the Middle Ages, which has thawed out and become a devastating flood.

29[211]

Every philosophy must be able to do what I demand, that is, to concentrate a man – but now none is able to do it.

29[221]

It must be seriously considered whether there are any foundations left for a developing culture. Can philosophy be used as such a foundation? – But it *never* was that.

My confidence in religion is infinitely small: the receding waters can be seen after an enormous flood.

29[223]

On the purpose of the philosopher

There is something impractical[17] that must be laid at the door of nature. It becomes evident when one asks: What is a work of art for? Who is it for? For the artist? For other people? But the artist has no need to make an image that he sees visible, and to show it to others. In any case the artist's happiness in his work, just as his understanding of it, is greater than the happiness and understanding of all the others. It is this disproportion that I find impractical. The cause should correspond to the effect. That is *never* the case with works of art. It is stupid to start a great avalanche in order to push away a little snow, or to slay a man in order to kill a fly on his nose. That is what nature does. The artist is a proof against teleology.

The philosopher even more. For whom does he philosophise? For himself? For others? But the former would be a senseless extravagance of nature and the latter, again, impractical. The usefulness of the philosopher affects only a few individuals and not the people in general; and it affects those few less strongly than the philosopher himself.

---

[17] *Unzweckmässiges.*

For whom does a master builder build? Should the manifold unequal reflex, the repercussion of his work in many souls, be the intention of nature? I believe he builds for the next great master builder. Every work of art tries to procreate and searches for receptive and procreative souls. So does the philosopher.

Nature proceeds unintelligibly and not skilfully. The artist, like the philosopher, discharges his arrow into the throng. It is bound to land somewhere. They do not bother to take aim. Nor does nature take aim and it misses countless times. Artists and philosophers perish if their arrows do not hit the target.

In the realm of culture nature proceeds just as wastefully as in that of planting and sowing. It fulfils its purposes in a clumsy and universal manner. It sacrifices far too much strength for disproportionate purposes. The artist and his connoisseurs and devotees relate to each other as a big gun does to a number of sparrows.

Nature is charitable but does not always use the best and most effective means. There is no doubt that it tried to help the others through the artist and the philosopher: but how disproportionately small and how accidental is the effect in comparison with the causes (the artist, the work of art)! The case of the philosopher is particularly baffling: the path leading from him to the object on which he is supposed to have an effect is quite accidental. The exercise fails innumerable times. Nature is wasteful, albeit not out of extravagance but out of inexperience: it is likely that if it were a human being it would never cease to be annoyed with itself.

29[224]

I hate the habit of skipping this world by condemning it wholesale: art and religion have their origin in this world. – O, I so understand this flight, out and across into the peace of the One!

O, this lack of love in these philosophers who only ever think of the chosen and who have so little faith alongside their wisdom. Wisdom must shine for everybody like the sun; and a pale ray must be able to plunge even into the lowest soul.

To promise men *one possession*! Philosophy and religion are a longing to *own* something.

29[230]

The philosopher

1st Chap. Medical morality.
2nd   Excessive thinking is ineffective. Kleist.[18]
3rd   The effect of philosophy, at other times and now.
4th   Popular philosophy (Plutarch, Montaigne).[19]
5th   Schopenhauer.
6th   The clerics' quarrel between optimism and pessimism.
7th   Primeval times.
8th   Christianity and morality. Why not the strength of the ancients?
9th   Young teachers and educators as philosophers.
10th   Veneration of ethical naturalism.
     Tremendous operations: but nothing comes of them.

---

[18] A German dramatist and author of a number of extremely finely chiselled and haunting short stories (1777–1811). In 1801 he suffered a crisis resulting from a reading of Kant's *Critique of Pure Reason* which had convinced him of the impossibility of attaining a morally relevant form of knowledge of the world.

[19] Plutarch (born AD 45) was an extremely prolific author of essays on a variety of topics, and, in particular, of a series of biographies of famous men, who was highly regarded by Nietzsche. Michel Eyquem de Montaigne (1533–92) was the first to use the title 'Essays' (*Essais*) for his reflections on human life.

Notebook 30, autumn 1873 – winter 1873/1874

30[5]

What is wisdom? As opposed to science. |Preface.
Is there a striving for wisdom today? No. |Main part.
Is a striving for wisdom necessary, a need? – No. But perhaps it will soon
be a need.
When? Description. |Afterword.

30[8]

The happiness of the individual in the state is subordinated to the common
good: what does that mean? Not that the minorities are used for the good
of the majorities. Rather that the individuals are subordinated to the
good of the *supreme individuals*, the good of the supreme specimens. The
supreme individuals are the creative men, be they the best in a moral sense
or the best and most useful in some other important sense, that is, the
purest types and improvers of mankind. The goal of the polity is not the
existence of a state at all costs, but the possibility for the supreme specimens to live and work in it. This is also the foundation on which states
come into being, although people have often had a wrong idea of who the
supreme specimens were: often conquerors, etc., dynasts. If it is no longer
possible to maintain the existence of a state in which the great individuals
can live and work, a terrible state based on necessity and robbery comes
into being: a state in which the *strongest* individuals take the place of the
best. The task of the state is not to enable as many people as possible to
lead good and moral lives in it. Numbers do not matter: what matters is

that a good and beautiful life as such should be possible in a state; that the state should provide the foundation of a *culture*. In short: the goal of the state is a nobler humanity. The state's goal is beyond the state: the state is a *means* to an end.

Today the element that binds all the partial forces together is missing: and so we see that everything is hostile to everything else and all the noble forces are engaged in a mutually devastating war of annihilation. I will demonstrate this by means of philosophy, which *destroys* because it is bound by nothing. The philosopher has become a *public menace*. He annihilates happiness, virtue, culture, and finally himself. – To avoid this, philosophy must *be an ally* of the binding *force, a physician of culture.*

30[15]

The Affliction of Philosophy

A. The need of the time, the demands on the philosopher.
  1. Haste.
  2. No building for eternity (the new houses).
  3. Religion worn out.
  4. Medical morality. Naturalism.
  5. Logic weakened (by history, science).
  6. Lack of educators.
  7. Useless and dangerous *complexity* of needs and duties.
  8. Volcanic soil.

B. Attacks on philosophy.
  1. Distrust of more rigorous methods.
  2. History deprives the systems of validity.
  3. The church has seized all popular influence.
  4. The state demands living in the moment.

C. Image of the philosopher.
  1. Worn out – excessive thinking ineffective (Kleist).[1]
  2. They find the point where erudition begins.
  3. Clerics' quarrel.

---

[1] See above, Notebook 29, footnote 18, p. 185.

4. Primeval times.
5. Lack of great moral models.
6. Conflict between life and thought tolerated everywhere.
7. Defective logic.
8. The nonsensical education of university students.
9. The life of philosophers and their genesis.

D. Philosophy – can it be the foundation of a culture? Yes – but now no longer: it is too refined and over-subtle; one can no longer be guided by it. In fact philosophy has allowed itself to be drawn into the current of today's education, rather than dominating it. At best it has become science (Trendelenburg).[2]

Image of Schopenhauer. The contrast between his eudemonological practice (the worldliness of over-ripe ages such as that of the Spaniards) and his solely intuitive deeper philosophy. He condemns the present from two sides. For the time being I see no other possibility than Schopenhauer's worldliness for practical living and his wisdom for deeper needs.

Those who do not want to live with this contradiction must fight for an *improved physis* (culture).

---

[2] See above, Notebook 29, footnote 15, p. 182.

Notebook 31, autumn 1873 – winter 1873/1874

31[4]

Those who know ancient morality are surprised to see how many things were then regarded in a moral light that are today treated by medical means; how many disorders of the soul, of the head, that were then referred to the philosopher are now handed over to be cured by the physician, and how the nerves in particular are now calmed by alkalis or narcotics. The ancients were much more moderate, and deliberately so, in their everyday lives: they knew how to abstain and how to exercise self-denial, so as not to lose self-control. Their statements about morality always derived from the living example of those who lived in accordance with the wording of these statements. I do not know what remote and rare things modern ethicists talk about: they take man for a strangely spiritualistic being, and they seem to believe it indecent to treat man in such a nakedly ancient way and to talk about his many essential, albeit low, needs. This modesty goes so far that one would think that modern man has only an apparent body. I think that the vegetarians, with their rule of eating less and simpler food, have done more good than all the new moral systems put together: a little exaggeration does not matter. There is no doubt that future educators will once more prescribe a stricter diet to men. Modern men are supposed to be made healthy by fresh air, sunshine, shelter, travel etc., including medicinal stimuli and poisons. But all those things that men find difficult are no longer prescribed: to be healthy and ill in a pleasant and comfortable manner seems to be the maxim. And yet it is precisely the continuous failure to be moderate in *small* matters, i.e. the lack of self-discipline, that ultimately reveals itself as universal haste and *impotentia*.[1]

31[7]

If philosophers today were to dream up a polis it would certainly not be a Platonopolis, but an Apragopolis (a town of idlers).

[1] powerlessness, inability; lack of self-control, lack of moderation.

Notebook 32, beginning of 1874 – spring 1874

32[44]

Wagner's art is excessive and transcendental: what can our poor German baseness do with it? It has something like an escape from this world, it negates and does not transfigure this world. That is why it has neither a direct moral nor an indirect quietistic effect. We see Wagner busy and active only in order to prepare a place for his art in this world: but what business of ours is a Tannhäuser, a Lohengrin, a Tristan, a Siegfried?[1] Yet, in a present such as ours, the destiny of art seems to be to assume part of the power of a dying religion. Hence the alliance between Wagner and Schopenhauer. This alliance reveals that perhaps soon culture will exist only in the form of sects living in monastic seclusion and rejecting the world around them. It is here that Schopenhauer's 'will to life' obtains its artistic expression: this dreary bustle without a purpose, this ecstasy, this despair, this tone of suffering and desire, this accent of love and ardour. Rarely a serene sunbeam, but a great deal of magical lighting.

Both the strength and the weakness of art lie in this position: it is so hard to return from there to the simple life. The goal is no longer to improve the real but to destroy or hide it. The strength lies in the sectarian character; it is extreme and demands from man an absolute decision. – Can a man be improved by this art and by Schopenhauer's philosophy? Certainly, with regard to truthfulness. If only, in an age in which lies and conventions

[1] Heroes respectively of Wagner's operas: *Tannhäuser*, *Lohengrin*, *Tristan und Isolde*, and *Siegfried*, and *Götterdämmerung*. Although they might originally have been historical personages it was an integral part of Wagner's aesthetics that his music dramas were based on *myth*, not history. Only an appropriately 'mythic' work. he thought, could hope to be of universal significance, and he defined 'myth' in opposition to 'history'.

are so boring and uninteresting, truthfulness were not so interesting! So entertaining! Aesthetically attractive!

32[45]

The artistic force ennobles the unbridled drive, restricting and concentrating it (into the desire to make this work as perfect as possible). It ennobles Wagner's entire nature. It constantly reaches for higher and higher goals, as high as he can see: these goals become better and better and finally also more and more definite and as a result closer and closer. Thus today's Wagner no longer seems to correspond to the Wagner of *Opera and Drama*, the socialist:[2] his earlier goal seems higher, but is only more distant and indefinite. His current idea of life, of Germany, etc. is more profound, although it is much more conservative.

32[52]

According to Wagner the error in the genre of opera is that a *means of expression*, the music, is turned into the purpose, and the purpose of the expression into the means.[3]

So he regards music as a means of expression – very typical of the actor. Faced with a symphony, one must ask: if the music here is a *means of expression* what is the purpose? The purpose cannot be the music, because that which by its nature is a means of expression must have something to express: Wagner has the drama in mind. Without the drama he regards the music on its own as an absurdity: it raises the question 'what is all the racket for?'. That is why he regarded the 9th Symphony as Beethoven's real feat, because by adding the words he had given the music its purpose, to be the means of the expression.[4]

The means and the purpose – music and drama – old doctrine.
The *universal* and the *example* – music and drama – new doctrine.[5]

---

[2] Wagner was theoretically committed to socialism and took an extremely active part in the (failed) revolution of 1848/9. After the failure of the revolution a warrant was issued for his arrest and he had to flee to Switzerland, one step ahead of the police. The relation of these beliefs to his actual cultivation of European royalty, e.g., King Ludwig of Bavaria, later in life is unclear.

[3] GSD 3.231.

[4] See passages from Wagner cited in Notebook 12, footnote 10, p. 89.

[5] This refers to an apparent change in Wagner's aesthetics between the early period (up to and including *Oper und Drama* 1852) and later works such as *Beethoven* (1870) and *Über die Bestimmung der Oper* (1871).

If the latter is true the universal must in no way depend on the example, i.e. absolute music is in the right, and the music of a drama must also be absolute music.

However, this is still rather a parable and image – it is not entirely true that the drama is only an example of the universality of the music: genus and species, but in what sense? As a movement of sounds in contrast to the movement of characters (to speak only of mimic drama at this point).

But the movements of a character can also be the more universal element: for they express internal states which are much richer and more nuanced than a man's external movements resulting from them: which is why we so often misunderstand a gesture. Moreover, all gestures carry an infinity of conventions – an entirely free man is a phantasm. But if we abandon the movements of the characters, and instead speak of the movement of emotions, the music should be the more universal element, and the movements of this or that character's emotions the specific. But music is precisely the movement of the musician's emotions, expressed in tones, that is, the emotions of an individual. And that is how it has always been (if one disregards the purely formalistic theory of tonal arabesques). Here we have the entire contradiction: a quite specific, quite definite, expression of emotions as music – and next to it the drama, the assembled expressions of the quite definite emotions of the dramatic characters through words and movements. How could these ever coincide? The musician may be able to empathise with the process of the drama and render it as pure music (*Coriolan Overture*).[6] But then this image amounts to a generalisation of the drama; all the political motives and reasons are omitted and only the stupid will speaks. In any other sense dramatic music is bad music.

Now for the demand for *simultaneity* and the most accurate parallelism of the entire process, in the musician and in the drama. There the music gets in the way of the dramatist, because it needs time to express something, often a whole *symphony* for a single emotion of the drama. Meanwhile what does the drama do? For that purpose Wagner uses the dialogue, or *language* as such.

Now a new power and difficulty is added: language. Language speaks in concepts. These too have their own *temporal* laws: briefly

---

[6] Overture by Beethoven, Opus 62 in C minor.

the mime alone expresses the underlying feeling	each at a different
the world of concepts	speed.
music	

Verbal drama is ruled by that power which needs the most time, the concept. That is why the action is often in repose, sculptural, groups. Particularly in antiquity: sculpture in repose expresses a condition. Therefore the mime is to a large extent determined by the verbal drama.

The musician needs quite different times and, strictly, cannot be prescribed any laws: an emotion once triggered may be long in one musician, short in another. What a demand then that the language of concepts and the language of notes should go side by side!

But language itself contains an element of music. A strongly felt sentence has a melody which is at the same time an image of the most universal movement of the will. The artist can use and interpret this melody into infinity.

It seems impossible to unite all these factors: one musician will render single moods aroused by the drama and be completely baffled by most of the drama: hence probably the recitative and the rhetoric. The writer will not be able to help the musician and thus himself: he wants to write only as much as can be sung. But of that he has only a theoretical awareness, not an internal one. The actor, above all as a singer, must do many things that are not dramatic, open his mouth wide etc.; he needs conventional manners. Everything would change if the actor for once became both musician and writer at the same time.

He uses gesture, language, melody of language and in addition the *recognised symbols* of musical expression. He assumes a very richly developed music, which has already gained a firm, recognisable and recurrent expression for a multitude of emotions. By means of these musical quotations he reminds the listener of a certain mood in which the actor wants to be imagined. Now the music has really become a 'means of expression': it is therefore on a lower artistic level because it is no longer organic within itself. At this point the musical master will still be able to interweave the symbols in the most skilful manner; but because the true context and design of his work is located beyond and outside the music, the music cannot be organic. However, it would be unfair to blame the dramatist for this. He has the right to use the music as a means for the benefit of the drama, just as he uses painting as a means. Such music, pure in itself, is comparable to allegorical painting: the true meaning does not consist in the picture and can therefore be very beautiful.

32[67]

On time.

Nature is not good – counter-dogma against false, feeble opinions and secularisation.

The meaning of life is not found in the preservation of institutions or in their progress, but in individuals. These are to be broken.

If a man takes on the task of justice life will teach him its meaning.

Life must not be organised as comfortably and as tolerably as possible, but strictly. In every way one must hold on to the metaphysical meaning.

The great instability of things makes teaching easier. Nothing must be *spared*, the truth must be told, for better or worse.

Our task is to find our way out of all obfuscations and half-measures and not to deceive ourselves about life. For the whole of mankind now has *succumbed to trivialisation* (naturally including the religious parties. Even the Ultramontanes,[7] who are dishonestly defending a mythical expression as if it were true *sensu proprio*,[8] in order to maintain their external power).

Goethe's Hellenism is firstly historically wrong and secondly too soft and unmanly.

There is no danger of slackening: justice is one of the hardest obligations and pity a great stimulator.

If it were our task to skim over life as much as possible, there are recipes, particularly Goethe's.

It is pleasant to *contemplate* things, but terrible to *be* them.

The voluntary suffering of truthfulness, to *accept* personal injuries.

Suffering is the meaning of life.

---

[7] A party within French and German Catholicism, which presented itself as 'traditionalist' and was characterised by its advocacy of extreme subordination to the Pope (i.e., a prelate who lived literally 'beyond the mountains', in Rome).

[8] in the proper sense.

The many whims we are wrapped in, and to that extent our ignorance about our own nature, also deceive us about the meaning of life: *the same courage that it takes to know oneself also teaches us to look at life without whims*: and vice versa.

32[72]

Time

– Destruction of enlightenment.
– Recovery of the metaphysical meaning of existence.
– Hostility to Christianity because it ignores existence.
– Against the ideas of the revolution.
– Not aiming at *happiness*: the 'truth', not in comfortable repose but heroic and hard.
– Against the overestimation of the state, the national element. J[acob] B[urckhardt].[9]
– Schopenhauer *misunderstood.*
– Loveless or only briefly loving.

32[73]

The education of the philosopher.

To be desensitised to nationalism through early travels.
To know men, to read little.
No culture of sitting at home.
To take the state and duties lightly. Or to emigrate.
Not donnish. No universities.
Nor history of philosophy; he should seek the truth for himself, not in order to write books.

---

[9] Jacob Burckhardt (1818–97), a cultural historian who was Nietzsche's colleague and friend in Basel and who influenced him deeply.

Notebook 34, spring – summer 1874

34[34]

What could we admire about ourselves, what could stand firm for us? Everything is small. The utmost that we can achieve is truth towards ourselves: for most people cheat themselves. A hearty self-contempt raises us to our highest level: we see how despicable the objects and products of such people are and we no longer allow masses to deceive us.

Pessimism. – The depth of self-contempt: Christianity is too narrow.

Why should destruction be a negative business? We clear away our apprehensions and seductions.

34[36]

Chapter 3/4. Schopenhauer is the *genius of heroic truthfulness.* The chapter about the dangers demonstrates how he educated himself. But *by what means* did he achieve this?

By striving to be *true.*

It is a *corrosive,* destructive striving; but it makes the individual *great* and *free.* He may perish externally in the process, but not internally.

Chapter 4. Schopenhauer as a *liberating destroyer* in his time. Nothing deserves to be spared any longer. Everything is lacking and rotten.

Chapter 5. He has the same stance towards *German culture.* The liberating destroyer.

Chapter 6. The continuation of his work. This requires the education of a generation of philalethes.[1] How will they be educated?

---

[1] lovers of truth.

34[39]

This activity of the philosopher does not stand on its own, but is part of a cycle.
Culture. Chief character.
Pseudo-culture.
   Taken into service
      by commerce
      by the state.
   Beautiful form, deception.
The prevailing mood from which true culture evolves.

34[40]

This is an ideal that makes the individual feel ashamed. How does he achieve a natural *active* relationship with it? How can the road to education be found?

   This mood of the individual is *used* by secularised culture, whose aims are closer at hand and do not place such a burden on the individual.

   The metaphysical meaning of true culture must be *established*. The first proposition of education.

   The education of the genius is the *practical* task.

34[41]

   An ideal.
Objection: it forces one to live a double life, no connecting activity is found.
   Those who are more consistent retreat to a lower goal.
   However: it is part of a circle of ideas, culture.
That lower goal is not a step along the road but a different, hostile point of view.
Given the magnitude of the picture, there are two kinds of danger:
1) the great goal is abandoned (culture straying from its path)
2) the goal is retained but no activity connecting us with it is found. The weaker natures are defeated: that is why Schopenhauer is only for the most active.

The meaning of the culture that has strayed from its path.

The attempt to derive *duties* from the full concept of that culture.

At some moments we stand within it.

It is necessary to find that lower level on which we are really able to stand, where we do not stumble.

34[43]

Beginning.

It is precisely this problem that needs considering in more detail: how could Schopenhauer bear living in his age without making any attempt to be its reformer?

And did not the weakness of the modern age weaken his image of life?

Against 1) He is the liberating destroyer. The free spirit.

Against 2) He engages himself as a genius against the weakness of his age and thus knows nature in its entire strength.

34[44]

Last chapter.

How do we educate the philosopher?

Him who makes justice his banner!

34[45]

Odysseus made sacrifices in order to - - - the shadows.[2]

Let us make a similar sacrifice to the spirit of Schopenhauer by saying: *Philosophia academica delenda est.*[3]

[2] See above, Notebook 19, footnote 1, p. 93.

[3] Cato the Elder was a Roman politican known for his inflexibility and old-fashioned 'virtue', who was also an implacable enemy of Carthage. It is reported (e.g., in Cicero's *De Senectute* 6.18) that he would always end his speeches in the Senate, regardless of the ostensible topic of debate, with the phrase: *Ceterum censeo Carthaginem esse delendam*: 'And in addition it is also my opinion that Carthage must be destroyed.' Nietzsche transforms this well-known expression into: 'Academic philosophy must be destroyed.'

Notebook 37, end of 1874

37[6]

All interaction between human beings is based on the ability of one man to read the soul of another; and a common language is the audible expression of a common soul. The more intimate and delicate that interaction becomes, the richer the language, which grows – or atrophies – together with the universal soul. Essentially, when I speak I am asking my fellow-man if he has the same soul as I; the oldest sentences seem to me to be interrogatives, and I suspect that the accent is the reverberation of those oldest questions addressed by the soul to itself, albeit in a different shell. Do you recognise yourself? – this feeling accompanies every sentence of the speaker, who is attempting a monologue and dialogue with himself. The less he recognises himself the more silent he becomes, and in the enforced silence his soul becomes poorer and smaller. If one could force men henceforth to be silent one could reduce them to horses and seals and cows; for these creatures show what being unable to speak means: namely the same as having a dull soul.

Indeed many people, and sometimes the people of whole epochs, have something of the cow about them; their soul rests dull and uncaring within itself. They may skip and graze and stare at each other, but they have only a miserable residue of soul in common. Consequently their language *must* be impoverished or become mechanical. For it is not true that language is created by need, the need of the individual. If at all, it is created by the need of a whole herd, a tribe, but in order for this need to be perceived as the common factor, the soul must have become wider than the individual. It must travel and *want* to find itself again, it must *want* to speak before it speaks; and this will is nothing individual. If one imagined primal man in the form of a mythical primal being with a hundred heads and feet and hands it would be speaking to itself; and it was not until it realised that it could speak to itself as to a second, third, indeed hundredth being that it allowed itself to disintegrate into its parts, the human individuals, because it knew that it could not entirely lose its unity: for the unity lies not in space as does the multiplicity of these hundred people, but when they speak the mythical monster again feels whole and one.

And does the glorious tonal system of a language really sound as if need were the mother of language? Is not everything born with joy and luxuriance, free and bearing the signs of contemplative profundity? What has apelike man to do with our languages? A people that has six cases and conjugates its verbs with a hundred forms has a full, communal and over-flowing soul; and the people that has created such a language for itself has poured out the abundance of its soul over all posterity. In a later age the same forces projected themselves into the form of poets and musicians, actors, orators and prophets, but when they were still bursting with their first youth they produced creators of languages. These were the most fertile men of all ages and they were distinguished by what distinguishes those musicians and artists in all ages: their soul was greater, more loving, more communal, and almost more alive in all than in a single dim corner. In them the universal soul spoke to itself.

Notebook 3, March 1875

3[63]

Most people obviously do *not* regard themselves *at all as individuals*; this is shown by their lives. The opposite of the Christian demand that *everybody* should seek his own bliss, and his own bliss *alone*, is human life in general, where everybody lives only as one point between points, not only entirely as the result of earlier generations, but also solely with regard to future ones. In three forms of existence only does man remain an individual: as philosopher, saint and artist. Just consider how a scholarly man whiles his life away: what does the study of Greek particles have to do with the meaning of life? – So here too we see how innumerable people really only live in preparation for a real man: e.g. philologists in preparation for the philosopher, who knows how to use their antlike labour in order to make a statement about the *value of life*. Of course, without *direction*, the *greatest part* of that antlike labour is simply *nonsense* and superfluous.

3[64]

Most people are obviously in the world *by chance*: no necessity of a higher order reveals itself in them. They are busy doing this and that, but their talent is mediocre. How strange! The way they now live shows that they think nothing of themselves; they betray themselves by throwing themselves away on shabby pursuits (whether these are petty passions or the trivialities of an occupation). The so-called 'vocations' everybody is expected to choose imply a touching human *modesty*: in so doing we say that we are called to be of use and service to our equals, as is our neighbour also, and His neighbour likewise; and so everybody serves everybody else, nobody has the vocation of existing for his own sake rather than constantly for the sake of others; so we have one tortoise lying on top of another and that one again on top of another, and so forth. If everybody's purpose is in somebody else *nobody has a purpose of existence in himself*; and this *'existence for one another'* is the most comic comedy.

3[68]

My goal is to create total enmity between our current 'culture' and Antiquity. Whoever wants to serve the former must *hate* the latter.

3[69]

If we think back very accurately we realise that we are a multiplication of many pasts: how then could we also be an ultimate purpose? – Why not? But most of the time we do not even want to be; we immediately rejoin the ranks and work on a small corner, hoping that it will not be entirely lost for those who come after us. But that is really the sieve of the Danaids:[1] there is no way round it, we must do everything again for ourselves, and only for ourselves; e.g. we must measure science against ourselves, asking: what is science to *us*? But not: what are we to science? One really makes life too easy if one simply regards oneself in historical terms and places oneself in the service of others. 'Your own salvation comes before everything else,' one must say to oneself, and: 'there is no institution that you should hold in higher esteem than your own soul'. – But now man is getting to know himself: finds himelf pathetic, despises himself, and is glad to find something worthy of respect apart from himself. And so he throws himself away by fitting in somewhere, strictly doing his duty and serving out his existence. He knows that he is not working for his own sake; he will want to help those who dare to exist for their own sakes; like Socrates. Most people hang in the air like a lot of balloons, and each breath of wind moves them. – **Consequently**: the *scholar must be a scholar out of self-knowledge, that is, out of self-contempt: i.e. he must know that he is*

---

[1] Because of crimes committed during their lives, in the Underworld the daughters of Danaus were condemned to try to draw water using sieves.

the servant of somebody higher who will come after him. Otherwise he is a sheep.

3[75]

I will tell all the things I no longer believe – also what I believe.

Man stands in the great vortex of forces, imagining that that vortex is rational and has a rational purpose: wrong!

The only rational thing we know is man's little bit of reason: he must make it work very hard and it always leads to his undoing if, for example, he abandons himself to 'providence'.

The only happiness lies in reason; everything else in the world is dreary. I see the supreme reason in the work of the artist, and he can perceive it as such. There may be something that would generate an even greater sense of reason and happiness if it could be produced consciously: for instance the course of the solar system, or the creation and education of a man.

Happiness lies in speed of feeling and thinking: everything else in the world is slow, gradual and stupid. If anybody could feel the course of a ray of light he would be very happy because it is very fast.

Thinking of oneself yields little happiness: if one does experience a great deal of happiness in the process it is because basically one is not thinking of oneself but of one's ideal. This is far away and only the fast reach it and are pleased.

The amalgamation of a large centre of people for the creation of better people is the task of the future. The individual must be attuned to such demands, so that by affirming himself he will affirm the will of that centre, e.g. in relation to his choice of a woman or the way he educates his child. So far no individual has been free, or only the rarest, who were governed by such ideas among others, but by bad and inconsistent ones. The organisation of individual intentions.

Notebook 5, spring – summer 1875

5[22]

Signs and *wonders* are not believed; only a 'providence' needs such things. There is no help, either in prayer, or in asceticism, or in visions. If all this is religion then there is no longer any religion for me.

My religion, if there is anything left that I may call by that name, consists in working for the creation of the genius; education is all that can be hoped for, and all that gives comfort is called art. *Education* is the *love of what has been created*, an excess of love beyond self-love. Religion is *'loving beyond ourselves'. The work of art is the image of such a love beyond oneself and a perfect image.*

5[26]

The negation of life is no longer achieved so easily: be one a hermit or a monk – what is being negated there? Now this concept is becoming more profound: it is above all a *negation that knows*, a *negation that tries to be fair and no longer wholesale.*

A man who wanted to be good and holy today would have a harder time: in order to be good he could not be as *unfair* to *knowledge* as the earlier holy men were. He would have to be a holy man who knew, joining love and wisdom; and he would have to do nothing more with a belief in gods or demigods or providence, just as the Indian holy men had nothing to do with such a belief. In addition, he would have to be healthy, and keep healthy; otherwise he would begin to distrust himself. And perhaps he would not at all look like an ascetic saint, but more like a playboy.

5[30]

I dream of a collective of men who are absolute, who know no consideration, and who want to be called 'destroyers'; they apply the standards of their criticism to everything and they sacrifice themselves to the truth. They want the bad and the false to come to light! We do not want to build prematurely, we do not know whether we shall ever be able to build and whether it is not best not to build. There are lazy pessimists, people who resign – we do not want to be among those.

5[167]

The task would be to *overcome* Greek culture through action. But in order to do that one would have to know it! – there is a thoroughness that is only an excuse for inactivity. Imagine what Goethe knew about antiquity; certainly not as much as a philologist and yet enough to engage with it in a fruitful manner. In fact one *should* not know more about a thing than one would also be able to create. Moreover, the only way of truly *knowing* something is trying to *make* it. Try to live in an old-fashioned style – you will immediately be a hundred miles closer to the ancients than with all erudition. – Our philologists do not show that they are *emulating* antiquity in any respect – that is why *their* antiquity has no effect on their pupils.

   Study of *competition* (Renaissance, Goethe) and *study of despair*!

5[175]

The promotion of a science at the expense of men is the most harmful thing in the world. An atrophied man is a backward step of mankind; he casts his *shadow* into all times. The ethos, the natural intention of the individual sciences, degenerates; in the end the science itself perishes; it has been promoted, but has either no effect, or an immoral one, on life.

5[179]

The intellectual culture of Greece was an aberration of the enormous political drive for ἀριστεύειν.[1] – The πόλις[2] was extremely hostile to the new education. *Nevertheless*, culture existed.

[1] to be the best.
[2] city or city-state.

5[180]

The highest judgement of life can arise only from the highest energy of life, the mind must be at the greatest distance from *feebleness*.

Judgement will have been most correct in the *middle* period of world history because that was when the greatest *geniuses* existed.

The *creation of the genius* as the only man truly able to *appreciate* and to *negate* life.

5[183]

The feeble, the intellectually poor, *must not* sit in judgement over life.

5[188]

Goals.

The value of life can be measured only by the *highest intellect* and the warmest heart.

How can those highest intellects be created? –

The goals of *human welfare* are on the whole quite *different* from that of creating the highest intelligence. Good living is too highly esteemed and quite superficially understood, as are also schools and education.

The ideal state of which socialists dream destroys the *foundation* of the great intelligences, the powerful energy.

We must wish for life to preserve its *violent* character, for *wild* forces and energies to be aroused. Judgement about the value of existence is the highest result of the strongest *tension* in the chaos.

The warmest heart wants that violent, wild character to be obliterated, even though it had its own origin in that character! It wants its own foundation to be obliterated! Therefore it is not intelligent.

The highest intelligence and the warmest heart cannot be together in the same person. The highest intelligence is *higher* than all goodness, which is only an item to be *estimated* in the complete balance sheet of life; the wise man rises above it.

The *wise* man must *oppose* the ideas of unintelligent goodness, because his concern is the reproduction of his own type. At least he *cannot promote* the ideal state. – Christ helped to make men stupid; he impeded the creation of great intellect. How consistent! Its counter-image would perhaps obstruct the creation of Christ's. – *Fatum tristissimum generis humani!*[3]

---

[3] Most sad fate of humankind.

Notebook 6, summer ? 1875

6[3]

I must confess that *Socrates* is so close to me that I am almost always fighting a battle with him.

6[4]

Science and wisdom in battle.

Science (NB *before* it becomes a habit and instinct) comes into being
1) if the gods are not thought to be good. The great advantage of recognising anything as *firm*.
2) selfishness impels the individual to seek his profit through science in certain occupations, e.g. shipping.
3) something for classy people with time to spare. Curiosity.
4) in the wild to and fro of the opinions of the people the individual wants a firmer foundation.

What distinguishes this drive for science from the drive to learn and to accept things in general? Only the lesser degree of egoism or the greater extension of the same. *First*, a losing of the self in things. *Second*, selfishness reaching out beyond the individual.
Wisdom manifests itself
1) in illogical generalisation and flight to the ultimate goal.
2) in relating these results to life.

3) in the absolute importance attributed to one's soul. Only one thing is necessary.

Socratism is *firstly*   wisdom in taking the soul seriously.

       secondly   science as fear and hatred of illogical generalisation.

       thirdly   something peculiar owing to the demand for conscious and logically correct actions.

The result is damage to science and to ethical living.

6[7]

There is also a way of telling this story *ironically* and *mournfully*. In any case I want to avoid a serious and level tone.

Socrates *knocks everything over* at the moment when it has approached the truth *most closely*; this is particularly *ironic*.

Everything should be painted on a background of myth. The boundless uncertainty and instability of myth. One longs for certainty.

It is only where the ray of myth falls that the life of the Greeks sparkles; otherwise it is gloomy. These philosophers deprive themselves of myth; how can they bear this gloom? –

The individual who wants to stand *on his own* feet. *This requires ultimate knowledge*, philosophy. Other people need slowly growing science.

Or rather: it is necessary to believe that one possesses such ultimate knowledge. There will never again be such a degree of faith in one's own knowledge as the ancient Greeks had: but the difficulty and danger of knowledge did not yet confront their soul; they had a robust belief in themselves, through which they overcame all their neighbours and predecessors. Happiness in possessing the truth was never greater in the world, but neither were hardness, arrogance, *tyranny*. In his secret wishes every Greek was a tyrant; and anybody who could actually be a tyrant was one, with the possible exception of Solon, to judge by his own poems.[1]

Independence, too, is only apparent: ultimately everybody carries on where his predecessor left off. Phantasm after phantasm. It is funny to take everything so seriously.

[1] Fragment 32: see T. Bergk, *Poetae lyrici graeci*, 4th edn (Leipzig: Teubner, 1882), no. 32, or E. Diehl, *Anthologia lyrica graeca* (Leipzig: Teubner, 1954), no. 23.

All ancient philosophy is a curious progression of reason in a *maze*. One should strike up the tune of dreams and fairy tales.

6[12]

These philosophers prove *what dangers were inherent in Greek culture:*[2]

myth as an intellectual bed of sloth	– in contrast: cold abstraction and strict science. Democritus.
the flabby creature comforts of life	– in contrast: frugality, strictly ascetic outlook in Pythagoras, Empedocles, Anaximander.
cruelty in battle and argument	– in contrast: Empedocles with his reform of sacrifice.
lie and deception	– in contrast: enthusiasm for the truth regardless of the consequences.
suppleness, excessive sociability	– in contrast: the pride and loneliness of Heraclitus.

6[13]

These philosophers show the vitality of a culture which generates its own correctives.

How does this age die away? Unnaturally. Where are the germs of destruction hidden?

The flight of the better men from the world was a great misfortune. From Socrates onward: all of a sudden the individual became too self-important.

In addition there was the *plague*, for Athens.[3]

Then came the *downfall* through the *Persian Wars*. The danger was too great and the victory too extraordinary.

The death of great musical poetry and philosophy.

Socrates is the revenge for Thersites:[4] glorious Achilles slew Thersites, the ugly man of the people, out of fury over his words at the death of

---

[2] See above, Notebook 19,19[18], p. 97; 19[89], p. 120; 19[116], p. 127; 19[134], p. 132; Notebook 23, 23[8], p. 163.

[3] Nietzsche does not follow strict chronological order here. The 'plague' is the one that struck Athens early in the Peleponnesian war (430 BC, described by Thucydides, Histories II.47ff.). The Persian wars were earlier (480s BC) and ended in a victory for the allied Greeks.

[4] In the *Iliad* (Book II, ll. 225ff.) Thersites is described as a discontented loud-mouth, who is also 'the ugliest man who came to Troy' (and thus very similar to the notoriously chatty, disruptive, and ugly

Penthesilea.⁵ Socrates, the ugly man of the people, slew the *authority* of glorious myth in Greece.

6[14]

Early Greek philosophy was *throughout* a philosophy of *statesmen*. How paltry our statesmen are! Incidentally, that is the greatest difference between the Pre-Socratics and Post-Socratics.

Among them one does not find the 'revolting claim to happiness',⁶ as one does from Socrates onward. Not everything revolves round the condition of their soul: for that is something that one does not ponder without danger. Later the γνῶϑι σαυτόν⁷ of Apollo was misunderstood.

Nor did they *chatter* and *grumble* like that, and they did not *write* either.

Enfeebled Greek culture was Romanised, coarsened, made decorative, then accepted as a decorative culture by enfeebled Christianity as an ally and spread by force among uncivilised peoples – that is the history of Western culture. The stunt has been pulled, and the Greek and the sanctimonious brought together.

I will add Schopenhauer, Wagner and early Greek culture together: this presents a view of a magnificent culture.

6[15]

Comparison of early and post-Socratic philosophy.

1) early philosophy is related to *art*; in solving the riddle of the world it was repeatedly inspired by art. The spirit of music and visual art.
2) it is *not* the negation of the *other* life, but has *grown* out of it as a rare flower; it articulates the secrets of the other life. (Theory – practice)
3) it is *not* as *individually eudemonological*, it lacks the revolting claim to happiness.

Socrates). In an open assembly of the army, he reviles the leader of the expedition, Agamemnon, for his greediness, and is thrashed by Odysseus. The story about Penthesilea (see following footnote), and the story that Thersites was eventually killed by Achilles, are post-Homeric.
⁵ The Queen of the Amazons who came to the aid of Troy after the death of Hector, and was killed by Achilles.
⁶ Adapted from Schopenhauer, *Parerga and Paralipomena*, Book I, 'Aphorismen zur Lebensweisheit', ch. 5.
⁷ know yourself. One of the mottoes inscribed over the entrance to Apollo's oracle at Delphi.

4) These earlier philosophers themselves, in their own lives, have a higher wisdom and not the coldly clever virtue of later times. Their conception of life is richer and more complex, while the Socratics simplify and banalise.

6[18]

These early philosophers can be represented as men who experienced the Greek atmosphere and conventions as a *prohibition* and *barrier*: therefore they were self-liberators (the struggle of Heraclitus against Homer and Hesiod,[8] of Pythagoras against secularisation, of them all against myth, particularly Democritus). They have a gap in their nature, as opposed to the Greek artist and probably also to the Greek statesman.

I regard them as the **precursors of a reformation** of the Greeks: but not of Socrates. Rather, their reformation did not come, or remained sectarian with Pythagoras. All of a group of phenomena are bearers of this spirit of reformation – the *development* of *tragedy*. The *failed reformer* is **Empedocles**; when he failed only Socrates was left. Thus Aristotle's hostility to Empedocles is very understandable.

Empedocles – free state – modification of life – popular reform – an attempt with the help of the great Hellenic festivals. –

Tragedy was also a means. Pindar?

They did not find their philosopher and reformer; compare Plato: he is distracted by Socrates. An attempt at a characterisation of Plato *without* Socrates. Tragedy – profound conception of love – pure nature – no fanatical turning away: obviously the Greeks were *about to find an even higher type* of man than the previous ones; then the scissors snipped, and there remains only the *tragic age* of the Greeks.

6[20]

Passion in Mimnermus,[9] hatred of *old age*.

---

[8] DK 40, 56, 57; KR pp. 182, 218.

[9] A seventh-century (BC) poet from Colophon in Asia Minor who wrote about his fear of old age: 'Without blond Sex, what is life? What pleasure is there?/ Before I lose my libido, I'd rather die./ Secret snogs, sweet gifts, and climbing into the sack:/ Snatch it, ladies and gents, while you're still keen/ and bushy, for when old age arrives and bites, it makes/ a man disgusting to look at, and impotent ... ' (Elegy 1, ll. 1–6, translation, R. G.).

Profound melancholy in Pindar; it is only when a ray comes from above that human life sparkles.[10]

Understanding the world from the *angle of suffering* is the tragic element in tragedy.

6[21]

Thales – the unmythical.[11]

Anaximander – death and birth in nature in moral terms as guilt and punishment.

Heraclitus – conformity to laws and justice in the world.

Parmenides – the other world behind this one; this one as a problem.

Anaxagoras – master builder of worlds.

Empedocles – blind love and blind hate; the profoundly irrational in the most rational portion of the world.

Democritus – the world is entirely without reason and drive, thrown together willy-nilly. All gods and myths are useless.

Socrates: here I am left with nothing but myself; fear for oneself becomes the soul of philosophy.

Plato's attempt to think everything through to its conclusion and to be the saviour.

6[25]

With Empedocles and Democritus,[12] the Greeks were well on the way to *correctly assessing* human existence, its irrationality, its suffering; *but they never reached this*, thanks to Socrates. An unbiased view of men is missing in all the Socratics, who have terrible abstractions, 'the good, the just', in their heads.

[10] See previous footnote. This is a reference to his Fourth Pythian Ode, ll. 95ff.: 'Man is the dream of a shadow/ but when a ray from a god comes/ a bright radiance is upon men and an easy time of living.'

[11] See above, Notebook 19, 19[18], p. 97; , 19[89], p. 120; 19[116], p. 127; 19[134], p. 132; 23[8], p. 163; Notebook 6, 6[12], p. 211.

[12] Empedocles seems to have thought both that, although the world was always moved by the two forces of Love and Strife (see above), at any given period one or the other dominated, and that the period in which he lived was dominated by Strife, not Love (DK 26, 35; KR 345, 346). He also believed that man desperately needed 'purification' (DK 112, 124; KR 354–5). The young Nietzsche was a particularly keen student of Democritus' thought. For an interpretation (and collection of fragments) that makes the affinity between Democritus and the young Nietzsche especially clear, see *Demokrit: Fragmente zur Ethik*, ed. and trans. Gred Ibscher with an Introduction by Gregor Damschen (Stuttgart: Reclam, 1996).

Read Schopenhauer and ask why the ancients lacked such a deep and free outlook – *had* to lack it? I do not understand that. On the contrary. They lose their unbiased attitude through Socrates. Their myths and tragedies are much wiser than the ethics of Plato and Aristotle; and their *'Stoic* and *Epicurean'* men are *poor* in comparison with their earlier poets and statesmen.

6[26]

The effect of Socrates:

1) he destroyed the spontaneity[13] of ethical judgement,
2) destroyed science,
3) had no understanding of art,
4) ripped the individual out of the historical nexus,
5) promoted dialectical chitchat and loquacity.

6[27]

I no longer believe in the *'natural development'* of the Greeks: they were far too gifted to be *gradual* in the step-by-step manner of rocks and stupidity. The Persian wars are their national misfortune: their success was too great, all evil drives erupted, a tyrannical craving to dominate the whole of Hellas came over single men and single cities. Together with the rule of Athens (in the intellectual sphere) a great many forces were crushed; just consider how unproductive Athens was in philosophy for a long time. Pindar would not have been possible as an Athenian. Simonides shows this.[14] And neither would Empedocles, or Heraclitus. Almost all the great musicians come from outside. Athenian tragedy is not the highest form imaginable. Its heroes are too short of the Pindaric element. How terrible that the struggle had to break out between *Sparta* and *Athens* of all places – this cannot be contemplated deeply enough. *The intellectual domination of Athens*

---

13 *Unbefangenheit.*
14 It is not exactly clear what this might mean, but one possibility is that Simonides, a fifth-century choral poet who spent some time in Athens, was a much more strikingly 'intellectualist' poet than Pindar, but also one who is aesthetically inferior. See the discussion of one of his poems in Plato's *Protagoras* 339–49. Simonides' poetry lends itself to this kind of discussion because of its sententiousness. Given the spiritual atmosphere of Athens, Simonidean poetry was the best that could be expected there.

prevented the reformation. One must imagine oneself in a situation in which this domination did not yet exist at all: it was not necessary, and became so only after the Persian wars, i.e. only after the physical political power had shown it. Miletus,[15] e.g., was much more talented, Agrigento[16] too.

6[28]

The tyrant who can do what he feels like, i.e. the Greek who is not restrained by any power, is a being that knows no bounds: 'he overturns the customs of his fatherland, violates women and kills people as he pleases'.[17] The tyrannical freethinker, of whom the Greeks are also afraid, is equally licentious. Hatred of kings – sign of a democratic mentality. I believe that the reformation would have been possible if a tyrant had been an Empedocles.

Plato, with his demand for the philosopher on the throne, expressed an *idea* that was once *possible*; he hit upon the idea when the time to realise it had gone. Periander?[18] –

6[29]

Without the tyrant Pisistratus,[19] the Athenians would have had no tragedy: for Solon was against it, but the taste for it had been awakened. What did Pisistratus want to achieve with these great arousals of grief?

---

[15] A city in Asia Minor that was the birthplace of Thales, Anaximander and Axaximenes, and thus an early centre of philosophy.

[16] A city in Sicily that was the home of Empedocles, and a centre of Greek culture in the sixth and fifth centuries BC.

[17] Herodotus, *The Histories* III.80: 'he changes the customs of our fathers, uses force against women, and kills men without trial'. See also Plato, *Gorgias* 466b9–c2; 469c2–e7.

[18] An extremely powerful tyrant of Corinth (and apparently patron of the arts) in the early sixth century BC, i.e. about 200 years before Plato. He is often listed as one of the Seven Wise Men; see above Notebook 19, footnote 3, p. 95.

[19] Solon (see above, Notebook 19, footnote 3, p. 95) was an early sixth-century Athenian political figure who succeeded in defusing a situation of great social tension by abolishing existing debts and reforming Athenian law. He wrote a certain amount of poetry but was a notorious enemy of (incipient) tragedy. Solon's slightly younger contemporary Pisistratus was able to establish himself as tyrant, and seems to have been an active patron of Thespis, the first actor recorded to have performed tragedies in Attica. See Plutarch, *Life of Solon* 29–30; DL I.59–60.

Solon's aversion from tragedy: think of his restrictions on funeral celebrations, the prohibition of *threnoi*.[20] The μανικὸν πένθος[21] of Milesian women is mentioned.

According to the anecdote it is the *dissimulation* that Solon dislikes; the unartistic nature of the Athenian manifests itself.

Cleisthenes,[22] Periander and Pisistratus are the promoters of tragedy as a popular entertainment, the enjoyment of μανικὸν πένθος.[23] Solon wants moderation.

6[30]

The centralising tendencies generated by the Persian wars: they were appropriated by Sparta and Athens. In contrast, none of these existed between 776 and 560: the culture of the polis flourished. I believe that without the Persian wars the idea of centralisation would have been obtained through a *reformation of the mind* – Pythagoras?

What mattered then was the unity of celebrations and worship: and this is where the reform would have begun. The *idea of a panhellenic tragedy* – out of this an infinitely richer force would have been developed. Why did it not happen after Corinth, Sicyon[24] and Athens had developed this art?

6[34]

It is a beautiful truth that a man for whom improvement or knowledge has become a goal in life is served for the best by all things. But this is only true within limits: a man who wants to know is forced to undertake

[20] ritual lamentation. See Plutarch, *Life of Solon* 21.12.

[21] excessive grief. It was an important part of the ideology of the Greek city-state to contrast the self-controlled moderation of the male citizen with the excess of women and 'barbarians' (non-Greeks, especially Orientals). Miletus in Asia Minor, though a Greek city, could because of its location plausibly have been thought to be more open to 'Oriental' influences than some other Greek cities.

[22] There were two important people with this name, a grandfather (an early sixth-century tyrant of Sicyon), and his grandson, an Athenian politician generally credited with introducing the institutional reforms that established the democracy. See Herodotus v.66ff.

[23] excessive grief.

[24] Dithyramb, often considered a precursor of tragedy, originated in Corinth under the tyranny of Periander (see Notebook 1, footnote 6, p. 11). Herodotus reports that the citizens of Sicyon used to celebrate their local hero with a 'tragic chorus' (v.67).

the most tiring work, a man who is improving is enervated and shattered by diseases! On the whole it may be correct that the apparent intentionality of fate is the deed of the individual, who arranges his life and learns from everything, sucking knowledge as the bee sucks honey. But a fate that strikes a people strikes a whole which cannot reflect on its existence and supply it with goals in the same way; thus the notion of intentionality in peoples was fabricated by daydreamers, and nothing is easier to show than the absence of intentionality, e.g. when a period of the fullest flowering is suddenly hit by a snowfall, so that everything dies. In this respect fate is just as stupid as nature. To a degree every people, even in the most unfavourable circumstances, achieves something that recalls its talent. But if it is to achieve its *best*, some accidents must not happen. The Greeks did not achieve their best.

The Athenians would also have become something higher without their political fury since the Persian wars: think of Aeschylus, who came from the pre-Persian age and who was dissatisfied with the Athenians of his own time.

6[35]

Through the unfavourable situation of the Greek cities after the Persian wars many favourable conditions for the emergence and development of great individuals were eliminated: and thus the production of genius indeed depends on the fate of peoples. The beginnings of genius are very frequent, but the concurrence of all the most necessary supports is very rare.

The reformation of the Hellenes of which I dream would have become a wonderful soil for the production of geniuses; nothing like it had ever existed before. This would need to be described. We lost something unutterable here.

6[39]

The seducers of philosophers are words, they wriggle in the nets of language.

6[41]

Science fathoms the course of nature, but can never *command* man. Inclination, love, pleasure, displeasure, elevation, exhaustion – science knows none of these. Man must *interpret* – and thereby assess – his life and his experiences from a specific point of view. The religions owe their strength to the fact that they are *criteria of value*, standards. Seen in myth, an event looks different. The interpretation of religions has the characteristic of judging human life according to ideals of a human kind.

Notebook 17, summer 1876

17[16]

A man is in a condition of genius when he loves and ridicules the same thing at the same time.

17[32]

The artist needs the infidelity of memory in order not to copy but to transform nature.

17[51]

The modern disease is an excess of *experiences*. Therefore everybody should go home on his own early so as not to lose himself to experiences.

17[64]

It is easy to break the habit of having religious opinions, if one just starts early enough.

17[90]

Lack of character can be a sign of preponderance of spirit.

17[100]

No *ethics* can be based on pure knowledge of things: for that purpose one must be like nature, neither good nor evil.

Notebook 19, October – December 1876

19[20]

The dramatic musician must have not only ears, but eyes in his ears.

19[37]

The only way of spreading morality is to ensure that what enlightens the intellect introduces the largest available number of new and higher possibilities of action and thereby offers a wide choice of motives; then to provide opportunities. Man is very often seized by a low motive only because he knew no higher one, and he remains mediocre and low in his actions because he was not given an opportunity to bring his greater and purer instincts to the fore. – Many men spend all their lives waiting for the opportunity to be good in *their* way.

19[69]

Those who think more sharply do not like the images of poets, because the images bring too many disparate things to their memory at one and the same time; likewise, those whose hearing is sharp hear the overtones of a tone as a jarring chord.

19[85]

The so-called metaphysical need proves nothing about any reality corresponding to that need: on the contrary, because we have this need we hear the language of the will, not that of the intellect, and we go astray if we believe this language. We would have to accept a god if he were demonstrable *without* being made to appear necessary to us by a need.

19[96]

Man has the tendency to give the most profound reasons for traditional things, if indeed he seeks any reasons. Sensing the enormously beneficent consequences, he seeks a profound intention full of wisdom in the souls of those who planted the traditions. – But the reverse is the case: the origin of god, or of marriage, is shallow and stupid, and the foundations of the tradition must be regarded as intellectually very low.

19[97]

By overthrowing a *belief* one does not overthrow the *consequences* that have grown out of it. These live on by virtue of tradition: tradition turns a blind eye to the association of belief and consequence. Consequence seems to exist for its own sake. Consequence disowns its father.

19[103]

One must acknowledge all that is useful to man in religion: it provides instant happiness and comfort. If the truth cannot be joined with usefulness its cause is lost. Why should mankind sacrifice itself for the truth? In fact it is not even able to do so. To this day all striving for truth has set its sights on usefulness: the distant usefulness of mathematics was what a father respected about his son, the student. A man who spent his time on something that yielded no profit, or even caused harm, would have been regarded as dim-witted. A man who spoilt the air that people were breathing would have been considered a danger to the public. If religion is necessary for living, a man who undermines it is a danger to the public: if the lie is necessary it must not be undermined. Therefore – is truth possible in connection with life? –

19[107]

It is the way of bound minds to prefer *any explanation* to none: in this they are easily satisfied. High culture demands that some things should be left unexplained: ἐπέχω.[1]

19[108]

A dark thing is regarded as more important and dangerous than a bright one. Fear lives in the deepest recesses of the human imagination. The ultimate form of the religious consists in the acceptance of dark, inexplicable areas; in these the mystery of the world is believed to reside.

---

[1] 'I withhold [judgement]'. Ancient sceptics thought there were equally strong (isosthenic) arguments on both sides of any theoretical disagreement, so the only way to attain tranquillity of mind was to 'refrain from judging' (or 'suspend judgement') on all theoretical issues.

Notebook 21, end of 1876 – summer 1877

21[11]

Mankind, an erratically functioning machine with enormous forces.

21[12]

On volcanic soil everything thrives.

21[40]

Love and hate are cataractic and one-eyed, likewise the 'will'.

21[45]

Those who can should follow me in being fair to different cultures.

21[46]

Philosophy is the mirage that falsely holds out the solution to the weary disciples of the sciences.

21[51]

Certain insights protect themselves by not being understood.

21[83]

Morality often depends on success.

Notebook 23, end of 1876 – summer 1877

23[9]

Why assume a *drive for self-preservation* at all? Among countless unsuitable[1] forms there were some capable of life, of *carrying on* life; millions of years of adaptation on the part of the individual human organs were needed until the current body could regularly come into being, and until those facts that are usually attributed to the drive for self-preservation began regularly to manifest themselves. Basically, what happens now is determined by chemical laws just as a waterfall is determined by mechanical laws. The pianist's finger has no 'drive' to hit the right keys but only the habit. In fact the word 'drive' is only a convenience and is applied wherever regular effects on organisms have not yet been traced to their chemical and mechanical laws.

23[10]

All man's goals and purposes were once also conscious to his ancestors, but they have been forgotten. The directions followed by man greatly depend on the past: the Platonic ἀνάμνησις.[2] The worm moves in the same direction even when its head has been cut off.

23[16]

The moment when airship travel is invented and introduced is favourable to socialism because it changes all concepts of landed property. Man is

---

[1] *unzweckmäßig.*
[2] recollection; see above, Notebook 2, footnote 3, p. 15.

everywhere and nowhere; he is uprooted. We must safeguard ourselves by means of societies, with strict mutual commitments and the *exclusion of all those who are not committed*. Otherwise all will take to the air and settle somewhere else if they cannot pay or do not wish to keep a commitment.

23[21]

If we seek an explanation of nature and man that corresponds to our highest and strongest moods we shall only come across metaphysical ones. How would men look without all these sublime errors – I believe, *like animals*. If we imagined an animal endowed with knowledge of a strict natural history it would not become a man as a result but would essentially continue to live as an animal, except that in its many hours of leisure, e.g. as a horse in front of a manger, it would read good books, which would make it understand that the *truth* and *animals* get on well together.

23[48]

Moral *introspection* is by no means sufficient today; it also takes history and knowledge of the peoples who have been left behind to recognise the complex motives of our actions. In these the whole history of mankind takes place, with all its great errors and false ideas woven into the fabric. Because we no longer share the latter we have ceased to seek them in the motives of our act[ions], but they still accompany them as mood, a colour and an overtone. It is believed that once man's motives have been classified in accordance with the *necessary* satisfaction of his needs all his motives have really been listed. But there were countless, almost unbelievable, indeed mad, needs that are not guessed so easily today: all these still have a contributory effect.

23[49]

Sometimes, for example in the deepest shock resulting from bereavement, betrayal or declaration of love, we are overcome by indignation when we hear the naturalistic historical explanation. But such feelings *prove* nothing; they can only be explained in their turn. The feelings have *become* – but have not always been – deep; and those supreme fervours have no corresponding grounds in reality, but are figments of the imagination.

23[59]

Those men who are conspicuously able to cut loose from inherited moral values and who lack 'conscience' can become like that only in the same way as freaks come into being; for growth and development continue after birth as a result of inherited habits and powers. In such cases one could therefore expand the concept of freak and talk about *malformations*. Against these the rest of mankind has the same rights as against freaks and monsters: it may destroy them so as not to foster the propagation of the retarded and the defective. E.g. the *murderer* is a malformation.

23[65]

The benefits and disadvantages of all martyrdom. – The many deaths of martyrs have become sources of strength for men, with regard to obstinacy out of conviction, not with regard to strict examination of the truth. Cruelties harm the truth but benefit the will (which manifests itself in belief).

23[135]

In former times men went in for definitions because they believed that every word and concept possessed a sum of predicates that needed merely to be extracted. But the word holds only a very vague suggestion of things: the sensible way with definitions is to use them only in order to say how one wants a word to be understood and to leave it to everybody to demarcate the meaning of a word afresh for himself: the word is not binding.

23[152]

Christianity says that 'there are no virtues but sins'. This slanders and poisons all human action and undermines confidence in men. Now even philosophy seconds Christianity in the fashion of La Rochefoucauld,[3]

---

[3] A French moralist (1613–80) whose aphoristic writings punctured moral pretensions and saw in most human action the pursuit of self-interest.

putting the celebrated human virtues down to paltry and ignoble motives. Thus it is a huge relief to learn that there are no actions that are good or bad in themselves and that, in the same way as the Christian maxim, it is also possible to put forward the opposite maxim of antiquity, which claims that 'there are no sins, but only virtues', i.e. actions appropriate to the point of view of the good (except that judgements differ as to what is good).[4] Everybody acts according to what is to his advantage, and nobody is deliberately bad, i.e. harmful to himself. It is a great step forward to learn that morality has nothing whatsoever to do with the thing-in-itself, but is opinion and belongs in the realm of the very changeable intellect. Admittedly, just as our ear has created our sense for music (which of course also does not exist in itself), so we have the moral sense as an elevated product of mankind to date. However, this sense is not based on the laws of logical thinking and rigorous observation of nature but, like the sense for the arts, on various wrong judgements and fallacies. Science cannot help uncovering this illogical foundation of morality, as it also does with art. It may therefore weaken the moral sense to some extent in the long run, but the *sense of truth* itself is one of the highest and most powerful *efflorescences of this moral sense*. This is where the compensation lies.

23[159]

To readers of my writings I want to declare unequivocally that I have abandoned the metaphysico-artistic views that essentially dominate those writings: they are pleasant but untenable. If one takes the liberty of speaking in public early one is usually obliged to contradict oneself in public soon after.

23[167]

If men had not built houses for gods architecture would still be in its infancy. The tasks man set himself on the basis of false assumptions (e.g. the soul separable from the body) have given rise to the highest forms of culture. 'Truths' are unable to supply such motives.

---

[4] See, e.g., Plato, *Protagoras* 352ff.

23[177]

Philosophy is not to be understood in religious terms. – To comprehend a philosophy through religious needs is totally to misunderstand it. A new belief, a new authority, is sought – but those who want belief and authority are more comfortable and safer with the traditional religions.

Notebook 27, spring – summer 1878

27[4]

The strong free man is a *non*-artist. (Against Wagner.)

27[17]

Men who try in vain to make a *principle out of themselves* (like Wagner).

27[19]

Dramatists are *constructive* geniuses, not original finders like epic poets. *Drama* is *lower* than the epic – coarser audience – democratic.

27[35]

Rhythm did *not* enter the poetry of the Greeks from dance. Dance and poetry are independent. **Therefore:** *music* and *dance* must have been *in*dependent for a long time.[1]

27[44]

My portrait of Wagner went beyond him; I had portrayed an *ideal monster*, but one which might be able to awaken artists. For me the real Wagner and the real Bayreuth[2] were like the bad last print of a copperplate

---

[1] A revision of Nietzsche's earlier view (following Wagner; see, e.g., GSD III.67)
[2] A small town in Bavaria in which Wagner built a special theatre to his own specifications for performance of his music-dramas, and established a music festival.

engraving on inferior paper. My desire to see real men and their motives was tremendously stimulated by this humiliating experience.

27[45]

Wagner recalls a flow of lava which impedes its own progress by solidifying and which suddenly feels obstructed by boulders formed by itself. No *allegro con fuoco*[3] in his case.

27[47]

His soul does not *sing*, it *speaks*, but it speaks as the supreme passion does. What is *natural* in him is the tone, the rhythm, the gestures of the spoken language; the music, on the other hand, is never quite natural, but a kind of *learnt* language with a modest stock of words and a *different* syntax.

27[50]

Wagner is *poor* in melodies and his melodies are poor in themselves. Melody is a *whole*, with many beautiful proportions, a reflection of an orderly soul. Wagner *strives* for this, but once he *has* a melody he almost crushes it in his embrace.

27[60]

In music too there is a *logic* and a *rhetoric* as stylistic opposites.
    Wagner becomes a rhetorician when he deals with a topic.

27[75]

Plato's envy. He wants to monopolise Socrates *for himself.* He puts a lot of himself into Socrates, and he believes that he is making him more beautiful, καλὸς Σωκράτης,[4] freeing him from the Socratics[5] and presenting him as if he were still alive. But he represents Socrates quite

---

[3] quickly with fire (a marking designating the way in which certain musical works are to be performed).
[4] beautiful Socrates.
[5] During his life Socrates accumulated a loose group of 'followers' (for whom he seems to have disclaimed responsibility, see Plato's *Apology* 23c–24b2), and after his death various different groups claimed to be Socrates' true philosophical heirs.

unhistorically and places him on the most dangerous edge (as Wagner does Beethoven and Shakespeare).

27[76]

The Greeks without a *sense of sin*. Orestes, the criminal,[6] is venerable. Madness, no desire for redemption.

27[81]

Whoever attacks his age can attack only *himself*: what can he see if not himself? Likewise one can glorify only oneself in others. Self-destruction, self-deification, self-contempt – that is our judging, loving, hating.

27[86]

What *use* are Wagner's follies and dissipations, and those of his party? Or should they be *made* useful? He carries them with him like a *noisy bell*. I do not wish him to be any different.

---

[6] Orestes murdered his mother Clytemnestra because she had killed her husband Agamemnon. See Aeschylus, *Oresteia*.

Notebook 28, spring – summer 1878

28[2]

Perennial distrust of so-called moral actions. Man acts as he feels best.
Exceptionally a defiant self-despising mountain-air sense of morality.

28[4]

I have never met a man with convictions who did not soon arouse irony in
me because of these convictions.

28[7]

As a child I saw God in his glory. – First philosophical paper about the
origin of the devil (God thinks himself, which he can do only by imagining his opposite). Melancholy afternoon – service in the chapel at Pforta,[1]
distant organ sounds.

28[9]

Daemonion[2] – the warning voice of the father.

---

[1] Nietzsche attended the old and distinguished Pforta school in Quedlinburg.
[2] That which is more than human. This is the term Socrates used in Plato's *Apology* (31d–32a) to
describe the voice he sometimes heard which, when he heard it, warned him against a course of
action he was about to undertake, but never gave him positive encouragement to any particular
action.

28[16]

My nature *reveals itself* – does it *develop*?

Ever since childhood I have been weighed down by an alien character and alien knowledge. I am discovering myself.

28[18]

Knowledge is *ossification* – acting is involuntary epilepsy. I am like a man shot with the curare arrow of knowledge: all seeing.

28[23]

I was wounded by him who awakened me.[3]

28[24]

Grotta di *Matrimonio*,[4] an idyllic picture of the unconscious life.

28[25]

Tiberius:[5] the madness of being able to act. Counterpart: the madness of being able to know.

28[26]

Nobody has insulted me; nevertheless, I part from men. No revenge.

28[35]

Did Christ really redeem the world? He must have failed in the attempt.

---

[3] This is what Brünnhilde says to Siegfried when he awakens her in Act III of Wagner's *Siegfried*.

[4] This grotto on the isle of Capri, which Nietzsche visited, was thought to have been a favourite haunt of the emperor Tiberius (42 BC–37 AD). The modern Italian name means literally 'grotto of matrimony', but this is most likely a distortion of 'grotto of Mitromania' (i.e., of the god Mithras who was worshipped by the sacrifice of a bull). See Suetonius, *Life of Tiberius* 40–4; 62.

[5] Tiberius lived during a volatile and extremely dangerous period of Roman history, was adopted by the emperor Augustus as his successor only rather late in life, and was said to have become increasingly suspicious, misanthropic and unpredictable in later life.

28[36]

Sowing on one's faults.

28[40]

To regain the ancient view of the world! The *Moira*[6] really above everything, the *gods* the representatives of real powers! To become one of the ancients!

28[41]

I need the ointment boxes and medicine bottles of *all* the ancient philosophers.

[6] fate.

Notebook 29, summer 1878

29[15]

Themes of a *tragic* view of life: the struggle of the non-victorious is glorified. Those who fail are in the majority. The terrible moves more deeply. Enjoying the paradox of preferring night to day, death to life.

Trag[edy] *and com[edy]* both supply a caricature, not an image, of life. 'Pathological'.

Goethe against the *tragic*[1] – why seek it out? – Conciliatory nature.

29[16]

Beings as gifted as I imagine geniuses to be have never existed.

29[45]

Why should one not be allowed to *play metaphysically*? And to expend a quite enormous creative force on it?

29[49]

Why are metaphysics and religion not accepted as a *game of adults*?

---

[1] In a letter to his friend Zelter of 31 August 1831 Goethe explains that tragedies deal with situations in which it is assumed that no 'reconciliation' between parties is possible, and that he believes that in our world a situation in which no reconciliation is possible (*'das Unversöhnliche'*) is 'absurd'. See *Goethes Werke*, Goethes Briefe, Weimarer Ausgabe, IV. Abteilung, 49. Band (Weimar: Böhlaus Nachfolger, 1909), p. 128.

29[50]

If one *gives seriousness away* for metaphysics and religion one will no longer have it for *life* and its tasks.

29[51]

Wagner's art is for those who are conscious of an essential *flaw* in their way of life: having either constricted a great nature through a low activity or wasted it through idleness or conventional marriages etc.

Here escaping from the world = **escaping from the self.**

Notebook 30, summer 1878

30[1]

My mistake was coming to Bayreuth with an ideal: as a result I experienced the bitterest disappointment. I was violently repelled by the over-abundance of the ugly, the distorted, the overseasoned.

30[38]

Since all want happiness, and the properties and affects are very diverse and hardly changeable, one must use *all* beginnings *ingeniously*. Ethics for the ingenious.

30[51]

At that time I believed that from the aesthetic point of view the world was a drama and meant as such by its author, but that as a moral phenomenon it was a *fraud*: therefore I came to the conclusion that the world could be justified only as an aesthetic phenomenon.

30[52]

When I listened to the total sound of the early Greek philosophers I thought I could hear tones that I had been accustomed to hearing from Greek art, and in particular tragedy. How far this was due to the Greeks or only to my own ears, the ears of a man in great need of art – that is something I still cannot say with any certainty.

30[56]

I would like fair-minded people to accept this book as a kind of atonement for my earlier encouragement of a dangerous aesthetic, which tried to turn all aesthetic phenomena into 'miracles' – – in so doing I caused some harm among Wagner's followers and perhaps to Wagner himself, who will accept anything that bestows a higher status on his art, however justified or unjustified this may be. Perhaps my approval since his treatise 'The Destiny of Opera'[1] has enticed him to be more decisive and introduced some untenable elements into his writings and activities. I regret this very much.

30[68]

How worm-eaten and full of holes, how well and truly built on deception and dissimulation, human life seemed to me to be. I felt that we owed everything uplifting – illusions, all enjoyment of life – to error and that therefore the origin of such a world must not be sought in a moral being, but perhaps in an artist-creator. At the same time I did not believe that such a being deserved any veneration in the Christian sense (which posits the god of goodness and love) and I did not even shrink from hinting that this idea could be ripped out of the German character as forcibly as it had been inoculated into it. I thought that in Wagner's art I had discovered the road to a German paganism, or at least a bridge to a specifically un-Christian view of the world and of men. 'The gods are bad and knowing: they deserve to perish; man is good and stupid – he has a more beautiful future and he reaches it once the gods have passed into their final twilight' – that is how I would have formulated my creed, whereas now – – –

30[110]

The total absence of morals in Wagner's heroes. He has a wonderful idea, which is unique in art: the reproach of the sinner addressed to the innocent: 'O King' – Tristan to Marke.[2]

---

[1] GSD IX.127–57.

[2] At the end of Act II of *Tristan und Isolde* King Marke discovers his wife, Isolde, having sex with Tristan in the forest, and asks Tristan why he has done this. Tristan tells Marke he will never understand the answer to that question, strongly suggesting that this is because of a failing on Marke's part, perhaps an incapacity to comprehend the 'marvellous realm of the night'.

30[111]

Listen to the second act of *Götterdämmerung*[3] *without* the drama: it is chaotic music, as wild as a bad dream, and so horribly clear as if it wanted to be clear even to the deaf. This *talking without saying anything* is frightening. The drama is pure deliverance. – Is it *praise* to say that on its own this music is unbearable (apart from some, deliberately isolated, passages) as a *whole*? – Enough, *without drama* this music is a constant negation of all the supreme stylistic laws of the earlier music: those who become fully *accustomed* to it lose their sense of these laws. But has the drama *gained* anything through this addition? It has been joined by a *symbolic interpretation*, a kind of philological commentary which banishes the ever *free imagination of understanding* – tyrannical! Music is the *language of the* explainer, who is continually speaking and leaves us no time; moreover in a difficult language which again demands an *explanation*. Those who have *separately* first mugged up the story (language!), then turned it into action by means of the eye, then sought out and understood the musical symbolism, and fully empathised, indeed fallen in love with, all three – they will have exceptional pleasure. But how *demanding*! But it is impossible, except for some brief moments – because it is too relentless, this tenfold comprehensive attention of the eye, ear, intellect and emotion, this extreme act of reception without *any* productive reaction! – This is done by the fewest; but where does the effect on *so many* come from? Because our concentration is *intermittent* and flags over whole stretches, because we pay attention now to the music, now to the drama and now to the scenic effects, each *on its own* – that is, we *dismantle* the work. – This condemns the *genre* out of hand: the result is not the drama, but a moment or an *arbitrary* selection. Here the creator of a *new genre* must be careful! Not the *constant juxtaposition of the arts* – but the *moderation* of the ancients, which is suited to human nature.

30[122]

There is *always* something in Wagner's work that arouses interest, allowing now the emotion, now the intellect to rest. This total relaxation and arousal of our nature is what we are so grateful for. In the end we

---

[3] The fourth and final music-drama in Wagner's cycle *Der Ring des Nibelungen*.

are inclined to praise his faults and deficiencies, because they make us productive for our part.

30[125]

The *critique of morality* is itself a high *degree* of morality – but, like all criticism, it is fused with vanity, ambition and the enjoyment of victory.

30[139]

We are experiencing the downfall of the **last** *art* – Bayreuth convinced me of this –

30[157]

To suffer from life neither so violently nor so feebly and impassively as to make Wagner's art *necessary* for us as a medicine. – This, rather than any impure motives, is the main reason for our **antagonism**: we cannot hold something to which we are not driven by a necessity, which we do not *need*, in such high esteem.

30[183]

The effects of Wagner's rhetoric are so violent that our intellect takes *revenge* afterwards – as with a conjurer. We criticise Wagner's *means* of achieving his effects **more severely**. Basically we are annoyed because Wagner did not find it *necessary* to use *more subtle* means to catch **us**.

Notebook 33, autumn 1878

33[2]

Against Socrates it can now be said that human virtue is nothing, but human wisdom a great deal.

Notebook 40, June – July 1879

40[3]

I conclude: *Restricting* our *needs*. With regard to these (e.g. our food, clothing, shelter, heating, climate etc.) we must *all* make sure that we become *experts. Building our lives on as many or as few foundations as we can adequately judge* – that is how we promote general morality, i.e. we force every craftsman to treat us *honestly* because we are *experts*. If we do not want to become experts in any one need we must *deny* that need to ourselves: this is the new morality.

Expertise in relation to the persons we use is the first *surrogate*. That is, understanding people where we cease to understand things.

Thus: acquiring a very different kind of *knowledge* based on our *needs*.

Notebook 41, July 1879

41[3]

We strive for independence (freedom) for the sake of *power*, not the other way round.

41[5]

Purposes make life quite nonsensical and *untrue.* Do we work *in order* to feed ourselves? Do we eat *in order* to live? Do we live *in order* to leave children (or works) behind? These likewise – etc. and finally *salto mortale?*[1] Rather, *in* working, eating etc. the *end* too is always present: with purpose we tie 2 ends together. I eat in order to eat *and* in order to live, i.e. in order to eat again.

The action wants to be *repeated* because it is pleasant. Everything pleasant is the end. Do plants exist *in order* to be eaten by animals? There is *no purpose.* We *deceive* ourselves. – I dip my pen *in order* to - - -

41[15]

The brain is growing. Only the youngest parts have an accompanying consciousness. The older ones work without this *controlling light.*

The goal: man as a great unconscious purposive activity, like the nature of the plant.

---

[1] a highly dangerous leap, somersault.

41[51]

Against Wagner one easily proves too right.

41[53]

The different kinds of *imagination* have a different power to *enlarge*. The imagination makes *fear* very *great* – that is why the would-be-powerful count on it first of all.

41[54]

Something that we *know* seems to us to have greatly risen in value as a result. For a while...

Notebook 42, July – August 1879

42[15]

We *need* food, but the *needs* of our taste are different: first compulsion, then habit, then a pleasure that wishes to be repeated (need). It is the same as with the moral sense, which is as differentiated as taste but the purpose it serves is almost identical (the preservation of man *by means of,* and against, men).

The moral sense is a *taste* with definite needs and aversions: the original *causes* of each need are forgotten, and the moral sense operates as taste, *not* as reason.

Taste is a *specific* and *selective hunger.* Morality likewise. (A hunger that wants to be satisfied in a certain way, not chemically. –) Thus, by virtue of the moral sense, we do not want to preserve ourselves by means of, and against, men in *every possible way.*

42[52]

In the world of *art* there is *no progress* over the millennia. But in morality there certainly is, because there is in knowledge and science.

42[57]

St Paul – who is one of those great immoralities in which the Bible is richer than one imagines.[1]

---

[1] Presumably a reference to the 'antinomian' strand in the writings of Paul, the emphasis on 'faith', 'love', and 'spirit' as against 'the letter of the law' (see Roman 3.27–30; 2 Corinthians 3.6–7).

Notebook 47, September – November 1879

47[3]

For the *people* Christianity as a muzzle! – So say many educated men, who do not count themselves among the people, to each other. They may not say it out loud; fear of the people is their muzzle.

47[5]

Schopenhauer's fundamental blunder is not to have seen that desire (the 'will') is only a *kind of knowledge* and nothing else.

47[7]

Shame on this lofty semi-idiotic seriousness! Are there no little lines around your eyes? Can't you lift a thought on your fingertips and flick it up in the air? Does your mouth have only this one pinched, morose expression? Do your shoulders never shake with laughter? I wish you would once in a while whistle and behave as if you were in bad company, instead of sitting together with your author in such a respectable and unbearably demure way.

On the Pathos of Truth (1872)

Preface

Is fame really nothing but the most delicious mouthful of our self-love? – After all, as a desire, it is attached to the rarest of men and again to their rarest moments. Those are the moments of sudden illumination in which man stretches his arm out imperiously, as if to create a world, drawing light out of himself and spreading it all round him. At those moments he is imbued with the blissful certainty that what has thus raised and transported him to the farthest distance, that is, the height of this *one* sensation, must not be withheld from posterity. It is in the eternal need of all future generations for these rarest illuminations that man recognises the necessity of his fame: mankind, for all time to come, needs him. And just as that moment of illumination is the distillation and quintessence of his most particular nature, so he believes himself to be immortal as the man of this moment, while he throws off everything else as dross, corruption, vanity, bestiality or pleonasm, and surrenders it to transience.

We see any disappearance and demise with dissatisfaction, and often with surprise, as if we were experiencing something essentially impossible. The fall of a tall tree upsets and the collapse of a mountain torments us. Every New Year's Eve night makes us feel the mystery of the contradiction between being and becoming. But the idea that a moment of supreme universal perfection[1] should disappear, as it were, without any posterity and heirs, like a fleeting beam of light, offends the moral man most of all. His imperative runs: what existed *once* in order to propagate

---

[1] *höchste Welt-Vollendung*

248

the concept of 'man' more beautifully must be eternally present. That the great moments form a chain, that they join mankind together through millennia like a mountain range, that what was greatest in a past age is also great for me, and that the visionary belief of the desire for fame will be fulfilled – that is the fundamental idea of *culture*.

The terrible struggle of culture is ignited by the demand that what is great should be eternal: for everything else that lives cries No! The habitual, the small, the common, filling all the nooks and crannies of the world, like the heavy earthly air that we are all condemned to breathe, shrouds greatness in clouds of smoke and, obstructing, impeding, stifling, confounding, deceiving, blocks the path that greatness must walk to immortality. The path leads through human brains! Through the brains of wretched, short-lived beings who, at the mercy of their petty needs, surface again and again to the same needs and ward off their ruin for a short time with difficulty. They want to live, live for a while – at any price. Who would suspect among them that gruelling torch race which alone assures the continuing existence of greatness? And yet, again and again some awaken who, faced with that greatness, are filled with such delight as if human life were a glorious thing and as if the finest fruit of this bitter plant must be the knowledge that once one man walked through this life proudly and stoically, another with profundity, a third with pity, but that all left *one* lesson behind: that those who live life most beautifully are those who do not respect it. While common men take such a dolefully serious view of this short span of life, those on their journey to immortality were able to rise to Olympian laughter or at least to a sublime scorn. They often stepped into their grave with irony – for what was there to be buried about them?[2]

The most daring knights among these fame addicts, who believe that they will find their coat of arms hanging on a constellation, must be sought among *philosophers*. Their work is not directed to an 'audience', to the excitement of the masses and the rapt applause of their contemporaries: following the road in solitude is part of their character. Their talent is the rarest and in a certain respect the most unnatural in nature; indeed it is exclusive and hostile even towards talents of the same kind. The wall of their self-sufficiency must be made of diamonds if it is not to be razed and smashed, for everything, man and nature, is in motion against them.

[2] See Plato, *Phaedo* 115c1–116a1; 118a7–8.

Their journey to immortality is more exhausting and obstacle-ridden than any other, and yet nobody can believe more firmly than the philosopher that it will lead him to his destination, because he has no idea where to stand if not on the widely outspread wings of all times; for disregard of the present and the momentary is inherent in the nature of philosophical contemplation. He has the truth; may the wheel of time roll where it likes, it will never be able to escape the truth.

It is important to learn that such men once lived. One would never be able to imagine as an idle possibility the pride of the wise Heraclitus,[3] who shall be our example. In itself, any striving for knowledge seems unsatisfied and unsatisfying by its nature. Therefore nobody who has not been taught by history will believe in such a regal self-esteem, such an absolute conviction of being the only favoured suitor of the truth. Such men live in their own solar system: that is where they must be sought out. A Pythagoras[4] and an Empedocles[5] too held themselves in a superhuman esteem, indeed in an almost religious awe, but the bond of compassion, linked to a great conviction of the transmigration of souls and the unity of all living things, led them back to other men and their salvation. The sense of loneliness that permeated the hermit of the Ephesian temple of Artemis[6] can only be surmised as one stands petrified in the wildest mountain wasteland. He exudes no overpowering sense of compassionate impulses, no desire to help and save: he is like a star without an atmosphere. His eye, blazing and inward-looking, merely pretends to be fixing a faded and icy gaze on the world outside. All round him waves of delusion and perversity break directly against the fortress of his pride: he turns away in disgust. But even men with feeling hearts avoid such a tragic mask; such a being may seem more understandable in a remote shrine, among images of gods, next to coldly magnificent architecture. Among men Heraclitus as a man was unbelievable; and if he was seen watching the play of noisy children, he was in any case thinking about something that no mortal ever thought about on such an occasion – the

---

[3] See above, Notebook 19, footnote 6, p. 97.

[4] See above, Notebook 19, footnote 9, p. 97. There is no reliable evidence for Nietzsche's specific claim about Pythagoras here.

[5] See above, Notebook 19, footnote 8, p. 97. See also DK I. (Empedocles) 112; KR pp. 354–5.

[6] He was said in antiquity, very unusually, to have taken up residence in the Temple of Artemis, for reasons that are unclear. Nietzsche's suggestion here is that this was a sign of his sense of his own isolation and of his superiority to his fellow citizens, a sense amply documented in the extant fragments. See DK I.121, 125a; DL IX.1.

play of the great world-child Zeus and the eternal joke of the destruction and the creation of a world.[7] He had no need of men, not even in order to acquire knowledge: he set no store by anything that could be ascertained, or that other sages before him had tried to ascertain, from them. 'I sought and explored myself',[8] he said in a phrase that was used to describe the exploration of an oracle: as if he, and none other, were the man who truly fulfilled and consummated the Delphic proposition 'Know thyself'.

But what Heraclitus heard from this oracle he regarded as an immortal wisdom, worthy of being interpreted for all eternity, in the sense in which the prophetic speeches of the sibyl are immortal. It is enough for the most distant generations of men, so long as it is interpreted for them like the sayings of an oracle, the same way as Heraclitus, like the Delphic god himself, 'neither tells nor conceals'. Although he proclaims it 'without laughter, without frills and the odour of ointments', but rather, as it were, with a 'foaming mouth', it *must* penetrate to the future thousands of years ahead.[9] The world has an eternal need for the truth and therefore it has an eternal need for Heraclitus, although he has no need for the world. What does *he* care about his fame? 'Fame among mortals who are constantly draining away',[10] as he exclaims scornfully. That is something for singers and poets, and also for those who became known as 'wise' men before him – they may swallow the most delicious mouthful of their self-love, but for him this fare is too common. His fame is the business of other people, not his. His self-love is the love of truth – and this truth tells him that it is the immortality of mankind that needs him and not he who needs the immortality of the man Heraclitus.

The truth! The rapturous delusion of a god! What business of men is the truth?

And what was the 'truth' of Heraclitus?

And where has it gone? A vanished dream, wiped from the faces of mankind, together with other dreams! – It was not the first!

---

[7] DK 1.52; see also BT § 24.

[8] DK 1.101, KR p. 212. No existing English translations were used for the short quotations from Heraclitus in this and the next paragraph as Nietzsche's own quotations in German differ somewhat from the standard version in DK.

[9] DK 1.92, 93; KR pp. 211–12.

[10] Apparently not a strict quotation, but a conflation of DK 1.29, KR p. 213 ('the best men choose one thing rather than many, everlasting fame among mortals') and the general Heraclitean idea of the universal flux of all things.

Perhaps a callous demon would have no more to say about all that we describe by such proud metaphors as 'world history' and 'truth' and 'fame' than this:

'In some remote corner of the universe poured out into countless flickering solar systems there was once a star on which some clever animals invented *knowledge*. It was the most arrogant and most untruthful minute of world history, but still only a minute. When nature had drawn a few breaths the star solidified and the clever animals died. It was time, too: for although they prided themselves on knowing a lot, they had finally discovered, to their great annoyance, that they knew everything wrongly. They died and as they died they cursed truth. That was the way of those desperate animals that had invented knowledge.'

This would be the fate of man if he were in fact nothing but a knowing animal. He would be driven to despair and destruction by the truth, the truth that he is eternally condemned to untruth. But for man the only fitting belief is the belief in the attainable truth, in the illusion that approaches him trustfully. Does he not really live *by* being continually misled? Does nature not conceal most things from him, even the closest things, e.g. his own body, of which he has only a deceptive 'consciousness'? He is locked up in this consciousness, and nature has thrown away the key. Oh, the disastrous curiosity of the philosopher who desires for once to peer out and down through a crack in the chamber of consciousness: he might then suspect that man, in the indifference of his ignorance, rests on the greedy, the insatiable, the disgusting, the merciless, the murderous, as if he were hanging in his dreams from the back of a tiger.

'Let him hang,' cries *art*. 'Wake him,' cries the philosopher, in the pathos of truth. But while he believes that he is shaking the sleeper, he is himself sinking into an even deeper magic slumber – perhaps dreaming of 'ideas' or of immortality. Art is more powerful than knowledge, because *it* wants life, while knowledge achieves as its ultimate goal nothing but – destruction.

On Truth and Lie in an Extra-Moral Sense (1873)

In some remote corner of the universe poured out into countless flickering solar systems there was once a star on which some clever animals invented knowledge. It was the most arrogant and most untruthful minute of 'world history'; but still only a minute. When nature had drawn a few breaths the star solidified and the clever animals died. – One could invent such a fable, but one would still not have sufficiently illustrated how pathetic, how shadowy and volatile, how useless and arbitrary the human intellect seems within nature. There were eternities in which it did not exist; and when it is gone nothing will have happened. For this intellect has no further mission leading beyond human life. It is human and only its owner and creator treats it as solemnly as if the hinges of the world turned on it. But if we could communicate with a gnat we would hear that it swims through the air with the same solemnity and also feels as if the flying centre of this world were within it. There is nothing so reprehensible or low in nature that it would not immediately be inflated like a balloon by a small breath of that power of knowledge; and just as every porter wants to have his admirer, so the proudest of men, the philosopher, believes that the eyes of the universe are trained on his actions and thoughts like telescopes from all sides.

It is remarkable that this is accomplished by the intellect, which is at best assigned as an aid to the most unfortunate, most delicate and most transitory beings in order to detain them for a minute in life, from which they would otherwise, without this extra gift, have every reason to escape as fast as Lessing's son.[1] Thus the arrogance connected with knowledge

---

[1] The only son of Gotthold Ephraim Lessing (1729–81), a major figure of the German Enlightenment, died immediately after birth.

and sensation, covering the eyes and senses of men with blinding mists, deceives them about the value of life by carrying within it the most flattering evaluation of knowledge itself. Its most universal effect is deception, but even its most particular effects carry something of the same character about them.

The intellect, as a means of preserving the individual, unfolds its main powers in dissimulation; for dissimulation is the means by which the weaker, less robust individuals survive, having been denied the ability to fight for their existence with horns or sharp predator teeth. In man this art of dissimulation reaches its peak: among men deception, flattery, lying and cheating, backbiting, posturing, living in borrowed splendour, wearing a mask, hiding behind convention, play-acting in front of others and oneself, in short, constantly fluttering around the single flame of vanity, is so much the rule and law that there is hardly anything more incomprehensible than how an honest and pure drive for truth could have arisen among them. Men are deeply immersed in illusions and dreams; their eye glides only along the surface of things and sees 'forms'; their feeling nowhere leads to the truth, but is content to receive stimuli and, as it were, play blind games on the back of things. In addition man, in his dreams at night, allows himself to be lied to all his life, and his moral sense never tries to prevent this, although men are said to have stopped snoring by sheer strength of will. What does man really know about himself? Indeed, would he ever be able to perceive himself completely, as if he were laid out in an illuminated glass case? Does nature not keep him in ignorance about most things, even about his own body, in order to detain and lock him up within a proud deceitful consciousness, removed from the coils of the intestines, the rapid flow of the bloodstream, the intricate vibration of the fibres? It has thrown away the key, and woe betide the disastrous curiosity which could one day peer out and down through a crack in the chamber of consciousness and suspect that man, in the indifference of his ignorance, rests on the pitiless, the greedy, the insatiable, the murderous, as if he were hanging in his dreams from the back of a tiger. Given this constellation, where on earth does the drive for truth come from?

To the extent that the individual wants to maintain himself against other individuals, in the natural state of things he has used the intellect mostly for dissimulation alone; but since man, out of necessity as well as boredom, wants to live in a society or herd, he needs a peace settlement and he tries to make at least the most brutal *bellum omnium contra omnes*[2] vanish from his world. This peace settlement entails something that looks like the first step towards attaining that mysterious drive for truth. At this point what is henceforth to be called 'truth' is fixed, i.e. a universally valid and binding designation of things is invented and the legislation of language supplies the first laws of truth. For it is here that the contrast between truth and lie first comes into being. The liar uses the valid designations, the words, in order to make the unreal appear as real: he says, for example, 'I am rich', when the correct designation of this condition would be 'poor'. He misuses the firm conventions by arbitrarily exchanging or even reversing the names. If he does this in a selfish and incidentally harmful way society will no longer trust him and he will be excluded as a result. What men shun in this case is not so much being deceived, but rather being harmed by the deception. At this level too they do not really hate the deception, but the bad, hostile consequences of certain kinds of deception. Only in a similarly restricted sense does man want the truth. He desires the pleasant, life-preserving consequences of truth; he is indifferent to pure knowledge without consequences, and even hostile to harmful and destructive truths. Moreover: how about those conventions of language? Are they perhaps products of knowledge, of the sense of truth: are designations and things congruent? Is language the adequate expression of all realities?

Only through forgetfulness can man ever come to believe that he is in possession of a truth in the degree just described. If he is not content with truth in the form of tautology, i.e. with empty shells, he will for ever be trading truths for illusions. What is a word? The portrayal of a nerve stimulus in sounds. But to infer from the nerve stimulus the existence of a cause outside us is the result of a false and unjustified application of the principle of sufficient reason. If the only decisive factor in the genesis of language had been truth and in the designation of things certainty, how could we say that stone is hard, as if 'hard' were known to us in any form other than that of a totally subjective irritation? We divide things by genders, designating trees as masculine and plants as feminine.[3] What arbitrary transferences! How far flown beyond the canon of certainty! We talk about a snake: the designation refers only to its winding motions

---

[2] See above, Notebook 10, footnote 12, p. 73.
[3] 'Tree' is masculine in German (*der Baum*), and 'plant' feminine (*die Pflanze*).

and could therefore also apply to worms.[4] What arbitrary demarcations, what one-sided preferences, now for one property of a thing and now for another! A juxtaposition of the different languages shows that what matters about words is never the truth, never an adequate expression; otherwise there would not be so many languages. To the creator of language too, the 'thing-in-itself' (which would be precisely the pure truth without consequences) is quite incomprehensible and not at all desirable. He only designates the relations between things and men, and to express them he resorts to the boldest metaphors. A nerve stimulus first transformed into an image – the first metaphor! The image then reproduced in a sound – the second metaphor! And each time a complete overleaping of the sphere concerned, right into the middle of an entirely new and different one. Think of a man who is stone deaf and has never felt the sensation of sound and music: imagine how he gazes in astonishment at Chladni's[5] sound figures in the sand and, realising that they are caused by the vibration of the string, swears that he now knows what men mean by 'sound'. This is the situation in which we all find ourselves with regard to language. We believe that we know something about the things themselves when we talk about trees, colours, snow and flowers, and yet we possess nothing but metaphors for things which do not correspond in the slightest to the original entities. Just as the sound appears as a sand figure, so the mysterious X of the thing-in-itself appears first as a nerve stimulus, then as an image and finally as a sound. In any case the emergence of language is not a logical affair, and if all the material with which and in which the man of truth, the scientist or the philosopher, later works and builds does not come from cloud-cuckoo-land, neither does it come from the essence of things.

Let us now think in particular of how concepts are formed: every word immediately becomes a concept precisely because it is not intended to serve as a reminder of the unique, entirely individualised primal experience to which it owes its existence, but because it has to fit at one and the same time countless more or less similar cases which, strictly speaking, are never equal or, in other words, are always unequal. Every concept comes into being through the equation of non-equal things. As certainly as no leaf is ever completely identical to another, so certainly the concept

---

[4] 'Snake' is *Schlange*, from *schlingen* (bend, wind around, curve about).
[5] See above, Notebook 19 footnote 41, p. 118.

of leaf is formed by arbitrarily shelving these individual differences or forgetting the distinguishing features. This is what gives the impression that in nature, apart from leaves, there is such a thing as the 'leaf', a kind of prototype from which all leaves were woven, drawn, delineated, coloured, ruffled, painted, but by clumsy hands, so that not one specimen has turned out to be a correct, reliable and truthful image of the prototype. We call a man honest. Why has he behaved so honestly today, we ask. Our answer is usually: because of his honesty. Honesty! This again means that the leaf is the cause of the leaves. We know nothing at all about an essential quality called honesty, but we know of many individualised and therefore unequal actions, which we equate by omitting the inequalities between them and which we now describe as honest actions; it is out of them that we finally formulate a *qualitas occulta*[6] called honesty.

We obtain the concept, as we do the form, by overlooking the individual and the real, while nature knows no forms or concepts and therefore no species either, but only an X which, for us, is inaccessible and undefinable. For our contrast between the individual and the species is also anthropomorphic and does not stem from the essence of things, even though we dare not say that it does not correspond to it, because that would be a dogmatic assertion and as such just as unprovable as its opposite.

What then is truth? A mobile army of metaphors, metonymies, anthropormorphisms, in short, a sum of human relations which have been poetically and rhetorically intensified, transferred, decorated and which, after lengthy use, seem firm, canonical and binding to a people: truths are illusions that are no longer remembered as being illusions, metaphors that have become worn and stripped of their sensuous force, coins that have lost their design and are now considered only as metal and no longer as coins. We still do not know where the drive for truth comes from: for so far we have heard only of the obligation that society, in order to exist, imposes on us – the obligation to be truthful, i.e. to use the customary metaphors or, to put it in moral terms, the obligation to lie in accordance with a firm convention, to lie in droves in a style binding for all. Of course man forgets that this is his predicament and therefore he lies, in the manner described, unconsciously and according to the habit of hundreds of years – and arrives at a sense of truth precisely *by means of this unconsciousness*, this oblivion. The sense of being obliged to call one thing

---

[6] hidden property.

red, another cold, a third mute, awakens a moral impulse related to truth: by the contrast with the liar, whom nobody trusts and whom everybody excludes, man demonstrates to himself the venerable, trustworthy and useful quality of truth. Now he submits his actions as a *rational* being to the rule of abstractions: he is no longer prepared to be carried away by sudden impressions, or intuitions, but he generalises all these impressions to form less colourful, cooler concepts, to which to harness the vehicle of his life and actions. All that distinguishes man from animals depends on this ability to dissipate intuitive metaphors into an abstract pattern, that is, to dissolve an image in a concept. For in the domain of those abstract patterns something is possible that would never work under the intuitive first impressions: the construction of a pyramidal order according to castes and degrees, that is, the creation of a new world of laws, privileges, subordinations and border demarcations, which now confronts the intuitive world of first impressions as something more solid, more universal, more familiar, more human and therefore as the regulating and imperative force. While every intuitive metaphor, being individual and without an equal, can avoid all classification, the large edifice of concepts shows the rigid regularity of a Roman *columbarium*⁷ and in logic exhales the severity and coolness characteristic of mathematics. Those who feel a breath of this aloofness will hardly believe that the concept too, bony, octagonal and movable like a die, endures only as the *residue of a metaphor*, and that the illusion of the artistic transference of a nerve stimulus into images is, if not the mother, at least the grandmother of every concept. But in this dice game of concepts 'truth' means using every die as it is marked; counting its dots accurately, establishing correct categories and never breaching the caste system and the order of the ranks and classes. Just as the Romans and Etruscans carved up heaven by rigid mathematical lines and enclosed a god within each section as in a *templum*,⁸ so every people has above it such a mathematically divided conceptual heaven and now understands the demand of truth to mean that every conceptual god must be sought in *his own* sphere only. Here man may well be admired as a tremendous

⁷ Originally a dovecote, then a catacomb with niches at regular intervals for urns containing the ashes of the dead.
⁸ There is some reason to believe that the Latin word *templum* (temple) is etymologically connected with the Greek τέμνω (to cut), and that the original meaning of *templum* is the designated, 'cut-out', region (especially of the sky) within which an augur intended to look for signs. The Romans thought the Etruscans were particularly good at this.

architectural genius, who succeeds in piling up an infinitely complicated cathedral of concepts on moving foundations and, as it were, running water. Admittedly, in order to find support on such foundations, it must be like a structure made of spiders' webs, delicate enough to be carried along by the waves, firm enough not to be blown apart by the wind. This raises man, as an architectural genius, high above bees: a bee builds out of wax it collects from nature, while man builds out of the far more delicate material of concepts which he has first to manufacture out of himself. Here he is much to be admired – but by no means because of his drive for truth or for a pure knowledge of things. If a man hides something behind a bush and seeks and finds it in the same place, there is not much to praise about this seeking and finding, and the same holds for seeking and finding the 'truth' within the domain of reason. If I think up the definition of a mammal and then, after inspecting a camel, explain 'look, a mammal', this does bring a truth to light, but one that is of limited value. I mean that it is entirely anthropomorphic and does not contain a single point which would be 'true in itself', i.e. real and universally valid apart from man. Basically, the searcher for such truths seeks only the metamorphosis of the world into man; he struggles for an understanding of the world as something resembling humans and he achieves at best a sense of assimilation. Like the astrologer who regards the stars as being in the service of men and connected to their happiness and sorrow, such a researcher regards the whole world as an attachment to man, as the infinitely refracted echo of a primal sound, man, or as the multiple copy of the one primal image, man. His method is to set man up as the measure of all things, but he makes the mistake of believing that he has these things directly in front of him as pure objects. He forgets that the original intuitive metaphors were in fact metaphors and takes them for the things themselves.

Only oblivion of that primitive world of metaphors, only the congealment and solidification of what was originally a hot and liquid mass of images pouring out of the primal force of human imagination, only the invincible belief that *this* sun, *this* window, *this* table is a truth in itself – in short, only forgetting that he is himself a subject, and an *artistically creative* subject at that, enables man to live with a degree of peace, certainty and consistency. If he could escape from the prison walls of this belief for one moment his 'self-assurance' would immediately come to an end. But he even finds it hard to admit to himself that the world perceived by an insect or a bird is completely different from that perceived by man, and that it would be quite pointless to ask which of the two perceptions of the world is more correct, because the answer would require the prior application of the standard of *correct perception*, i.e. a *non-existent* standard. In fact, correct perception – which would mean the adequate expression of an object in the subject – seems to me a self-contradictory absurdity: for between two absolutely different spheres, as between subject and object, there is no causality, no correctness, no expression, but at most an *aesthetic* attitude: by this I mean an allusive transference, a halting translation into an entirely foreign language, which in any case demands a freely creative and freely inventive intermediate sphere and mediating force. The word 'appearance' contains many enticements, which is why I avoid it as far as possible: for it is not true that the essence of things appears in the empirical world. A painter without hands who tried to express the image in his mind by means of song would still reveal more about it by this transposition of the spheres than the empirical world reveals about the essence of things. Even the relation of a nerve stimulus to the image it produces is not in itself a necessary one. But if the same image is produced millions of times and transmitted through many generations, until in each case it finally appears to the whole of mankind as an effect of the same cause, it will ultimately acquire for man the same meaning as if it were the only necessary image and as if the relation of the original nerve stimulus to the conventional image were a strictly causal one; just as a dream, eternally repeated, would be perceived and judged as absolutely real. But the congealment and solidification of a metaphor by no means guarantees the necessity and exclusive justification of that metaphor.

Anybody who is used to such reflections has certainly felt a deep distrust of any idealism of this kind every time he clearly recognised the eternal consistency, ubiquity and infallibility of the laws of nature. He has concluded that in nature, as far as we can penetrate to the heights of the telescopic world or the depths of the microscopic, everything is so certain, complete, infinite, regular and without gaps that science will be able to dig in these shafts successfully for ever, and all its findings will harmonise and not contradict each other. How little this resembles a product of the imagination: for if it were that, it would necessarily betray the illusion and the unreality at some point. Against this it must be said, first: if we all still had different sense perceptions; if we could only perceive now as a bird, now as a worm, now as a plant; or if one of us saw the same stimulus as red, another as blue, and a third even heard it as a sound; then nobody would talk about such a regularity of nature, but would understand it only as a highly subjective construct. And second: what is a law of nature really to us? We do not know it in itself, but only in its effects, i.e. in its relations to other laws of nature, which again we know only as relations. Therefore all these relations refer only to each other, and they are thoroughly incomprehensible to us in their essence. All we really know about them is what we add to them: time and space, that is, relationships of succession and numbers. But everything miraculous that astonishes us in the laws of nature in particular, everything that demands our explanation and that might seduce us to distrust idealism, lies precisely and exclusively in the mathematical rigour and steadfastness of our representations of of time and space. But these representations are produced in us and out of us by ourselves with the same necessity as a spider spins its web. If we must understand all things in these forms alone, then it is no longer a miracle that what we really understand of all things are only these forms: for they must all carry the laws of number with them, and number is the most astonishing feature of things. The regularity that impresses us so much in the movement of the stars and in chemical processes basically coincides with those properties that we ourselves bring to things, so that ultimately we are impressed by ourselves. But this in turn means that the artistic creation of metaphors, with which every perception begins within us, already presupposes, and is thus implemented in, these forms. The unyielding persistence of these primal forms alone explains the possibility of subseqently building a conceptual edifice out of the metaphors themselves. For such an edifice is an imitation of the temporal, spatial and numerical relations on the foundation of metaphors.

2

As we have seen, the construction of concepts is originally a labour of *language*, in later ages *science*. Just as the bee builds cells and fills them with honey at one and the same time, so science works inexorably on the great *columbarium* of concepts, the burial place of intuition, building new and ever higher storeys, propping up, cleaning and renovating the old cells and, above all, striving to fill that colossal, soaring frame by fitting the whole empirical world, i.e. the anthropomorphic world, into it. Even if the man of action ties his life to reason and its concepts, in order to avoid being swept away and losing himself, the scientist builds his hut close to the tower of science, in order to be able to assist with the construction and to find shelter for himself under the existing bulwark. And he does need shelter, for he is continually besieged by terrible forces that counter scientific truth with quite different 'truths' bearing the most diverse insignia on their shields.

The drive to create metaphors, that fundamental drive of man which cannot be calculated away for a single moment because in the process man himself would be calculated away, is not truly defeated but barely tamed by constructing for itself, out of its own evaporated products, the concepts, a world as regular and rigid as a prison fortress. It seeks a new territory and a new channel for its operation, which it finds in myth and in art as a whole. It continually confuses the conceptual categories and cells by introducing new transferences, metaphors and metonymies, and it continually reveals the desire to make the existing world of waking man as colourful, irregular, free of consequences, incoherent, delightful and eternally new, as the world of dreams. In fact waking man realises that he is awake only thanks to the rigid and regular web of concepts, and that is precisely why he sometimes believes himself to be dreaming when this web of concepts is torn apart by art. Pascal is right in saying that if we had the same dream every night we would be as much exercised by it as we are by the things that we see every day: 'If an artisan were sure to dream for twelve hours every night that he was king, I believe', says Pascal, 'that he would be just as happy as a king who dreamt for twelve hours every night that he was an artisan.'[9] Owing to what myth assumes to be the continuous operation of a miracle, the waking day of a people in a state of mythical arousal, e.g. the ancient Greeks, is indeed more like a dream than the day of a thinker under the sobering influence of science. If every tree can speak like a nymph, or a god in the guise of a bull carry off virgins, if the goddess Athene herself, accompanied by Pisistratus, is suddenly seen driving through the markets of Athens in a beautiful horse and carriage[10] – and the honest Athenian believed this – then anything is possible at any moment, as it is in a dream, and all nature swarms around

---

[9] Adapted from Blaise Pascal, *Pensées* (VI. 386), trans. Martin Turnell (London: Harvill, 1962).
[10] See Herodotus I.60.

man as if it were only the masquerade of the gods, who were amusing themselves by deceiving man in all their different shapes.

Man himself has an, invincible tendency to be deceived and is almost spellbound by happiness when the rhapsode tells him epic fairy tales as if they were true, or when the actor in a drama plays the king even more regally than he is in reality. The intellect, that master of deception, is free and released from its habitual slavery so long as it can deceive without *causing harm*; it is then that it celebrates its Saturnalia,[11] and is never more luxuriant, richer, prouder, more adroit and more daring. With creative relish, it muddles up metaphors and shifts the boundary stones of abstraction, e.g. describing a river as a moving road that carries man to places to which he normally walks. Now it has thrown off the signs of servitude: while at other times it glumly strained to show a poor individual craving for existence the way and means, or set out like a servant in search of prey and booty for his master, it has now become the master and may wipe the expression of neediness from its face. No matter what it does now, in comparison with its earlier activity everything bears the marks of dissimulation, just as its earlier actions bore those of distortion. It copies human life, but takes it for a good thing and seems to be quite satisfied with it. For the liberated intellect, the huge structure of concepts, to whose beams and boards needy man clings all his life in order to survive, is only a scaffolding and a toy with which to perform its boldest tricks: by smashing, jumbling up and ironically reassembling this structure, joining the most alien elements and separating the closest, it demonstrates that it can do without those makeshift resources of neediness and is now guided not by concepts but by intuitions. From these intuitions there is no regular road leading to the country of ghostly schemata, of abstractions: the word is not made for them, and man falls silent when he sees them, or he speaks in nothing but forbidden metaphors and outrageous combinations of concepts, in order to live up to the impression of the powerful present intuition in a creative manner, at least by shattering and deriding the old conceptual barriers.

There are eras in which rational man and intuitive man stand side by side, the one fearful of intuition, the other scornful of abstraction. The latter is just as irrational as the former is inartistic. Both desire to dominate life: the former by knowing how to meet the greatest needs with

---

[11] See above, Notebook 19, footnote 19, p. 104.

foresight, prudence and regularity, the latter by being an 'over-joyous hero'[12] who does not see those needs and who regards life as real only when it is disguised as make-believe and beauty. Where intuitive man, as for instance in ancient Greece, wields his weapons more powerfully and more victoriously than his opponent, if conditions are favourable, a culture can evolve and the rule of art over life establish itself. All the manifestations of such a life are accompanied by dissimulation, the denial of neediness, the splendour of metaphorical intuitions and, in particular, the immediacy of illusion. Neither their house, nor their gait, nor their clothing, nor their clay jug betrays the fact that it was invented by a need; it seems as if all these things were meant to express a sublime happiness, an Olympian cloudlessness and, as it were, a play with seriousness. While man guided by concepts and abstractions can only ward off unhappiness and strive for the greatest possible freedom from pain without wresting any happiness for himself from these abstractions, intuitive man, rooted in the middle of a culture, apart from warding off evil, reaps from his intuitions a continuous flow of illumination, comfort and redemption. Of course, *when* he suffers he suffers more violently; and he also suffers more often because he is unable to learn from experience and keeps falling into the same pit into which he has once fallen. In grief he is then as irrational as in happiness; he cries out loud and cannot be consoled. How differently does the stoic man, who has learnt from experience and who controls himself by means of concepts, face the same misfortune! This man, who usually seeks nothing but sincerity, truth, freedom from illusions and protection from beguiling attacks, now, in misfortune, delivers his masterpiece of deception, just as the other man does his in happiness. He wears no twitching and changeable human face but, as it were, a mask dignified by a symmetry of features; he does not shout or even alter his voice. If a real storm cloud empties itself over him he wraps himself in his coat and with slow steps walks away from beneath it.

---

[12] A phrase used of Siegfried in Wagner's *Götterdämmerung* (Act III).

Index

Cambridge Texts in the History of Philosophy

Titles published in the series thus far

Aquinas *Disputed Questions on the Virtues* (edited by E. M. Atkins and Thomas Williams)

Aquinas *Summa Theologiae, Questions on God* (edited by Brian Davies and Brian Leftow)

Aristotle *Nicomachean Ethics* (edited by Roger Crisp)

Arnauld and Nicole *Logic or the Art of Thinking* (edited by Jill Vance Buroker)

Augustine *On the Trinity* (edited by Gareth Matthews)

Bacon *The New Organon* (edited by Lisa Jardine and Michael Silverthorne)

Berkeley *Philosophical Writings* (edited by Desmond M. Clarke)

Boyle *A Free Enquiry into the Vulgarly Received Notion of Nature* (edited by Edward B. Davis and Michael Hunter)

Bruno *Cause, Principle and Unity* and *Essays on Magic* (edited by Richard Blackwell and Robert de Lucca with an introduction by Alfonso Ingegno)

Cavendish *Observations upon Experimental Philosophy* (edited by Eileen O'Neill)

Cicero *On Moral Ends* (edited by Julia Annas, translated by Raphael Woolf)

Clarke *A Demonstration of the Being and Attributes of God and Other Writings* (edited by Ezio Vailati)

Classic and Romantic German Aesthetics (edited by J. M. Bernstein)

Condillac *Essay on the Origin of Human Knowledge* (edited by Hans Aarsleff)

Conway *The Principles of the Most Ancient and Modern Philosophy* (edited by Allison P. Coudert and Taylor Corse)

Cudworth *A Treatise Concerning Eternal and Immutable Morality* with *A Treatise of Freewill* (edited by Sarah Hutton)

Descartes *Meditations on First Philosophy*, with selections from the *Objections and Replies* (edited by John Cottingham)

Descartes *The World and Other Writings* (edited by Stephen Gaukroger)

Fichte *Foundations of Natural Right* (edited by Frederick Neuhouser, translated by Michael Baur)

Fichte *The System of Ethics* (edited by Daniel Breazeale and Günter Zöller)

Hamann *Philosophical Writings* (edited by Kenneth Haynes)

Heine *On the History of Religion and Philosophy in Germany and Other Writings* (edited by Terry Pinkard, translated by Howard Pollack-Milgate)

Herder *Philosophical Writings* (edited by Michael Forster)

Hobbes and Bramhall on Liberty and Necessity (edited by Vere Chappell)

Humboldt *On Language* (edited by Michael Losonsky, translated by Peter Heath)

Hume *Dialogues Concerning Natural Religion and Other Writings* (edited by Dorothy Coleman)

Hume *An Enquiry concerning Human Understanding* (edited by Stephen Buckle)

Kant *Anthropology from a Pragmatic Point of View* (edited by Robert B. Louden with an introduction by Manfred Kuehn)

Kant *Critique of Practical Reason* (edited by Mary Gregor with an introduction by Andrews Reath)

Kant *Groundwork of the Metaphysics of Morals* (edited by Mary Gregor with an introduction by Christine M. Korsgaard

Kant *Metaphysical Foundations of Natural Science* (edited by Michael Friedman)

Kant *The Metaphysics of Morals* (edited by Mary Gregor with an introduction by Roger Sullivan)

Kant *Prolegomena to any Future Metaphysics* (edited by Gary Hatfield)

Kant *Religion within the Boundaries of Mere Reason and Other Writings* (edited by Allen Wood and George di Giovanni with an introduction by Robert Merrihew Adams)

Kierkegaard *Fear and Trembling* (edited by C. Stephen Evans and Sylvia Walsh)

La Mettrie *Machine Man and Other Writings* (edited by Ann Thomson)

Leibniz *New Essays on Human Understanding* (edited by Peter Remnant and Jonathan Bennett)

Lessing *Philosophical and Theological Writings* (edited by H. B. Nisbet)

Malebranche *Dialogues on Metaphysics and on Religion* (edited by Nicholas Jolley and David Scott)

Malebranche *The Search after Truth* (edited by Thomas M. Lennon and Paul J. Olscamp)

Medieval Islamic Philosophical Writings (edited by Muhammad Ali Khalidi)

Medieval Jewish Philosophical Writings (edited by Charles Manekin)

Melanchthon *Orations on Philosophy and Education* (edited by Sachiko Kusukawa, translated by Christine Salazar)

Mendelssohn *Philosophical Writings* (edited by Daniel O. Dahlstrom)

Newton *Philosophical Writings* (edited by Andrew Janiak)

Nietzsche *The Antichrist, Ecce Homo, Twilight of the Idols and Other Writings* (edited by Aaron Ridley and Judith Norman)

Nietzsche *Beyond Good and Evil* (edited by Rolf-Peter Horstmann and Judith Norman)

Nietzsche *The Birth of Tragedy and Other Writings* (edited by Raymond Geuss and Ronald Speirs)

Nietzsche *Daybreak* (edited by Maudemarie Clark and Brian Leiter, translated by R. J. Hollingdale)

Nietzsche *The Gay Science* (edited by Bernard Williams, translated by Josefine Nauckhoff)

Nietzsche *Human, All Too Human* (translated by R. J. Hollingdale with an introduction by Richard Schacht)

Nietzsche *Thus Spoke Zarathustra* (edited by Adrian Del Caro and Robert B. Pippin)

Nietzsche *Untimely Meditations* (edited by Daniel Breazeale, translated by R. J. Hollingdale)

Nietzsche *Writings from the Early Notebooks* (edited by Raymond Geuss and Alexander Nehamas, translated by Ladislaus Löb)

Nietzsche *Writings from the Late Notebooks* (edited by Rüdiger Bittner, translated by Kate Sturge)

Novalis *Fichte Studies* (edited by Jane Kneller)

Plato *The Symposium* (edited by M. C. Howatson and Frisbee C. C. Sheffield)

Reinhold *Letters on the Kantian Philosophy* (edited by Karl Ameriks, translated by James Hebbeler)

Schleiermacher *Hermeneutics and Criticism* (edited by Andrew Bowie)
Schleiermacher *Lectures on Philosophical Ethics* (edited by Robert Louden, translated by Louise Adey Huish)
Schleiermacher *On Religion: Speeches to its Cultured Despisers* (edited by Richard Crouter)
Schopenhauer *Prize Essay on the Freedom of the Will* (edited by Günter Zöller)
Sextus Empiricus *Against the Logicians* (edited by Richard Bett)
Sextus Empiricus *Outlines of Scepticism* (edited by Julia Annas and Jonathan Barnes)
Shaftesbury *Characteristics of Men, Manners, Opinions, Times* (edited by Lawrence Klein)
Adam Smith *The Theory of Moral Sentiments* (edited by Knud Haakonssen)
Spinoza *Theological-Political Treatise* (edited by Jonathan Israel, translated by Michael Silverthorne and Jonathan Israel)
Voltaire *Treatise on Tolerance and Other Writings* (edited by Simon Harvey)